Quest for Love in Central Morocco

Gender, Culture, and Politics in the Middle East
miriam cooke, Simona Sharoni, and Suad Joseph, *Series Editors*

For a full list of titles in this series,
visit https://press.syr.edu/supressbook-series/gender
-culture-and-politics-in-the-middle-east/.

Quest for Love
in Central Morocco

Young Women
and the Dynamics
of Intimate Lives

Laura Menin

Syracuse University Press

∞ The paper used in this publication meets the minimum requirements
of the American National Standard for Information Sciences—Permanence
of Paper for Printed Library Materials, ANSI Z39.48-1992.

For a listing of books published and distributed by Syracuse University Press,
visit https://press.syr.edu.

ISBN: 9780815638292 (hardcover)
9780815638308 (paperback)
9780815657033 (e-book)

Library of Congress Cataloging in Publication Control Number: 2023043563

Manufactured in the United States of America

To the girls and their mothers and grandmothers, who have accompanied my days in al-Azaliyya, for having shared with me their time, thoughts, stories, desires, hopes, sorrows, and fears, as well as listened to mine. I do hope that, somehow, this book might live up to their beauty.

Contents

Acknowledgments

Writing this book has been a long journey punctuated by memorable encounters and unexpected events, numerous breaks and difficult restarts. Many people have accompanied my first steps in al-Azaliyya, listened to my doubts and ideas, suggested possibilities, and wisely guided and encouraged me in moments of hesitation and indecision. Their comments and criticisms have helped me call into question my certainties, develop my ideas, and, eventually, take a stand. My deepest thanks go to the young women and their mothers, relatives, and friends, whom this book talks about, for having opened their homes and hearts to me. Above all, fieldwork has been a totalizing human experience and an extraordinary opportunity for personal growth. Without the patience and friendship of those I spoke with, I would not have simply been able to write this book. All names of places and people in this book are anonymized, and the details of the subjects' lives are changed to protect their privacy. Since being away from home and loved ones for long periods can be difficult, I will forever be indebted to my host families and friends for having been a source of inspiration and loving support during my stay in al-Azaliyya.

The University of Milan-Bicocca provided me, via the Ministry of Education, with a scholarship and academic support during the four years of my PhD in the Anthropology of the Contemporary World program. I express my deepest gratitude to Ugo Fabietti, who left us too soon, Setrag Manoukian, and Mauro Van Aken for igniting my passion for North Africa and the Middle East. Alice Bellagamba not only supervised me as a graduate student and trusted me when I subverted my initial research project but also contributed significantly to my academic formation.

During my fieldwork in Morocco, Noureddine Harrami at the Moulay Ismail University of Meknes, who passed away prematurely in 2018, offered me fundamental material support and intellectual insights. I am particularly grateful to Abdelmajid Zmou at the Sultan Moulay Slimane University of Beni Mellal for his invaluable hospitality and generosity in sharing his immense knowledge about the Tadla.

While completing my dissertation and afterward, I benefited immensely from the stimulating intellectual environment at the Zentrum Moderner Orient in Berlin, where I could also carry out new research on Morocco's recent history, as well as write and discuss my work with scholars and colleagues. I am grateful to Yasmine Berriane, Ulrike Freitag, Sonja Hegazy, Kai Kresse, Saadi Nikro, and Samuli Schielke. Back in Italy, a postdoctoral fellowship within the project "Shadows of Slavery in West Africa and Beyond: A Historical Anthropology" (ERC Grant 313737) and, especially, a postdoctoral fellowship at the Department of Sociology and Social Research of the University of Milano Bicocca allowed me to do new research and rewrite and edit this book. Since 2008, first as a D.Phil. visiting student and later as a research associate, I have benefited enormously from the time spent at the Global Studies Department at the University of Sussex. I will be indebted forever to Filippo Osella for his unstinting support far beyond his role as a mentor. Without his constant presence and advice, I might not have found the energy to complete this book. The shared conversations and collaborative projects with friends and anthropology colleagues have been a vital source of professional growth and inspiration. I am grateful to Paola Abenante, Alessandra Brivio, Irene Capelli, Daniele Cantini, Lorenzo D'Angelo, Gaia Delpino, Alice Eliott, Mamdouh Fadil, Corinne Fortier, Marco Gardini, Aymon Kreil, Irene Maffi, Luca Nevola, Barbara Pinelli, Arianna Cecconi, Claudia Mattalucci. Special thanks go to Samuli Schielke, Paolo Gaibazzi, Elisabetta Costa, Simone Ghezzi, Vincenzo Matera, Valentina Duca, and Caroline Osella for having read and generously commented on this book or some of its chapters at the various stages of their evolution.

A previous version of chapter 4 was first published as "The Impasse of Modernity: Personal Agency, Divine Destiny, and the Unpredictability Of Intimate Relationships in Morocco" in the *Journal of Royal*

Anthropological Institute 21 (2015), while sections of chapter 7 first appeared as "Texting Romance: Mobile Phones, Intimacy, and Gendered Moralities in Central Morocco" in *Contemporary Levant* 3, no. 1 (2018). Thank you to everyone at Syracuse University Press for supporting this project from the outset. A special thank-you goes to miriam cooke, Suad Joseph, and Simona Sharoni for welcoming my work in the Gender, Culture, and Politics in the Middle East series and supporting my project throughout its many stops during the past five years. Laura Fish has always been present, providing essential support and responses to my queries. The three anonymous reviewers who generously engaged with my work have contributed to making it much better with their comments, suggestions, and criticisms. Any flaw is solely my responsibility.

Throughout my life, my family has been a loving presence and constant support. My parents have encouraged me unreservedly to pursue my passion for anthropology. Through all these years, I have had the privilege of sharing my life with Simone, who has been my refuge and eternal source of love and wonder. Amanda's arrival turned my life upside down, slowing down my work enormously, but every day makes me realize how much it was worth it. Without these people, I would stagger in the darkness.

Notes on Transliteration

Moroccan Colloquial Arabic (Darija maghrebiya), the language commonly spoken by my interlocutors, can vary significantly across different regions and zones, as well as in relation to class and education. The lack of a standardized written form makes transcription particularly tricky. For transcribing words and sentences in Moroccan Colloquial Arabic, I have followed the simplified rules of the *Georgetown Classic in Arabic Language and Linguistics on Moroccan Arabic* (Harrell and Sobelman 2004), but I have also simplified diacritics. I have decided to transcribe as /s/ both س and ص (respectively, s and ṣ in standard transliteration) and as /h/ both ه and ح (respectively, h and ḥ in standardized transliteration) while maintaining hamza (') and 'ayn ('). Concurrently, I have tried to respect as much as possible the sounds of Moroccan Colloquial Arabic words and people's speech style in the Tadla Plain by transliterating /e/ instead of /a/ for ‾ / ̩/ when necessary.

The sounds ث /th/, ذ /dh/, ظ /ẓ/ present in Modern Standard Arabic
    are not present in Moroccan Colloquial Arabic:
ق /q/ sometimes is pronounced as /g/ in Moroccan Colloquial
    Arabic;
غ /gh/ is similar to the French "r";
خ /kha/ is pronounced like the "ch" in the German "Bach."

When quoting other authors, I have maintained the original transliteration. I have left names of things, people, and places as they are commonly known in English (such as hammam or Casablanca).

Maps

SPAIN

ATLANTIC OCEAN

Tangier

Tétouan

Oujda

RABAT

Fès

Casablanca

Meknès

Beni-Mellal

Marrakech

Agadir

Canary Islands
(Spain)

ALGERIA

Laayoune

WESTERN

SAHARA

MAURITANIA

MALI

1. Morocco (elaboration by the author)

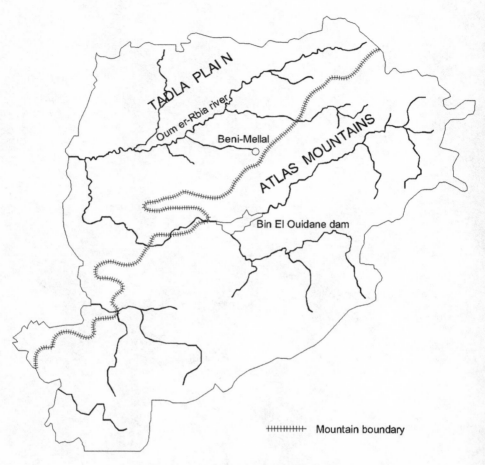

2. The Tadla-Azilal region (elaboration by the author)

Quest for Love in Central Morocco

Introduction

"Love is a problem in Morocco!"

One afternoon in May 2009, I was strolling along the main avenue of al-Azaliyya, a middle-sized town at the foot of the Moroccan Middle Atlas Mountains, with Najat, a bright middle-class university student in her early twenties. I had arrived there a few weeks earlier, and Najat was among the first girls I made friends with. That afternoon we found ourselves sharing our difficulties. I was grappling with the hot weather and the sense of unfamiliarity with the rules of everyday life there; Najat was battling her love troubles. "You know, love in Morocco is a big problem!" she said, taking off her sunglasses to wipe her misty eyes and fix the wisp of hair that had slipped out from her colored veil. Unwittingly, listening to her story, I found myself trying somehow to console her. At that time, I could not foresee the extent to which my involvement in her love troubles would reshape—and eventually entirely shift—the trajectory of my research in such an unpredictable way.

Six months before, Najat had met Abdelghani, a professional in his mid-thirties whose elegant manners had enchanted her from the outset. Overwhelming Najat with lavish attention, Abdelghani won her trust. They started dating secretly and exchanging romantic love letters and text messages, and, after a suitable period, Abdelghani suggested an informal meeting with her parents, to whom he declared his intention to marry their daughter. In Najat's eyes, this proved that he was a serious man (*m'aqul*), and that his love was sincere. Just when she thought that her romance was about to develop into marriage, however, her fiancé became erratic. He continued to declare his love for Najat while remaining elusive about

1

his commitment to her. In their mobile phone conversations, he hinted at problems with his family, who did not support their union, and concluded that their marriage "was not written by God"—in other words, it was not destined to be. While the subtle meanings of Abdelghani's statements remained unclear, they marked for Najat the end of her conjugal dreams. Witnessing Najat's desperation, her mother jumped to the conclusion that her daughter had lost her virginity with him and imposed on her a virginity test. As Najat explained, the future groom's family may ask for a certificate of virginity (*shahada al-ʿuzuba*), which socially embodies the girl's honor and respectability and that in turn reflect—and are reflected in—that of her entire family. The test proved that she had protected her sexual honor (*sharaf*), as a "respectable" girl is expected to do.[1]

Najat had many dreams indicating that another woman had come between her and Abdelghani.[2] Even though he denied any such involvement, Najat learned through her female networks that her dreams had indeed been true. Trying to make sense of her fiancé's misbehavior, she speculated that his lover must have bewitched him by the use of his sperm to bind him to her sexually and emotionally.[3] "I'm both a modern and religious girl," Najat said, "and I could not seek the help of a sorceress (*shuwwefa*) to counter the magic spell." Reflecting on his behavior, she added: "Love in Morocco breeds only problems, especially for girls like me. I love him to distraction, like in a novel. But men love differently. They don't respect women and think they are superior to them." Only praying and dancing, she said, could alleviate her suffering.

1. This expression refers to Najat's virginity. The expression *ʿandha sharaf*, literally meaning that she has honor / is a virgin, reveals the intimate bond between female honor and virginity.

2. My interlocutors think there are various types of dreams: those engendered by concerns, ruminations, and thoughts of everyday life, and those associated with revelation and premonition (*ro'ya*). The latter are produced by the roaming of the soul (*ruh*), which travels around outside the body and may anticipate forthcoming events. See, for example, Pandolfo (1997) on Morocco, and Mittermaier (2011, 2012) on Egypt.

3. Like personal belongings and bodily substances such as hair, sweat, or spittle, sperm is an ingredient of love filters and potions (Rausch 2001).

By introducing me to the slippery worlds of human passions and transcendental powers, Najat's story captured my attention in a way that I could only understand after several months of fieldwork, when I realized that it was far from unique. Narratives of passionate love and unfulfilled promises of marriage, of family's opposition and men's deceit, serve not only as powerful tropes in oral traditions and literary imaginations in Morocco, but they also punctuate parts of the secret dynamics of premarital love in al-Azaliyya, as experienced and narrated by my female interlocutors. Najat's quest for love, however, also speaks of a more recent history, which evokes new ways of imagining and enacting one's intimate future. More than in its most private and ineffable dimensions, the significance of her love story rests precisely on the specific ethnographic and theoretical questions it compels us to ask: What is "love" for young women like Najat, and why is it a problem? What kind of intimate exchanges are taking shape in secret and public dynamics? Why do my interlocutors use the religious vocabulary of destiny to make sense of unexpected twists in their intimate lives, and why is Islam regarded as the solution for love troubles, as for other problems? And, finally, what is the space for choice and freedom in a world where personal desire and intentionality encounter greater powers?

This book ventures into the quest for love of young women like Najat, whose lives unfolded in the low-income (sha'bi) and lower-middle-class neighborhoods of al-Azaliyya, where I conducted fieldwork between 2009 and 2014.[4] By attending to the ways in which these young women seek, imagine, and experience love in heterosexual relationships, the book unravels the complex expectations and unexpected outcomes love triggers at a historical time when demands of ethical reform interweave with subterranean youth cultures in which premarital relations are reinvented and practiced in varied, unexpected ways. Compared with the Moroccan big cities, which have been the focus of much literature on love and intimacy,

4. The young women in this book were aged between their early twenties and mid-thirties. As unmarried women are named *bnat* (sing. *bnt*, contextually translatable as "daughter," "girl," "virgin," "female child," "unmarried woman") in Moroccan Arabic, regardless of their age, I use both the terms "young women" and "girls" to refer to my interlocutors.

everyday life and possibilities are limited in a middle-sized town like al-Azaliyya, where life in public is shaped by rigid control on male-female socializing, and gossip runs quickly from mouth to mouth.[5] This journey into the intimate worlds and imaginations of young Moroccan women, however, will reveal unexplored dynamics marked by rapid and contradictory trajectories of change. Unlike their illiterate or poorly educated mothers, the generation of women in this book attended university or high school. They could experience new freedoms in the definition of their life trajectories and new modes of dating and digitally mediated intimate communication, way beyond the experience of previous generations of women. Together with new freedoms, they encountered moral and existential anxieties intimately connected with these generational changes, the delay of marriage, and significantly widened horizons of professional work and conjugal intimacy. Moving between public and secret dynamics, between online and offline realms, this book looks closely at the creative ways young women craft themselves and their affective worlds by navigating competing desires and moralities. In so doing, this ethnographic inquiry into love, and into the imaginative and social worlds shaping it, hopes to provide the ground for expanding anthropological reflections on emerging gendered selves and intimate dynamics in a Moroccan town and beyond.

"Love" as an Ethnographic Object and a Theoretical Question

This venture into a young women's quest begins with the problems of delineating "love" as an object of anthropological inquiry. Until relatively recently, love as an anthropological object in its own right has been overlooked (Lindholm 2006; Venkatesan et al. 2011). The dearth of love as a subject area in anthropology can be connected with the biased assumption that love is a "modern" Western invention or can be explained through a combination of disciplinary taboos and "the anthropologists' cultural sense of what topics are taboo" (Wynn 2015, 234). Not only did the classic

5. See Dialmy (1988, 2003, 2014, 2017); Namaane-Guessous (1991); Bakass and Ferrand (2013); Cheikh (2009, 2020a); and El Aji (2018).

anthropological focus on kinship, social organizations, and political systems leave little room for the analysis of love, but the sphere of feelings was also regarded as "too ineffable and private" to be investigated anthropologically (Pussetti 2005, 5). Since the 1980s, anthropologists have begun to explore emotions as sociocultural constructs (e.g., Rosaldo 1984; Abu-Lughod 1986; Luz and Abu-Lughod 1990; Lutz and White 1986; Reddy 1999; Andrew 2013; Beatty 2014). Lila Abu-Lughod's seminal book *Veiled Sentiments: Honor and Poetry in a Bedouin Society* (1986) has opened up an avenue for love as a topic of anthropological inquiry. Abu-Lughod's exploration of love poetry (*ghinnawa*) among the Awlad Ali Bedouins in Egypt has brought into focus a discourse on feelings of love, loss, and vulnerability that did not find expression in the gendered vocabulary of honor and modesty—two opposing discourses that together constitute the complexity of the Bedouin experience of morality. In addition to the contextual study of emotion, anthropologists influenced by sociobiology have argued for the universality of romantic love, assessing its existence and ethnographic manifestations cross-culturally. Conceptualizing love as a universal experience, William Jankowiak and Edward Fischer (1992, 150; Jankowiak 1995) have defined passionate love as "an intense attraction that involves the intrusive thinking about one person within an erotic context" (2008, 13) by distinguishing it from "companionate love," which entails the amity and affection between two persons whose lives are deeply intertwined. Moving in a different direction, Charles Lindholm (1988; 2006, 15) has delineated an "anthropology of romantic love" based on structural and comparative analysis. Investigating where and under what social conditions what he calls "romantic complexes" (21) can be found, Lindholm has correlated different types of romantic love, and its relations with marriage and sexuality, with different social organizations. Another strand of research, inspired by Nancy Scheper-Hughes's notion of the "political economy of emotion" (1992), has contended that cultural meanings and practices of love are also shaped by broader economic and social transformations (Padilla et al. 2007, xiii). Combining a structural analysis with a focus on people's intimate experience, scholars have traced the changing dynamics of love and intimacy in the contexts of globalization, global capitalism, and market liberalization (e.g., Rebhun 1999; Ahearn 2001; Hirsch and Wardlow 2006; Palilla et al. 2007). Moving the analysis beyond the focus on the contemporary dynamics of globalization and neoliberalism, other studies have explored, through a historical perspective, how African people have imagined and negotiated love in colonial times (Cole and Thomas 2009; Decker 2015). By developing different lines of inquiry, this scholarship has conceptualized love as a complex cultural and historical phenomenon, shaped at the intersection of socioeconomic and political developments, but has generally neglected North Africa and the Middle East. This neglect reflects a lacuna within scholarship on Arab-majority societies, where, as Lara Deeb and Jessica Winegar (2012, 550) note, there is too little research on love.

In central Morocco, as in North Africa and the Middle East, the historical depth of ideas and vocabularies of love testifies to a centuries-old history comprising religious texts and manuals, Arabic and Persian poetry, prose and oral traditions, songs, and proverbs. However, as Marcia Inhorn (2012, 95) has noted, the absence of love in anthropological reflection on the region was particularly striking, considering that past and contemporary Middle Eastern cultures are imbued with love. In addition to Abu-Lughod's (1986) seminal work on love poetry, the anthropological and sociological literature on love and sexuality in Morocco that has developed since the eighties constitutes an important exception. While Susan Schaefer Davis and Douglas Davis (1989, 1995a, 1995b) have explored the changing ideas and experiences of premarital love among Moroccan adolescents in the 1980s vis-à-vis mass schooling and emerging global media horizons, sociologists Soumaya Naamane-Guessous, author of *Au-delà de toute pudeur. La Sexualité féminine au Maroc* (1991), and Abdessamad Dialmy (1988) began to examine young Moroccans' intimate and sexual lives. Remarkably, these works are rarely mentioned in regional scholarly literature on love, thus making Morocco/Maghreb look like a virgin scientific territory. In general, however, love has been subsumed within the realms of marriage, gender, and family (S. Davis 1983; Haeri 1989; Hoodfar 1997; Joseph 1999; Hasso 2010; Inhorn 2012), rather than being tackled as an ethnographic object in its own right. The predominating vision of North Africa and the Middle East as dominated by kinship/tribalism, sexual segregation, patriarchy, and Islam (Abu-Lughod 1989) has long represented these societies as incompatible with a Western idea of "modern love" based on a free choice outside the realms of kinship alliance and instrumentality. Even though postcolonial and feminist scholars, drawing attention to the complexity of Muslim women's lives, have complicated classic theories on kinship, patriarchy, and political powers (e.g., S. Davis 1983; Abu-Lughod 1993; Altorki 1986; Friedl 1989; Boddy 1989; Maher 1989; Hoodfar 1997; Kandiyoti 1996; Wikan 1996), similar biases have continued to surface in popular imaginations and political debates.

Especially when it comes to questions of freedom, love, and sexuality, we often encounter powerful orientalist fantasies (Said 1978; Mernissi 2001) and fearful imaginations around women's bodies and lives (Keddie 1989; Kahf 1999). The image of Muslim women as "victims to be saved" (Abu-Lughod 2013)—rooted in the history of colonial encounters—legitimized the "civilizing mission" of the colonial powers in the late nineteenth and twentieth centuries (Ahmed 1992) and has more recently surfaced in the American and European involvements in a "war on terror" in the post–9/11 world (Billaud 2015). On the other hand, popular academic and journalism writings, drawing on the experience of secular elites and youths in big cities, romantically search for possibilities of emancipation and a sexual revolution in the Middle East (Mahdavi 2009; El Feki 2012; Eltahawy 2015). Both narratives fail to capture the emotional possibilities and tensions running through young women's intimate and affective worlds in al-Azaliyya. By attending to desires, aspirations, and dreams, this book, in contrast, foregrounds young women's agentive capacities without losing sight of the working of powers in their everyday lives. It not only shows that "modern love" does exist along with family allegiances and the search for pious lives, but it also interrogates what love, choice/freedom, and modernity mean for a generation of women who pursue complex hopes and navigate even more complex realities. This book, rather than providing an a priori definition of "love" or assuming its universality, takes love as a fundamental ethnographic and theoretical question and contextualizes the shifting meanings, emotions, and expectations associated to it across generations. As will become evident, however, putting the idea of love under ethnographic scrutiny goes beyond the question of defining its semantic and experiential boundaries. On the contrary, probing what quest for love, in the first place, *is* and *means* for my young interlocutors opens up a number of ethnographic and theoretical questions, which I begin to delineate in this introduction.

Love as a Quest

In al-Azaliyya, *l-hobb* (Modern Standard Arabic *al-hubb*) is the general term for "love," which comprises the love for God as well as family ties, affection, and amity (Mernissi 2011), while the term *'ishq* (verbal form *kan-'ishqk*, "I love you"), laden with mystical connotations in Sufi traditions, expresses potent and passionate love for a lover.[6] *Kan-bghik* may be the most common way to say "I love you" in Moroccan Arabic, together with several idiomatic expressions that connect passionate love to death, madness, and irrationality, such as *kan-mut 'alik* ("I would die for you"), and *kan-hammaq 'alik, kan-hbal, kan-tsaty*, all translatable as "I am mad for you," or "I love you to craziness." Other times, love is named *hawa*, with the verbal form *kan-hawak*, which also means "air" and evokes the roaming of one's head in the clouds. More refinedly, some educated girls talk of love as *hoyam*, the feeling that comes from the heart and makes the mind stop thinking while the imagination (*khayal*) wanders, conferring on love a dreamlike, textured quality. The vast range of vocabularies associated with love points to its semantic and experiential complexity. Beyond the definition of its semantic fields, drawing the conceptual boundaries of love takes us to the heart of the specific tensions and imaginative possibilities that constitute the very texture of the quest for love in central Morocco. As Najat's story powerfully illustrates, love is not only about dreams, passions, and the "aspiration for a narrative about something to share" (Berlant 1998), but also about dangers and loss, pain and disillusionment. Love promises an exclusive relationality between two individuals, but often delivers the unsettling experience of its absence or even impossibility.

---

6. For a comparative analysis of notions of *hubb* and *'ishq*, see also Nevola (2016) on Yemen, and Marsden (2007) on Pakistan.

Variously described as a sublime feeling and an irrational force, a dangerous emotion that brings dishonor and vulnerability, a form of madness, or even the fruit of magic, love was not considered conventionally the proper basis for marriage in al-Azaliyya. As happens in other societies, sex/romance and marriage/family are seen as very different things, associated with diverse types of affective, ethical, and pragmatic reasoning. Traditionally, the idea of love as dangerous created a split between marital love and carnal passion and legitimized parental opposition to love marriages (Mernissi 1975; Maher 1974, 149–62). More than the private choice of two individuals bonded by love, marriage is a focal event in people's lives that marks the entrance into social adulthood for both girls and boys. Even though, as in other Muslim-majority settings, kin should not be necessarily set in opposition to love marriage (Allouche 2019a), and couples often seek to combine romance and kin approval (Hart 2007; Maqsood 2021), marriage in al-Azaliyya remains an important family business that needs validation by the two families (Newcomb 2010, 116–17). Some parents do support a love match, and others tolerate their daughters' premarital romance as long as it remains secret and unspoken. However, dating—the social practice of going out with a young man for romantic reasons—is considered unacceptable for "good girls" in the poor and lower-middle-class neighborhoods where I carried out a large part of my fieldwork. While marriage has strong public dimensions, premarital love is experienced in the social spheres of secrecy and discretion (Carey 2010). It is just its intrinsic secret quality that renders the quest for love a thrilling and potentially dangerous enterprise. While talking passionately of love, young women often connect physical and emotional intimacy to the dangers of men's deceit and loss of respectability. Laden with risks and possibilities, the quest for love manifests itself as an exciting adventure whose outcome often remains, as in Najat's story, unpredictable. This complexity is precisely what makes love both a vital emotion and a deeply ambivalent experience in my young interlocutors' lives and words.

Bringing into focus young women's journey into love, this book hopes to contribute to literature in the anthropology of the Middle East that, especially in the past decade, has explored the changing dynamics of love, desire, sexuality, and intimacy (e.g., Beaumont, Cauvin Verner, and

Pouillon 2010; Deeb and al-Kassim 2011; Fortier, Kreil, and Maffi 2016, 2018; Zengin and Sehlikoglu 2016; Costa and Menin 2016; Ozyegin 2016). Inspired by the work of historians Afsaneh Najmabadi (2005) and Dror Ze'evi (2006), some scholars have examined intimacy in relation to and beyond the domains of sex and sexuality, by tracing its everyday enactments, definitions, and transformations across the Middle East (Zengin and Sehlikoglu 2015, 2016). Other studies have included explorations of love and intimacy in connection to the growing influence of the Islamic revival and the emergence of pious desires (Smith-Hefner 2005, 2019; C. Osella 2012). Authors have highlighted the troubles that love triggers in contexts where premarital intimacy confronts social and family expectations and the constructions of respectable gendered and religious selves (Fortier, Kreil, and Maffi 2016; Schielke 2009, 2015). While these works emphasize the ambivalence and "fractured desires" (Ozyegin 2015) that love produces in young people, another strand of research has pointed to the way digital technologies help people combine competing aspirations (Lee Bowen, Green, and James 2008; Perl Kaya 2009; Costa 2016a, 2016b; Nevola 2016a; Menin 2018). Precisely because of the complexity of premarital dynamics in contemporary Muslim contexts, love becomes a crucial site for the theorization of morality and ethical reasoning (Marsden 2007; Schielke 2009). Samuli Schielke (2009), in particular, shows that young Egyptians' engagement with love opens space for ethical reflection marked by moral ambivalence, which is stimulated by the coexistence of competing moral drives in people's lives. Attention to moral ambivalence has offered a counterpoint to the ethnographic and conceptual focus on discursive traditions and religious virtuosi proposed by Saba Mahmood (2005) and Charles Hirshkind (2006) and has continued to stimulate lively anthropological debate on the relations between Islam and the everyday (Soares and Osella 2009; Zyskowski 2014; Fadil and Fernando 2015).

This book engages with recent anthropological debates on morality not only because any discussion of love entails considering closely local gendered ideas of honor, self, marriage, family, and respectability but also because, as Magnus Marsden (2007, 92) suggests, "discourses of sentiments" open "a window into the variety of levels at which moral choices are made." While following in the footsteps of works emphasizing moral ambivalence, this book also takes a different direction, one that fore-grounds the productive and creative dimensions of young women's engagement in a quest for love. It considers carefully how love is shaped by broader social, economic, and political transformations, while showing how love itself is a powerful trigger of social, intimate, and imaginative dynamics. Above all, one of the aims of this book is to bring into focus the idea of love as a *quest* that generates specific expectations and quandaries, conjugal hopes and digital intimacies, moral discipline and experiences of destiny and freedom. Unpacking the complex and textured qualities of this quest entails, first of all, asking what this quest is about. The book's key idea is that young women's quest for love goes beyond the search for the beloved one; it becomes a quest for the self and for different modalities of intimate exchange. The ambivalence infusing this quest does not speak only of the tensions between personal desires and family/social/moral constraints, although these can be an important part of it; it is about young women's endeavors to rewrite conventional plots of tragic, unfulfilled love. As we will see, these endeavors engender both intimate experimentations and relational uncertainties, which result from the ongoing redefinition of gendered subjectivities and conjugal expectations in al-Azaliyya specifically and in Morocco more generally. Precisely because of its centrality in the ways my young interlocutors reflect upon themselves in relation to intimate others, a focus on love gives visibility to affective dimensions of the gendered selves that might be otherwise difficult to grasp. Crucially, what is at stake in the quest for love is not only the making of gendered selves and intimate relationships, but also the imagination of social and political life. As I will argue, the quest for love is also about personal and social transformation. This book shows how ethnographic attention to love is crucial in thinking through changes and debates occurring in central Morocco and the Middle East more broadly, and how young women engage with and reflect upon such transformations.

The Ambivalent Powers of Love

It is often through the language of power—the uncontrolled power of love and the social powers that seek to contain it—that young women narrate and reflect on their intimate worlds. This is perhaps because love itself is a potent feeling that infuses, acts upon, and even possesses people (S. Davis and D. Davis 1995b) in the form of the *jinniya* in the Moroccan imagination, 'Aisha Qandisha (Crapanzano 1975, 1977), a seductive and attractive woman who sexually enslaves males after being possessed (*mskun*, literally "inhabited").[7] Experienced and imagined as a potent and mysterious emotion, love is enmeshed with power relations, deeply imbricated in broader gender and sexual politics. Not surprisingly, it is also through "love" that my interlocutors subtly evoke or overtly discuss the powers shaping social and intimate dynamics of life in al-Azaliyya. The French distinction between *puissance* and *pouvoir* helps us capture love's dual relations with power: whereas *puissance* evokes great power, influence, energy, and potency, *pouvoir* refers mainly to "power" in a political and social sense.

Love's intimate enmeshment with social powers has long made feminist scholars reluctant to tackle love as an object in its own right. While sexuality became one focus of feminist theorization and political practice in the 1970s, love was disregarded as a privileged site for the reproduction of patriarchal ideology (hooks 2000b, 102) and heteronormativity (García-Andrade, Gunnarsson, and Jónasdóttir 2018). Love's centrality in making specifically gender and hetero subjectivities (Allouche 2019b; Sehlikoglu and Karioris 2019) is precisely what makes its everyday and ordinary unfolding a crucial site of analysis of gender and sexual (hetero)normative practices, affects, desires, institutions, and subjectivities.

The intimate relations of love and sex with power have been scrutinized by a generation of Moroccan sociologists (Dialmy 1985, 1988, 2005;

---

7. *Jinniya* is a female *jinn* (pl. *jnun*). In Islamic cosmologies, *jinun* are invisible to human beings and, like angels, humans, and animals, were created by God. The human body is conceived as an entity permeable to external forces and hence potentially vulnerable to encounters with *jinun*, which are thought to cause several diseases (Dieste 2013; Pandolfo 2018). Encounters between humans and *jinun* may also result in intimate, lifelong bondages conferring mystical powers, agency, and authority on marginal subjects (Crapanzano 1985; Kapchan 2007). The diverse practices surrounding *jinun* reveal the ambiguous status of spirit possession in Morocco.

Namaane-Guessous 1991) against the backdrop of the emergence of feminist movements in Morocco in the early 1980s. Their groundbreaking works investigated intimacy and sexuality in connection with issues of domination, the social construction of the female body, and the cultural ideas of shame and virginity. In dialogue with these works, this book looks closely at the ways in which love interweaves with power relations without reducing it to questions of power and patriarchal ideologies. At the same time, it joins the steps of recent sociological and anthropological scholarship in Morocco that departs from the previous focus on social and sexual repression and points instead to the ways young people creatively deal with sexual and gender norms. Sociologist Sanaa El Aji (2018), in particular, examines how young people in different Moroccan cities reckon with social, legal, and religious norms surrounding sexuality vis-à-vis prolonged celibacy and the delay of marriage. Moving beyond the questions of norms and normativity, Mériam Cheikh (2020) explores from an anthropological perspective the sexual practices of working-class young women in Tangier in connection with "economic intimacies" and emerging urban youth cultures. While this literature renews long-standing scholarly interest in sex and intimacy in Morocco, it fails to conceptualize love as a subject in its own right. This book, in contrast, disarticulates conceptually love from sexuality, even though my interlocutors themselves often use "love" (*l-hobb*, in French *l'amour*) to talk of sex. Moving beyond a conceptualization of love as gender and sexuality, it brings into focus the quest for love as a space for self-exploration and reflexivity, where conventional modalities of masculinities and femininities and intimate dynamics are reflected upon, called into question, and imagined in new ways.

A key idea guiding this book is that love, far from being just the site of reproduction of gendered norms, is also a crucial site of agency and imagination, where young women creatively inhabit the different modalities of femininity available in their society and carefully navigate everyday norms. As I will show, within the dynamics of seduction and romance, gender, hetero, and sexual norms are embodied and reproduced as well as practiced and reimagined in a multiplicity of ways. This is perhaps because the quest for love entails strivings, hopes, and desires, all dimensions that are produced by power and that, simultaneously, escape the determination of power. This theoretical perspective diverges from analyses informed by Foucauldian and Bourdieusian frameworks, with their emphasis on the dynamics of repetition, subjection, and incorporation of norms. Taking inspiration from feminist scholars highlighting the productive dimensions of agency and self-crafting (McNay 2000; Moore 1994, 2007, 2011), my analysis foregrounds the imaginative, aspirational, and dreamlike qualities of the quest for love, not as an illusory relationship with reality, but rather as a particular way of engaging the everyday. Young women's encounters with the different social powers hindering their romantic dreams stimulate a reflection on their relationships with men and their place in the family and society. This space of reflexivity, opened up by the quest for love, contains within it the possibility to envision new modalities of (gendered and generational) relationality. This is not only because, as Lindholm (2006, 27) argues, "human beings always want to exceed their concrete lives and be more than rational maximizers of cultural goals," but also because young women's engagement with love enables them to envision, and want, a world (Berlant 2011, 687).

By creatively inhabiting the imagination and vocabulary of love, my interlocutors give voice to a demand for "choice" and self-determination in their intimate lives, a demand that opens up relational possibilities without denying family connectivity (Joseph 1999). Their quest takes the shape—at least partially—of a demand for intimate and social freedom, conceived of as a vernacular concept with specific meanings and impacts. However, as with Najat's story, destiny (in Arabic, *qadar* or *maktub*) relocates human strivings, desires, and intentionalities in a broader cosmological order. A powerful reminder that major elements in human life, including marriage, are predestined by God, destiny is often evoked in discussing the unpredictability of intimate relationships, and of life itself (Menin 2015). In addition to providing a theory of failure (Schielke 2015; Nevola 2018), evocations of destiny give voice to the tension between young women's desire to take their lives into their hands and the encounters with broader social-cum-transcendental powers. Perhaps most importantly, this tension is not conceived here in terms of an opposition between the liberal binary concepts of individual freedom and social constraints (Povinelli 2006), nor as an opposition between modernity and tradition

(Uberoi 2006). It is a generative tension, one that triggers, among my interlocutors, a reflection on the very possibilities of human choice and freedom in the face of bigger powers. In this sense, I do not conceive love just as freedom and choice, but as a space that opens key ethical and cosmological questions, with which people work out their relationships, desires, and dilemmas. Unpacking the tensions at the heart of the quest for love in al-Azaliyya—between destiny and choice/freedom, public and secret, and between desires and social bonds—will offer insights into the changing gendered dynamics in central Morocco as well as into the changes young women want in their intimate and social worlds.

A Horizon for Transformations

Beyond being an ideal of intimate attachment and gendered subjectivity, love is imagined as a horizon for transformation. Crucially, the idea of "transformation" (*tghriyr*) acquires different meanings for different social actors and is imagined as moving in radically different directions. In al-Azaliyya, "transformation" is connected with historical processes of modernization and a local conceptualization of "modernity" as a move away from "tradition," although what these terms mean in this specific ethnographic and historical context deserves our full attention.

The relation between love and modernity has been at the core of Anthony Gidden's influential book *The Transformation of Intimacy: Sexuality, Love and Eroticism in Modern Societies* (1992) and of a growing stream of anthropological works which emerged against the backdrop of a "love turn" in social sciences in the 1990s. Moving beyond the idea that modern love spreads from the West (Palilla et al. 2007), scholars have offered nuanced analyses of the variety of ways in which people engage with love as a particular modality of inhabiting modernity in both the colonial times (Cole and Thomas 2009) and the contemporary contexts of modernization and neoliberal economies (Rebhun 1999; Ahearn 2001). The work of historians has deepened further the relations between modernity and love, sex and (homo)sexualities in Middle Eastern societies (Ze'evi 2006; Babayan and Najmabadi 2008; Habib 2007; Afary 2009; Najmabadi 2005; Al-Samman and El-Ariss 2013) by recovering "the deliberate forgetting of the homoerotic past" (Babayan and Najmabadi 2008, 4). Afsaneh Najmabadi (2005, 160–61) has delineated the heteronormalization of love and sexualities in the making of Iranian modernity and has traced the emergent ideal of companionate marriage in the nineteenth and twentieth centuries. Similarly, in Egypt the reconceptualization of marriage as a romantic union turned love into a project of social reform and modernization of gender relations (e.g., Baron 1991; Ahmed 1992, chap. 7; Abu-Lughod 1998; Cuno 2015).

The idea of marriage as a choice based on love surfaced in postcolonial Morocco. As Fatima Mernissi (2008, 165–85) argues, the generation of Moroccan intellectuals who were adolescents at the dawn of independence in 1956 envisioned a marriage based on love as a political critique of Moroccan "custom and tradition ('adat wa t-taqalid)," arranged marriage, the patriarchal and political establishment upon which their society relied. Against the global backdrop of the political and student movements that culminated in the May 1968 student uprisings in France and the Chinese Cultural Revolution, many students and activists in the left-wing circles of the 1960s and 1970s experienced new gender relationships as political and social change. For example, the Moroccan former Marxist prisoner Nour-Eddine Saoudi (2007, 77) writes in his memoirs that his political engagement led him to question the interplay of gendered and generational hierarchy and to refuse the patriarchal and authoritarian masculinity that he felt was embodied by his father and his generation. In the 1980s context, marked by growing access to education and exposure to globalized media cultures, Susan and Douglas Davis (1989, 1995) trace how adolescents in a Moroccan town aspired to a love match as part of imagining themselves as "modern subjects."

Cognizant that the encounter of love, choice, and marriage has a long history in North African and Middle Eastern engagements with modernity and its historical permutations, nevertheless I do not conceive love just in terms of modernity; rather, I trace how the quest for love opens up a horizon for transformation at the core of alternative imaginations of modernity itself. The young women in this book came of age in a period of rapid socioeconomic transformations and witnessed crucial political changes. Toward the end of his reign, King Hassan II (1961–99) initiated a political opening up after thirty years of violent repression of all the political forces opposed to his regime (Slyomovics 2005). The accession of his son Mohammed VI in 1999, celebrated as the "king of the poor," was presented in the national and international media as the beginning of a "new era" (Vermeren 2002, 31). While emphasizing the continuity of the monarchy, Mohammed VI encouraged expectations of social and political changes (Hegasy 2007; Vermeren 2002, 2006, 2009). First, he allowed the return of the exiled Marxist leader Abraham Serfaty (1926–2010) and removed from the Ministry of the Interior Driss Basri, who embodied the symbol of the "Years of Lead" during the former reign; Mohammed VI also created an Equity and Reconciliation Commission (Instance Equité et Réconciliation) in 2004 to investigate past state abuses and compensate the victims (Slyomovics 2005). Second, the king reformed the press and allowed freedom of speech, which, in turn, encouraged the emergence of a vibrant cultural landscape (Orlando 2009) and the proliferation of local NGOs and associations (Berriane 2013). Third, he announced a set of political and juridical reforms to improve the rights of ethnic minorities (notably, the Amazigh population) and to fight against unemployment and social injustice, poverty, and illiteracy. One of the most significant reforms concerns the Personal Status Law (in Arabic, *Mudawwana al-ahwal al-shakhsiyya*), confirming the centrality of the questions of marriage, family, and gender relationships in the establishment of a modern reign.

The 2004 Personal Status Law reform resulted from a two-decade-long confrontation between the left-wing parties and social movements—including feminist and human rights groups—and the Islamist PJD (Islamist Parti de la Justice et du Développement) and Islamist movements (Buskens 2003; Salime 2011). Crucially, the societal confrontations and debates that culminated in the reform of the Mudawwana reveal how these questions have been turned into a battlefield for competing projects of modernity upheld by political actors who aim to orient social change in radically different directions.[8] Both Islamist and "progressive" and fem-

---

8. The struggle over the definition of authenticity has long been integral to the perennial debates on modernity in the social and political history of Morocco and the Middle East more generally. Stefania Pandolfo (2000) offers fascinating insights into Moroccan

inist women (neither of which is a homogeneous group) affirm a need to move away from tradition. However, whereas the former promotes a progressive (*tqaddumiyya*) vision of society and interprets modernity in terms of "moving forward," an Islamic vision of modernity emerges from its major theorists as "moving back" toward the authenticity of the Prophetic model. Especially in the past two decades, the revivalist movements have provided alternative imaginations of modern lives, selves, and marital relationships. These different positions do not simply reveal a tension between two irreconcilable religious and secular sensibilities (Mahmood 2009; Hafez 2011), nor are their views more or less "authentic." They are the outcomes of historical encounters and circulations of heterogeneous ideas, thoughts, and philosophical currents that are part and parcel of the complexity of Morocco's postcolonial condition.

The 2004 Mudawwana reform was acclaimed internationally as a major step toward gender equality within an Islamic framework, although scholars have underlined its shortcomings and contradictions (Cavatorta and Dalmasso 2009; Salime 2009; Žvan Elliott 2015). For example, in her work on the impact of women's rights and legal reforms in southern Morocco, Katja Žvan Elliott (2015, 173) argues that, far from ameliorating female conditions tout court, the 2004 Mudawwana reform ends up reaffirming patriarchal gender and marital relations in contexts where "family dictates the roles, life choice, as well as the behavior of its members". Žvan Elliott (2015, 176–97) contends that the reformed Mudawwana provides women with additional legal options in marriage and divorce, but fails to grant them, especially adult girls, actual rights insofar as their recognition depends on the law application in different jurisdictions as well as on the women's family and their social milieu. Women and girls in the Tadla acknowledged that the 2004 reform enhanced women's rights in marriage

---

debates on modernity through an exploration of the writings of Driss Chraibi and Abdellah Laroui; in these authors' reflections, modernity remains a "cut": both a watershed and a laceration in the history of Morocco. From a materialist perspective, Jafaar Aksikas (2009) discusses liberal, nationalist, and Islamist perspectives on modernity through the works of Abdellah Laroui, Mohammed Abd al-Jibri, and Abdessalam Yassine.

and divorce, but some also claimed that equality between the sexes is yet to be achieved.

The national developments traced so far have affected the local dynamics in al-Azaliyya (which I describe in chapter 1) and marked generational ruptures in my interlocutors' imaginations of intimate, social, and political life. This book shows not only that broader sociopolitical processes contribute to shaping young women's vision of love, but also that love itself is central to the ways in which they think through and engage with transformations and debates underway in Morocco and the Middle East more broadly. Going beyond the boundaries of marriage, and its association to ideas of "freedom," their quest for love takes us into the midst of current societal dynamics and debates.

The 2011 Protests

A short time after I left Morocco in the autumn of 2010, protests and demonstrations led to the fall of authoritarian regimes in Tunisia, Libya, and Egypt. "Bread, freedom and social justice" (Mittermaier 2014) emerged as critical dimensions of people's political horizons and collective actions after decades of despotic rule and corruption, triggering major historical changes: Tunisian president Ben Ali left the country on January 13, 2011, and Egyptian president Hosni Mubarak was ousted on January 25. Moroccans demonstrated in support of Tunisians and the Tahrir Square protesters in Cairo before giving birth to what later became the February 20 Movement (or 20F, named after the day on which it began). From the initial cyberactivism to sit-ins and demonstrations across the country demanding "dignity, freedom and social justice" (karama, hurriya, 'adala ijtima'iyya), the February 20 Movement was able to involve secular, progressive, and Islamist groups, and youth sections of political parties (Laouni 2022). Speaking out about the humiliation (hogra) felt by many youths, the movement claimed equal access to education, health services, and upward social mobility, as well as constitutional reform to redefine the role of the monarch (Hoffman, König 2013). Within protests and uprisings across North Africa and the Middle East, gender and sexual orders have been challenged in novel ways (Hasso and Salime 2016; Salime 2014; Singerman 2013; Hafez 2014). In Morocco, young women's presence in the protests contributed to "turning squares and streets into new gendered spaces" (Pepicelli 2016, 419). While the arrival of Mohammed VI fostered great expectations among young Moroccans (Hegasy 2007), neoliberal reforms initiated under the Structural Adjustment Programs (1983–93) in the fields of education, public sector employment, and health care have continued to sharpen class divisions and inequalities (Cohen 2003, 2004; Cohen and Jaidi 2006; Newcomb 2017). Instead of radically changing the previous style of governance, the new king's influence has remained pervasive across most political and economic sectors of society (Cohen and Jaidi 2006: 6; Cavatorta 2016). To undermine the momentum of the protests, King Mohammed VI announced on television on March 9, 2011, his intention to set up a commission for constitutional reform (Maghraoui 2011; Benchemsi 2012, 58). Against the backdrop of social tensions and violent state repression, on June 17, 2011, the king presented the draft of the Constitution on television and announced an imminent referendum on July 1. Despite the February 20 Movement activists' campaign to boycott the referendum, the new Constitution was approved with a 98.7 percent majority. In the general election on November 25, 2011, the Islamist Justice and Development Party (Parti de la Justice et du Développement, or Hizb 'adala wa tanmiya) won more than 40 percent of the seats in the parliament, becoming the first Islamist government in Morocco's modern history.

Political power in Morocco was not overturned, and, as Béatrice Hibou (2011) notes, "the politically thinkable remained defined by the *Makhzen*" (translation mine).[9] While the international media celebrated the "Moroccan exception" as the tangible proof of the "democratic transition" underway under Mohammed VI's reign, the February 20 Movement voiced discontent over the reforms undertaken by the king. Ultimately,

9. In the precolonial period, *makhzen* indicated the centralized power of the sultan, the army, and its officers (Pennel 2000, 12) and today refers to the centralized power, the system, the political and economic elites who revolve around the king, and the state bureaucratic and repressive apparatus.

the king was able to retain fundamental economic and political powers despite the 2011 constitutional reform (Benchemsi 2012, 60) and succeeded in containing the protests through a mixture of repression and reform (Badran 2022). The wind of change was blowing in the streets of al-Azaliyya, expanding the horizon of the possible and the sayable. People demonstrated in the streets against government corruption, social injustice, and bureaucratic bribery, and, I was told, "the police let them speak out." Even though the young women in this book are not activists, their desires for change in many ways anticipated some of the instances animating protests in Morocco and beyond.

During and after the 2011 protests, new discussions of freedom in political, religious, and intimate spheres of life emerged in Morocco's public sphere, as also happened in other Middle Eastern countries. Public events and debates organized by the February 20 Movement activists, human rights campaigns, the independent press, as well as movies, performances, and art exhibitions have addressed questions of gender equality, sexual violence, and freedom (Hasso and Salime 2016; Skalli 2014; Borrillo 2016).

In the aftermath of the suicide of Amina Filali in 2012, after she was married to her rapist under Article 475 of the Penal Code, online protests and mobilizations triggered a national debate and demanded the abrogation of the article.[10] The president of the Moroccan Association for Human Rights, Khadija Riadi, along with other activists, ignited discussions on the abrogation of Article 490 of the Moroccan Penal Code, which punishes consensual sexual relations outside marriage with imprisonment between one month and one year. This instance is part of a growing discussion on individual liberties in Moroccan society in the past decade, in which "freedom" (*l-hurriya*; in French, *la liberté*) evokes a multiplicity of ideas and political demands, from political to religious and sexual freedoms. Since its creation in 2009 as a Facebook group, the Alternative

---

10. This process led in 2014 to the abrogation of the second clause of Article 475 of the Penal Code that allowed rapists to marry their victims in order to escape prison. For a discussion of the complexity of Amina Filali's tragic story beyond its mediatization, see Meshahi (2018).

Movement for Individual Liberties (Mouvement alternatif pour les liber-tés individuelles, or MALI) has been particularly active.

Even though protests and revolutions have opened up new horizons of transformation, this does not mean that various social strata and con-stituencies support premarital love and sex out of wedlock. On October 3, 2013, a couple of teenagers from Nador, northern Morocco, were picked up by police and placed in pretrial detention for posting on Facebook a photo of them kissing in the street, facing charges of outraging public morals under Article 484 of the Penal Code. Subsequently, the hashtag #FreeBoussa ("free kiss," in a mixture of English and Arabic) was launched on Twitter and Facebook by MALI activists, and, on October 12, 2013, a "kiss-in" was organized in front of the Moroccan Parliament of Rabat. In-terestingly, in 2014, a Facebook group organized a public kissing event in Kerala, South India, dubbed the "kiss of love," that began a protest spread-ing across the country (Devika 2021). In revealing the working of insti-tutions and constituencies in the ordinary regulation of sexuality, these events illustrate the extent to which the act of kissing in public, far from being a private issue, is a politicized question. In Morocco, as in other contexts, love and sex out of marriage are the battleground for competing ethics of the gendered subject, ideas of modernity, and political visions of society (Ilkkaracan 2007). Even though premarital love and sex are wide-spread, discussions on the topic and public displays of intimacy between unmarried couples trigger the opposition of various constituencies and components of society (El Guabli 2012). My young interlocutors often mo-bilized love as a political concept to discuss the institutions and powers that shape different scales of social and intimate life in al-Azaliyya. How-ever, their quest for love is not articulated through a feminist vocabulary, the international language of human rights, or the political imagination of the Arab revolutions, nor does it necessarily uphold progressive instances and politics. More than fueling desires for the revolution, my interlocu-tors' demand for choice and freedom, as I will show, generates specific modalities of intimate and secret actions as practical ways of reckoning with the malleability of the norms. Importantly, the quest for love is not set in contrast to Islam, nor is "freedom" opposed to religious values and norms. On the contrary, most of my interlocutors seek to combine piety and romance, eclectically moving between religious and worldly vocabularies to discuss love, sex, and gender relations.

The Book's Structure

This book is organized into seven chapters that explore different facets of love in al-Azaliyya. In tracing young women's quest for love and the troubles it triggers, this ethnography privileges a narrative approach based on stories and everyday conversations, because telling stories is a powerful tool for accounting for the complexities of flesh-and-bone people (Abu-Lughod 1993, 7–30). Women's narratives enable us to capture their perspective on the affective and power relations in which they are involved (Personal Narrative Groups 1989) and the meanings they find in their experiences (Bruner 1987; Ochs and Capps 2001), as well as how narrative sense-making connects to prospective social action (Andersen, Ravn, and Thomson 2020). Connecting the self and society, personal narratives and life stories are relevant for the windows they open on broader societal and historical dynamics (Franzosi 1998). Rarely did my interlocutors tell me their "own stories" during formal interviews; rather, the linearity of their narratives result from the artificial patching together of bits and pieces of dialogues, recollections, and reflections on past and present events that were invited in informal conversations or that emerged spontaneously in concrete life situations. While some chapters center on particular young women's life stories, other chapters focus more on their daily activities, following them in the places where they spend their spare time and search for love. Men, too, appear in the background as key actors in my interlocutors' lives, and, at times, their voices come to the foreground by offering different perspectives on love dynamics. However, they are mainly present through young women's eyes. This is, indeed, a consciously partial and situated ethnography of love as experienced and narrated by the heterosexual young women I met in a specific historical moment.

In chapter 1, in particular, I introduce the reader to al-Azaliyya and the neighborhoods where I carry out my research. Setting the scene for the chapters to follow, I provide the historical coordinates for understanding the complex intertwining of regional, national, and global dynamics shaping young women's everyday worlds and imaginations. A narrative description of al-Azaliyya and the regional history is combined with a reflection on the research methods and my positionality in the field. In chapter 2, I zoom in on Rabi'a, one of the two neighborhoods where I lived, and trace the sense of self of three generations of women: Hasna, her mother, and her grandmother. Delving into their affective biographies, I focus on the ways in which they craft themselves as gendered subjects in relation to intimate others and reflect on their affective worlds by resorting to shifting discourses on kinship, love, and marriage. The comparison between the three women reveals the gradual shift of intimacy and emotional investment from the birth family to the marital bond. Far from following a linear trajectory, I show that these transformations are laden with both possibilities and contradictions in the lives of young women like Hasna.

In chapter 3, I begin by tracing the slipping of a new religious horizon into young women's everyday life and examine the variety of ways in which they engage with revivalist projects of reform of the self, personal and social ties, as well as forms of sociality in al-Azaliyya. Taking the mosque and satellite television as two ethnographic points of departure, I illustrate how the weekly neighborhood mosque lessons, religious satellite broadcasts, romantic soap operas, charismatic preachers, and Islamic fashion offer grounds of self-making and imaginative resources with which young women craft themselves as consciously Muslim. In chapter 4, I dwell on the encounters between freedom and destiny in the personal narrative of Ghizlan, a professional woman in her thirties, and then trace how she moves between worldly and revivalist imaginations to make sense of tragic twists in her affective life. I show how Ghizlan's reflections on love and destiny interrogate the meanings of choice, freedom, and responsibility in a world where personal agency meets greater human and transcendental powers.

In chapter 5, I go on to explore ideas and practices of love by discussing the search for fun, freedom, and transgression undertaken by Sanaa and her gender-mixed group of friends. Following Sanaa and her friends, their consumption practices, their summer nights, and their daydreams of elsewhere, I discuss the gendered politics of fun, love, and sex in al-Azaliyya. I show how refined "etiquettes of transgression" enable young women to inhabit the malleability of the norms and carve out a space for enacting desires that do not conform to family and gendered expectations. In chapter 6, I concentrate on the meanings and conceptual possibilities of what a group of university students (both girls and boys) call "true love." Tracing how they use love as a political concept, I show that their quest for "true love" reveals a utopian vision that confronts the public secrets surrounding and constituting intimate and social lives in the town. Engaging love as a horizon for transformation, these young people not only envision a different relationality between the sexes and between the generations but also interrogate political and social orders.

Finally, in chapter 7, I focus on the key roles of mobile phones and internet platforms in expanding the social spheres of secrecy and invisibility, where romantic encounters take place, and the premarital dynamics unfold. By concentrating on the tensions between premarital love and marriage, the chapter offers insights into how gendered (Islamic) moralities and romantic desires, and social and transcendental powers are reckoned with and negotiated between the online and offline worlds. From different angles, the chapters foreground "love" as a crucial object of ethnographic exploration and anthropological theorization of the changing dynamics of intimate, social, and political life.

1

Encountering al-Azaliyya

Leaving behind the Atlantic coast, with the white fortified city (*qasba*) and the modern buildings of the capital Rabat, the coach travels for five hours toward the Middle Atlas Mountains of central Morocco along a road dotted with villages and towns and flanked by the cultivated wheat fields of the Chaouia-Ouardigha plain. From time to time, it stops at the coach stations in the main towns. A few beggars climb aboard to ask for alms while the vendors show the travelers their wares: chocolate, snacks, wipes, and natural products with allegedly therapeutic properties. As the journey proceeds, the phosphate plateau appears on the horizon, an immense expanse of yellow hills and arid steppes. The palm trees lining the modern streets of Khuribga, the administrative center of the phosphate plateau, built during the French Protectorate (1912–56), seem like a mirage in this lunar-like landscape. When the coach approaches the Tadla plain, this arid scenery gradually turns into a geometric sweep of irrigated farmland, one legacy of the colonial presence in the region.

The Tadla plain is a vast agricultural region extending to the feet of the Middle Atlas Mountains, central Morocco. The inhabitants of the big cities—the centers of cultural, economic, religious, and political life in Morocco—regard the Tadla as *l-ʿarobiya*, the countryside, a term indicating an ecological area while evoking the peripheries of the kingdom's modernity and urbanity.[1] For the French colonizers, it was a laboratory of modernity. On the colonial map, the Tadla was included in the category

---

1. In everyday conversations, the term *ʿaroby*, literally meaning "peasant," is also used to designate uncouth manners and an uneducated person.

26

of *le Maroc utile* (useful Morocco), which indicated the fertile and culti-vable lands rich in water, forests, and mineral resources (Vermeren 2002). The French established a protectorate in Morocco in 1912, but, because of the resistance of the local population, they were able to bring the Tadla region under their control only in 1934. They "fixed to the soil" the two main tribal groups who populated the plain, the Beni Amir and the Beni Moussa, through the geometrical division of their territories along tribal lines (Prefol 1986, 26–29). They promoted the "large dams policy" (*poli-tique des grands barrages*), the development of a system of irrigation for intensive agricultural production (Prefol 1986; Swearingen 1987; Troin 2002). With the development of modern agriculture, the French Protec-torate established the administrative, transport, and commercial sectors in the main towns of the Tadla.[2]

During the two decades of political turmoil that followed Morocco's independence in 1956, the population of the urban centers and the rural villages of the irrigated perimeters of the Tadla continued to grow, due to inward migration, until the 1970s (Recensement General de la Popula-tion et de l'Habitat 1982, 1994, 2004).[3] After the departure of the French in 1956, the lack of cultural elite trained in the modern French school system contributed to the inward migration of professionals from Mar-rakesh, Meknès, and Fez who entered the top echelons of the public sector.

2. It created, for example, the Office de l'Irrigation (Irrigation Office), and the Office de Mise en Valeur Agricole (Agricultural Development Regional Office) to manage the irrigation system, and the Office des Affaires Indigenes (Offices of Indigenous Affairs) to manage relations with the local populations (Prefol 1986, 71–78).

3. Morocco got its independence from France in 1956. After an initial struggle for power between the royal palace and the political and military forces that had fought for national liberation (mainly the Istiqlal Party and the Armée de Libération Nationale), Sultan Mohammed V was able to establish an authoritarian regime and in 1957 took the title of king. His successor Hassan II (1961–99) entrenched the king's constitutional posi-tion by co-opting some of his potential opponents while crushing opposition parties with repression and mass trials (Vermeren 2006, 19–30; Pennel 2000, 297–316; Saoudi 2004, 261–89). Morocco went through three decades of political turmoil, marked by the violent state repression of the political forces that contested the makhzen and two unsuccessful military coups (in 1971 and 1972), economic crisis, and rising inflation.

However, the majority who entered the public sector in postcolonial times in the main urban center of the Tadla were *petits fonctionnaires* (junior civil servants and administrators) and schoolteachers who had benefited from the national policy of mass education.

In the following decades, though, the trend of population growth changed because of the crisis of the nonirrigated agricultural sector, economic restructuring imposed under the Structural Adjustment Plan (1983–93), and the privatization of the agricultural sector and the disengagement of the state (Harrami and Mahdi 2006). Neoliberal reforms in the institutional, legal, and social sectors then imposed on Morocco ended the postindependence economy of domestic protection. In Morocco's economy—which mainly relied (and still relies) on tourism, migrants' remittances, and phosphates—neoliberal economic reforms (e.g., cutting social services, healthcare, and education) together with market liberalization have intensified the divide between the elites and the middle classes (Cohen 2004; Cohen and Jaidi 2006) and have had catastrophic impacts on poor and low-income families.

One important consequence of the liberalization of the agricultural sector was the development of agricultural credit and the demand for payment being imposed by the Agricultural Development Regional Office before the harvest was gathered (Troin 2002, 165). The need for cash, along with rising unemployment, led many people, including married men, to emigrate to Italy (Harrami and Mahdi 2006). Compared to the regions of Morocco with established connections to Europe, therefore, migration from the Tadla is a recent—albeit prominent—phenomenon (Troin 2002; Harrami and Mahdi 2006, 2008; Menin 2016; Elliot 2021). From being simply an essential livelihood strategy, it has also acquired a central place in young people's imagination and enactment of the future in a context where trajectories of upward social mobility based on education are increasingly unreliable. Researching the social and intimate dynamics triggered by migration was the reason why I was on a five-hour journey on an uncomfortable coach in the direction of al-Azaliyya, one of the medium-sized towns of the Tadla plain. When the high peaks of the Middle Atlas Mountains began to fill the horizon, I worked out that the coach was approaching my destination.

A Moroccan Boomtown

The Tadla's connections with the "outside world" permeate many aspects of the social and economic life of the town, but the architecture of one of its main centers, al-Azaliyya, reveals a much longer history than that. Al-Azaliyya developed around the fortified town (*qasba*) and the old city (*l-medina l-qadima*), which together continue to be the heart of the craftworking and commercial life of the town. The modern parts of the town developed around the administrative and residential sectors built for the French after the "pacification" (1934) of the Tadla in colonial times, where the main public institutions can be found, along with banks and offices, and today include the upper classes' residential neighborhoods. In the two decades following Morocco's independence, rapid and muddled urbanization contributed to the development of several new neighborhoods. Besides the job opportunities opened up by the public sector, many people migrated to al-Azaliyya after having left their home villages in the countryside and the mountains to flee famine or in search of a better life in what appeared as a modern boomtown. The poorest migrants built huts made of soil and straw in the slums (*bidonvilles*) that mushroomed messily on the outskirts of al-Azaliyya; these peripheral districts were replaced by low-income neighborhoods over time and progressively integrated into al-Azaliyya. Nowadays, among the modern houses of professionals and senior civil servants in the residential areas of the town, one can find extravagant villas built by the newly rich, successful migrants.

As has happened in other urban centers and the rural villages of the Tadla, migrants' remittances and their investments in land, construction, agriculture development, and local businesses have all contributed to the rapid growth of al-Azaliyya. The exotic names of Café Milano or Pizzeria Venisia, the secondhand European commodities that inundate the local weekly markets, the migrants' Italian-and Spanish-registered cars that fill the streets during the summer, make palpable the many stranded connections to southern Europe and the immense possibilities of "the outside" (*l-brra, l-kharij*), as people call migration destinations in Europe. Although increasingly restrictive migration policies in southern Europe and Morocco have rendered migration difficult and risky, the "outside

world" permeates life in the region in different guises (Elliot 2021).[4] Crucially, the outside world has also intruded into people's imaginations
through the spread of satellite television, the Internet, and communication technologies.

Climbing the upper part of the town, al-Azaliyya comes into view as
a large collection of houses dotted by hundreds of rooftop satellite dishes.
Since the late 1980s, the circulation of smuggled decoders and satellite
dishes and the increasing availability of pirated CDs of American, French,
and Arabic videos and movies in video shops have helped to loosen the
state's control over Moroccan public culture (Ossman 1994; Pennel 2000,
384–86).[5] Satellite channels such as CNN, the American all-news channel
established in 1980, and MBC (Middle East Broadcasting Center) burst
onto the scene in the early 1990s, giving people access to information
about sensitive political news and events that were censored and filtered
on state-owned television. Owning a satellite dish became legal in Morocco in 1992, but not all families in al-Azaliyya were able to have one
because of an exorbitant government tax (5,000 dirham) required (Sakr
2001, 18–19); when this was abolished in 1994, rooftop satellite dishes
began to fill the urban landscape. Today all families I know own a TV set
and a satellite dish. "Learning" and "understanding" are some of the terms

4. In 1990, Italy introduced visa requirement, and, in 1991, Spain ended the right of
Moroccan citizens to enter Spain without a visa, as a consequence of the "Schengeniza-
tion" of the Spanish-African border. Along with Morocco's partnership with Spain in military border control, in 2003 the government legislated a restrictive migration law (2002–3)
under Moroccan/Spanish bilateral agreements and international anti-terrorist policies.

5. During the reign of Hassan II (1961–99), television was under state control, and
both national and foreign programs and movies were—and still are—supervised and censored (Tozy and Hibou 2002). Aware of the fundamental role of television in the process
of nation-building, in 1962 Hassan II established and then developed further the national
broadcasting system Radiodiffusion et Télévision Marocaine (RTM), which he used as a
means of pro-regime propaganda against its political opposition (Orlando 2009). One of
the first private television stations in the Arab world, the predominantly French-language
private entertainment channel 2M SOREAD, was launched in 1989 and turned public in
1996. The accession of Mohammed VI in 1999 contributed to the liberalization of the
telecommunication sectors and to important changes in Moroccan TV production.

by which my young interlocutors describe the impact of the satellite dish on their lives and political awareness, as they feel they can have access to uncensored news.

Satellite television is also a central dimension of the subterranean youth culture of love and dating (*musahba*) that has developed in urban Morocco against the backdrop of increased female school attendance and the postponed age of marriage (Bakass and Ferrand 2013), which have all created new opportunities for gender-mixed socializing (Naamane-Guessous 1991, 40–41; S. Davis and D. Davis 1995; Bennani-Chraïbi 1995). Satellite television exposes young women's local worlds to Western cultural productions like European and American movies, and TV series, as well as to the entertainment and TV cultures of the urban Middle East: from reality television and Turkish soaps to the Saudi religious channels. Together with TV culture, the Internet and the mobile phone have become integral parts of the local youth cultures and sociality. Moroccans accessed the World Wide Web in the mid-1990s, and high-speed connection became available in 2004, but, because of its high cost, cybercafés mushroomed in every corner of the town until the spread of mobile Internet. Located in a two-three room or small apartments where the internet connection is available in neighboring computers under hourly payment, cybercafés are gender-mixed spaces where young people surf the Internet, listen to music, watch media content, and chat on platforms (Hassa 2012). With the widening of internet access, social media has boomed: from an estimated three million users in 2009 (Zaid and Ibahrine 2009) to over thirty-six million internet users in 2023, with a penetration rate of 98 percent of the population.[6] Initially, Yahoo, Messenger, chat rooms and Skype, and then Facebook, all opened up new opportunities for young women in al-Azaliyya to get in touch with friends and lovers.[7] With the spread of

6. Agence National de Réglementation des Télécommunications, Observatoire des abonnements a Internet au Maroc—Situation à fin de juin 2023, https://www.anrt.ma /sites/default/files/publications/observatoires_anrt_-_le_memo_-_t2-2023.pdf?csrt=156 93344966533434027 (accessed September 17, 2023).

7. For a comparative analysis of romance and love on Facebook across the Middle East, see Friedland et al. (2016), and Sotoudeh et al. (2017).

mobile connection in the past decade, WhatsApp has become the most popular messaging application among the youth in Morocco, and phone dating applications like Tinder are ubiquitously used for chatting, dating, and casual sex (Hayes 2019, 33, 43).

The mobile phone (in Arabized French, *l-tilifun portable*) began to spread in 2001, when competition among telecommunication companies made it increasingly affordable. Especially in the working-class neighborhoods of al-Azaliyya, where landlines are poorly developed, the mobile phone was the first home telephone communication device. Initially, families had a shared mobile phone, but in 2008 the young people I knew owned at least one, often with several SIM cards, depending on the special deals on offer and their varying social needs. The mobile phone has been rapidly incorporated into youth communication and sociability (Ilahiane 2019, 2022; Kriem 2009; Menin 2018). In 2010, the number of mobile phone subscribers reached twenty-seven million (85 percent of the population), and in 2015 mobile phone subscribers rose to about forty-four million. In 2014, some of the young women I knew could navigate on their smartphones and now have online platforms such as Facebook and WhatsApp installed on their mobiles. In turn, smartphones, the number of which reached fifty-four million in 2023, have contributed to the growth in the number of internet subscribers.[8] In addition to facilitating existing relationships, mobile phones have made possible novel dynamics of socialization and encounter. My female interlocutors would receive text messages from unknown numbers sent by men hoping that a female stranger would reply and engage in conversation with them, a practice also described by Maya Kriem (2009). Flirtatious games developed from this practice could evolve into sexual encounters (Carey 2012), but my interlocutors generally preferred on-phone relationships with young men they knew or had previously met in chat rooms, Facebook, and matrimonial websites. As has happened in other Muslim countries (Brinkman, de Bruijn, and Hisham

---

8. Agence National de Réglementation des Télécommunications, Observatoire de la telephonie mobile au Maroc—Situation à fin juin 2023, https://www.anrt.ma/sites/default /files/publications/observatoire_anrt_-_mobile_-_t2_2023.pdf?csrt=52067932363572 73368 (accessed September 17, 2023).

2009, 80; Costa 2016b, 204; Hijazi-Omary and Ribak 2008, 161–62; Walter 2021), digital technologies, including mobile phones, were often blamed for weakening parents authority over their children, increasing divorce rates, and changing the dynamics of female-male relationships (e.g., facilitating both premarital sex among young people and cheating between married couples). Hsain Ilahiane (2020, 197) reports that his Moroccan interlocutor claimed that "there are 70 Satans between a man and a woman and the mobile is number 71" to underline the widespread perception of mobile phones as perilous devices. Ilahiane (2019, 2020) also argues that mobile phones, as a means for creating new forms of gender switching, enable users to maintain social order and restore patriarchal morality.

A Religious Time in a Mundane World

During the warmer months, when the longer days prolong the rhythms of social life, a crowd fills the streets of al-Azaliyya in the chaotic swarm of merchandise, stalls, and the loud *sha'bi* music of the emigrants' cars with Italian and Spanish number plates that inundate the town in summer. The radios of the yellow cabs (*petit taxi*) that run back and forth across town play loud pop songs, or, depending on the taxi driver's religious feelings, the recorded Qur'anic recitations and CD sermons that increasingly fill the "ethical soundscape" (Hirschkind 2006) of the town. Young people promenade in same-sex groups of girls and boys exchanging flirting gazes (*nkkan*) in a subtle game of seduction. Women dressed in the colorful *jellaba* (the traditional loose-fitting outdoor dress with wide sleeves and hood) walk side by side with the fashionable young women and girls who have started wearing the veil in the wake of the Islamic revival.

The Islamic revival—or, more precisely, "the Islamic awakening" (*al-sahwa al-islamiya*)—is a movement that has characterized Muslim worlds since the 1970s and 1980s. In Morocco, different revivalist currents have contributed to the re-Islamization of the individual and society, promoting the purification of Islam through a move away from "traditional" practices, the remediation of the relationship between God and the believer, and the centrality of individual responsibility (Zeghal 2008; Spadola 2013). The encounter between global revivalist Islam and Moroccan

Islam, historically marked by Salafi rationalism and Sufi mysticism (Eick-elman 1976), should be situated within the recent history of Morocco and in relation to the peculiar position of the Moroccan king as "com-mander of the faithful."[9] From the early years of his reign, King Hassan II (1961–99) struggled to establish and maintain the monopoly of the re-ligious and political spheres. In 1977, during the so-called Years of Lead, he promoted the policy of Arabization of state education to undermine the basis of critical thinking that had formed generations of left-wing po-litical activists that challenged his regime (Vermeren 2006, 75). This fa-cilitated the penetration of Islamic ideas and influence in universities and high schools, which began to compete with socialist ideology. Unlike the nineteenth-century *salafiyya* that gained momentum within the national-ist movement, the groups that emerged as political actors during the 1980s represented a real political opposition to the monarchy and became the target of its violent repression (Slyomovics 2005; Zeghal 2008; Daadaoui 2011).[10] Among the emerging political actors of the period, Sheikh Ab-dessalam Yassine (1928–2012), the charismatic leader of the outlawed Jus-tice and Spirituality movement (*al-'adl wa al-ihsan*) (Tozy 1999; Bouasria 2015), formulated a radical critique of the existing political order.[11]

9. The king in Morocco is not only a political figure as the political leader of a com-munity of believers (*umma*). As a descendant of the Prophet, he is also the guardian of Islamic values and the spiritual leader of the kingdom, which he rules in the name of God.

10. The term *salafiyya* derives from *salaf*, the first three generations of pious an-cestors in the history of Islam, comprising the companions of the Prophet Muhammad. Beginning in the eighteenth century, *salafiyya* rested on the various religious reforms undertaken over different historical times and contexts that advocated the return to the written texts of the Qur'an and the Sunna (the words and deeds of the Prophet). Under the influence of the two main centers of religious reforms, Arabia and Egypt, the *salafiyya* developed in Morocco between the nineteenth and twentieth centuries.

11. In 1974 he addressed a letter to Hassan II, in which he overtly challenged the sacredness of the king and the legitimacy of his religious authority as the commander of the faithful, calling for his repentance. Subsequently, he was arrested and put into a psychiatric hospital without trial for three and a half years. Kept under house arrest until 2000, he continued writing books and delivering his message, which he then carried on until he died in 2012.

When Hassan II initiated the political opening up of the political sphere in the mid-1990s, he co-opted the moderate section of the Islamist movements by legalizing the newly born Justice and Development Party (PJD), which is the only legalized Islamist party in Morocco, in order to exclude from the electoral competition the dangerous competitors like Abdessalam Yassine (Daadaoui 2011).[12] One of the several modern revivalist movements in Morocco, the PJD emerged from an alliance of individuals with a range of religious and political views as "an unprecedented and atypical actor on the Moroccan political stage" (Zeghal 2005, 146). To accommodate its claims with the rules of a multiparty system, the PJD calls for the moralization of public life, by turning religion into social and political ethics, instead of overtly proclaiming an Islamic state. The strategy proved to be successful, as the PJD was able to position itself as a main political party throughout the 2000s elections, and since then has increased its political influence until 2021, winning the 2011 and 2017 parliamentary elections.

During my fieldwork, the presence of the "Islamic awakening" in al-Azaliyya was palpable in the spread of mosque reading groups and religious associations, which have all revived people's interest in religion in their everyday lives. A street corner Islamic market of CD sermons and Qur'anic recitations, booklets, and religious books is available. On satellite television, the proliferation of religious channels, where TV preachers call for a return to "true Islam," has made religious knowledge and teachings available to everyone (van Nieuwkerk 2008; Hroub 2012; Moll 2010, 2020). Another trait of the Islamic revival in al-Azaliyya has been the "sartorial reform" (Masquelier 2007, 58) that has brought about multifaceted Islamic

---

12. Under increasing pressure from the international press and the human rights activists who denounced the state violations, as well as because of diplomatic and economic interests, Hassan II initiated a process of political liberalization (1991–99) that culminated with a constitutional reform (1996) and the creation of "le gouvernement d'alternance" (1998–2002). For the first time in postcolonial Morocco, the opposition parties that formed the *bloc democratique* (Istiqlal, Union socialiste des forces populaires, and Parti du progress at du socialism) entered the government led by the exiled socialist leader Abdelrahman Youssoufi as prime minister.

fashion. Colorful veils and modest clothes have carved out their own space among the modern boutiques and the stands of secondhand European shoes and garments traded by migrants between southern Europe and Morocco. Zakia Salime (2016, 63) dates the emergence of an Islamic dress style in Morocco back to the 1980s in two main versions: the Islamic fashion inspired by the Iranian Revolution (the women's long jacket buttoned at the front, with a pair of long and large pants underneath) and the mandatory headscarf that covers the chest and the typical Moroccan jellaba. Looking at the family pictures in the homes of my female friends in various districts of the town, I was surprised to see that most of them were unveiled up to the late 1990s and early 2000s. The Western-style trousers, blouses, skirts, and miniskirts that they were wearing in the old pictures were replaced by colored veils and modest clothes hiding the female body from the gaze of men. Together with Morocco's long and rapidly evolving fashion handicraft tradition and industry (Jansen 2014), young women's sartorial practices tap into other centers of fashion influence. As has happened in other Muslim settings (Moors 2003; Osella and Osella 2007; Abaza 2007), Saudi garments such as the *khimar* (a long veil that extends over her top) and *'abeya* (the long, loose robe with wide sleeves covering the whole body) have been incorporated into local ways of dressing modestly and fashionably.

As this overview shows, in the past few decades the intertwining of historical and contemporary dynamics—marked by the town's encounters with transnational migration, globalization, neoliberal reforms imposed by the Structural Adjustment Plan (1983–93), and the increased influence of the Islamic revival—has turned al-Azaliyya into a place full of contradictions and possibilities. Within this bustling town, where worldly and spiritual invitations interweave in complex ways, we will see unfolding the social and intimate lives of the young women this book tells about.

Settling on the Field

I first encountered Morocco in 2008, when I spent three months in Meknes to study the Moroccan dialect, immersed in university student life. After a few short trips to al-Azaliyya, I moved there in 2009 to study the travels that Moroccans undertake to faraway countries, but I ended up working on how they journey through their intimate worlds on a quest for love. As will become clear, this shift is inextricable from the ethnographic relationships I have developed during my fieldwork during 2009–10. Especially when it comes to an exploration of love in a context where premarital dynamics belong to the social spheres of secrecy, the researcher's positionality, the permutations of the ethnographic encounters over time, and the anthropological knowledge constructed upon them (Rabinow 1977; Abu-Lughod 1986; Viswesvaran 1994) deserve close methodological attention. This is particularly true for a foreign researcher, a *gawriya* (a Western woman), as I was identified there, not acquainted with the subtitles of life there, and who did not fully master the Moroccan dialect (*darija*). Both native and nonnative ethnographers have to reckon with specific constraints and possibilities shaped by the shifting positionalities they come to occupy during fieldwork (Altorki and El-Solh 1988; Tsuda 2015), their contextual being seen as insiders/outsiders, and the closeness and distance they may experience in different ethnographic relationships. Beyond nationality, the ethnographic insight a researcher gets is also shaped by several factors such as class, gender, ethnicity, and social position, not to mention a variable degree of serendipity (Hannerz 2010; Fabietti 2012), a complexity that a feminist intersectional perspective captures better than a sharp native/nonnative opposition. In tracing my path into the field and the topic of love, I focus on the constraints and possibilities that have contributed to shaping my "situated gaze" (Haraway 1988) on such a slippery subject of ethnographic inquiry.

I settled in al-Azaliyya, thanks to the help of a respected university professor who found me a host family in hay el-Mounia, a lower-middle-class neighborhood, where I lived for some five months. Hay el-Mounia is located outside the ancient walls bordering the medina. One neighborhood born out of the inward migration of petits fonctionnaires and school-teachers, hay el-Mounia developed during the 1960s and 1970s, when a few lines of buildings began to fill and progressively replace the fields of olive trees. The neighborhood provides its inhabitants with all basic services (public schools, public steam baths, public ovens, and mosques). Along the lines of the three-story buildings that define a residential block (*bloc*), an administrative classification of the space within the neighborhood (*hay*), there are also clothes stores, beauty salons, dressmaker shops, téléboutiques (phone shops with coin-operated phones), and internet cafés (*cyber*). Once hay el-Mounia materialized the upward social mobility of diplomés with rural or humble backgrounds who could benefit from modern education, while today it is inhabited mainly by an aspiring lower middle class. The socioeconomic difference does exist within the neighborhood, but most of its inhabitants define themselves as *bin-w-bi*, to mean they are "in the middle" (neither poor nor rich) of the local class hierarchy. Some upper-class interlocutors perceive the neighborhood simply as low income (*sha'bi*). In winter, the cold climate drives inhabitants into their homes early. The heating is absent, and the front doors are locked at sunset. During the warmer months, in contrast, young men and boys stand around with their gangs until late, and their sisters and mothers go shopping with their female relatives and friends in the crowded streets of the medina or the main avenues of the town for their evening promenades. Even though residential proximity (*jora*) remains an important dimension in the construction of social ties, and women try to get on well with their neighbors, the older inhabitants of hay el-Mounia recall that in the past neighbors "gathered a lot" (*kay-tjam'o nas bzzef*), and that "people were close to each other" (*kano nas qrab 'ala ba'diyathom*). The sense that neighborly relationships have weakened over time is perhaps also connected with the mobility of its inhabitants. Some families who moved up the social ladder have relocated to residential areas, in the prestigious neighborhoods where the villas of cadres, professionals, and high state officials are located. On the other hand, many young people and families have migrated to Italy and return during the summer, when cars with Italian number plates multiply on the main paved roads and unpaved streets of hay el-Mounia. International migration, in turn, has brought about the social mobility of village families and individuals who have invested in small businesses and moved to the city.

Like many dwellers, my host family was originally from a village in the countryside and moved to al-Azaliyya when the patriarch, to whom we all would refer deferentially as 'Azizi (my darling/my beloved), began to work as a schoolteacher. By saving money, he could build a three-story building, where he now lives with his wife, Lella (lady), and his two un-married daughters: Ilham, aged twenty-six, and Leyla, aged thirty-five. The architecture of their home reflects the typical mixture of modern (big street windows with shutters) and traditional elements (inner courtyard and internal decorations with colorful tiles) that mark the new neighbor-hoods. 'Azizi's home has a bathroom with a shower, three furnished sitting rooms, a well-equipped kitchen with an oven, and a living room where meals are served and consumed around a small round table. On the roof-top, they keep a washing machine. Unlike 'Azizi and Lella, who have a pri-vate bedroom with a double bed, their daughters sleep on the sofas in two different sitting rooms. On the ground floor, there is a small apartment where one of 'Azizi's married sons, himself a schoolteacher, lives with his wife and his three kids, and the dressmaking shop set up by her daughter Leyla. Like 'Azizi's daughters, many women and girls in hay el-Mounia work within and outside the neighborhood as schoolteachers, civil ser-vants, or shop owners, while others are "just sitting at home" (*ghyr glsa f-dar*), as they say, meaning that they are not involved in formal jobs.

During the first two months of fieldwork, I spent my days in Leyla's dressmaking shop, watching Turkish soaps, practicing the Moroccan dia-lect, asking questions, taking notes, observing female clients coming and going, and waiting for something to happen. As the two sisters were very busy with housework and their business, going with Ilham to shop or run errands in the medina was our only leisure activity. Rarely did we meet female friends. My relationship with Ilham and Layla was facilitated by their command of English and French, respectively, and their mediation allowed me to get in touch with some girls, like Ghizlan, Sanaa, Amal, and others, who later became key interlocutors of mine, and who figure prominently in this book. Living with their family offered me a vantage point from which to observe the relationships between family members and enabled me to participate in their everyday routines. I could also get a sense of the gendered demands on my female hosts as soon as my position as the "special guest" shifted into an ordinary presence at home. As a girl, I became involved in time-consuming domestic routines such as preparing meals, cleaning house, shopping, and hand-washing dishes, which they considered female duties. Being part of a family (*'a'yla*), I was expected to respect the gendered practices that my hosts considered appropriate for a young woman, and this entailed limits on my comings and goings. My position as an unmarried *gawriya* alone placed particular responsibilities on my host family and me toward them. The expansion of my social world created tensions between the girls and me, and, when I felt that the surveillance of my relationships was undermining my research and well-being, I accepted the invitation of Hasna, a young woman with whom I had developed a friendship, to move to Rabi'a, to stay with her family for Ramadan.

Rabi'a is a low-income neighborhood located along the asphalt road that climbs up to the forests of the Middle Atlas Mountains. Old men in jellaba or *gandora* (traditional Moroccan gowns), their heads wrapped in turbans, sit in small groups in the shade of the olive trees while the children play football in the dirt field along the road. From the main road, a gravel path leads to the heart of Rabi'a, an intricate set of narrow alleys winding up and down a row of houses. During the 1950s, a few families built huts in Rabi'a, and gradually the area took shape as a squatter settlement for men and their families who had left behind their natal villages in the Middle Atlas Mountains and other regions of Morocco in search of a better life, or fleeing from famine and drought. Other families came from the countryside or the mountain areas to provide their children with a modern education, which was an important mechanism for upward social mobility. The oldest inhabitants cannot say when exactly they settled in Rabi'a and chronicle their arrival and that of the new settlers by referring to the Green March in 1975.[13] Only in 1992 was the neighborhood included in al-Azaliyya through a new urban plan.[14]

Rabi'a's geographical distance from the city center reflects the historical marginality of the neighborhood and its inhabitants, which results in a lack of prime-importance services, such as schools, public baths

13. Hassan II launched the Green March in 1975 with an impressive demonstration of around 350,000 Moroccans, in order to reoccupy Western Sahara, which was still under Spanish rule, and bring it under the unity of Islam and the Moroccan Kingdom.

14. Abdelmajid Zmou, Université Sultan Moulay Slimane, Beni Mellal personal communication, 2010.

(hammam), and public ovens for baking bread. Only in 1993 were two public fountains built, and, before running water came to the houses, women and girls used to fetch the water from the river for daily cleaning, cooking, and drinking. Two mosques provide literacy classes for women and, more recently, lessons of Qur'anic recitation for women, which has been the case for a long time in other parts of the city (see chapter 3). Compared with hay el-Mounia, only a few men are civil servants and schoolteachers, while the majority work as, for example, plumbers and mechanics, taxi drivers, retailers, shopkeepers, building-site workers, dustmen, and factory workers. Women and girls, too, contribute to family income, either by holding formal jobs or by participating in the informal economy organized within the neighborhood, selling homemade food and other handicraft products.[15] After having carried out the housework (e.g., cleaning the house, handwashing clothes, preparing the meals), women devote their spare time to cultivating relationships with female neighbors and friends. Although their networks are not limited to the neighborhood where they live, homes, alleys, and thresholds are the everyday sites of interactions and socialization where adult women and girls build their sense of self and their social worlds. Sitting on small wooden stools or the doorsteps in their doorways called *fum l-bab* ("the mouth of the door"), women and girls gather with close relatives and neighbors to chat and comment on the passersby while enjoying the evening breeze.

The social life in Rabi'a is intimately embedded within and continuously reshaped by the ties among its inhabitants and the everyday practices through which they gave birth to a community that continues to face social and economic marginality. People living in Rabi'a for generations feel they are part of a moral community that distinguishes themselves from the inhabitants of the modern and wealthy neighborhoods of al-Azaliyya, "where people live their lives on their own," as they say. Houses

15. One informal activity in which many women and girls are involved is handicraft decorations for jellaba, an activity that enables women and girls to earn a small amount of money respectably without altering the tempo of domestic work and childcare duties, as they can weave and knot colored silk-like threads to craft while watching their favorite TV program.

and their dwellers all along the same alley (*z-zanqa*) are connected and feel a relationship with each other. Many families in Rabiʻa are related to each other through interwoven kin ties, resulting from marriages amongst extended families and neighbors and breastfeeding (*radaʻa*, or Modern Standard Arabic *ridaʻa*).[16] The intricate interweaving of family and neighborly ties shapes women's perceptions of the spaces outside as a variable extension of their houses. Within the quiet alleys of Rabiʻa, women and girls feel free to step out dressed in pajamas or wrapped in a loose sheet to venture into the neighborhood out of sight of outsiders (*brrani*). They are aware that neighborly ties have loosened over time, but they say there are still good intentions (*baqy niya*), and that doors are kept open from dawn to sunset.

When I moved to Rabiʻa, I became part of a network of related families who were curious about the *gawriya* (Western woman) who tried to speak their language and was eager to learn about Moroccan "costumes and traditions" (*ʻadat wa t-taqalid*), as they put it. Hasna introduced me to her female cousins, friends, and neighbors, and soon I began to visit them autonomously. Fathers and brothers, male cousins and uncles were important presences, and with some of them I discussed several topics, from politics to love, although a respectful distance between us prevented them from speaking of love and sex at personal levels. I participated in the incessant flow of visits among relatives and neighbors, religious festivities, weddings, betrothal celebrations, birth-naming parties, and funerals that animated the social life there. Being part of their household also gave me a place in the neighborhood. Women and girls, who would initially refer to me, while talking with my hosts, as "that *gawriya*," started talking to

16. Milk kinship is one of the three types of kinship comprised in Islamic law, alongside blood (*nasab*) and affinity (*musahara*). Like the bonds established through marriage and filiations, breast milk has the legal power to engender kinship ties and marriage (and sexual) interdictions, but not descent or heritage rights. The four legal schools do not agree on the extent to which these should be applied (Altorki 1980), nor are the social practices related to milk-kinship the same everywhere; the latter vary considerably according to local contexts and social class.

me directly and inviting me for tea, to watch television or to do sport early in the morning. At times, the illusion of becoming "like a Moroccan"—as women and girls would say with pride—was crumbled by subtle remarks, which materialized the difference between us, including the fact that I could travel freely between Morocco and Italy, or the major freedom they assumed I enjoyed in my affective and sexual life. Having to reckon with distance and closeness was a constant dimension of my fieldwork (a point I discuss contextually in various chapters).

Girls and Love

In my host families' homes and within the relationships I have developed over time within and beyond the neighborhoods where I lived, the most important ties I created were with women and girls. Being a young woman made it easy for my female interlocutors to invite me to their homes to have tea or lunch, to stay overnight or even for a few days, and to travel with their families to visit distant relatives. With the young women, I shared their daily routines and leisure activities like watching television, surfing the Internet, promenading in the city center, visiting cafés and beauty salons, shopping in the new mall and the weekly secondhand Western clothes market, and meeting friends and lovers. Although, as we have seen, there is a palpable class difference between hay el-Mounia and Rabi'a, in terms of materiality and possibility, the young women in this book also share important similarities. The neighborhood is one central space where female interlocutors build their gendered and social identities. Compared to the older generations, the young women who study and work spend much time away from their homes, and have more opportunities to create bonds of friendship with both girl and boy friends beyond the boundaries of the neighborhood. As gossip spreads quickly, young women are careful not to be seen alone with male strangers in order not to compromise their reputation (*sum'a*). Beyond the smoky all-male cafés dotting the main avenues, there are several gender-mixed socializing places where young people can meet, flirt, and date, such as *laiteries* (in Arabic, *mahlaba*), snack bars, ice-cream parlors, internet cafés (*cyber*), and a recently built shopping mall, a place where consumer and romantic desires often interweave.[17]

Spending time together within and outside the home and the neighborhood, I could develop relationships of friendship and trust with some girls, and this gave me access to their viewpoints on family ties, love, and marriage. Right from the beginning, when I was collecting data on migration, I found myself involved in conversations about love or, as with Najat, about love troubles. Initially, I was confused by my interlocutors' different discourses on love. Some girls like Najat would talk passionately about love, even in gender-mixed groups of friends, sharing with both male and female friends their love troubles. Whereas for Najat being veiled did not preclude the yearning for premarital love, other religiously committed girls like Ilham claimed adamantly that love outside of marriage is forbidden (*haram*), remarking that, unlike in Europe, in Muslim countries a man should ask for a woman's hand, and afterward the marriage contract (*'aqd*) is signed before a notary. Some young women who were hurt by love claimed bitterly that "love does not exist in Morocco (*ma kensh l-hobb f-l-Maghrib*)." Some other girls said that they did not invest much in love and preferred to be pragmatic instead of relying on an unstable sentiment doomed to "run out in seven years," as a local saying goes. I realized that such diversity in part reflected the diverse religiosities and gendered subjectivities present in al-Azaliyya. Following these young women over time, I also worked out that silences and secrecy practices allowed them discreetly to navigate the gendered and social norms shaping their everyday world, making for a more nuanced reality than is suggested by normative discourses (to be discussed in chapter 5).

I returned to al-Azaliyya in 2010, determined to refocus my work on what by now had emerged as an important preoccupation. I rented a room in Rabi'a, while continuing to visit friends and key interlocutors in hay el-Mounia and other neighborhoods. I came back again in 2012, 2013, and 2014 for shorter periods, during which I could visit and spend

17. Originally, the term *mahlaba* referred to shops where fresh dairy products could be bought, but since the 1990s these shops have become also gender-mixed places where people can eat, either standing or sitting, milk pudding, fruit juices, cakes, and yogurt.

time with some of the young women in this book. Since then, I have continued to stay in touch with some of them and follow their lives through phone calls, WhatsApp, and Facebook. I collected data through surveys in hay el-Mounia and Rabiʻa regarding people's living arrangements, age at marriage, family composition, consumption, and lifestyle. I carried out in-depth interviews and informal conversations in English, French, Moroccan Arabic, or a combination. To grasp the generational dimensions of the intimate dynamics in the town, I worked with women of different generations asking questions on love and marriage that most of them judged naive, funny, trivial, or even impertinent. I also included interviews and conversations with women of different classes and cultural backgrounds. The tape-recorded interviews I collected were of paramount importance because they provided information on the informal and formal dynamics of marriage proposals, courtship rituals, and wedding ceremonies. However, I felt that the most important things I learned came from sharing time with the girls with whom I built up relationships of closeness and friendship.

As an ethnographic object, "love" itself is difficult to observe from the outside, and even problematic to define for my interlocutors. Even though occasionally I was asked to act as a go-between at romantic encounters, or I spent time with couples in cafés, love is impossible to participate in. "Love" emerges ethnographically in this work in and through the specific tensions and imaginative possibilities it stimulates in my interlocutors' lives. While this book makes extensive use of women's narratives, these were shared in specific contexts, often as reflections on the ambivalent qualities of love or commentaries on concrete occurrences. Over the years, I listened to young women's gossip and thoughts, their joys and concerns, and was often asked for advice. I could also follow how occasional encounters developed into years-long on-phone liaisons and then ended. I observed secret love relationships, including online relationships with a stranger met on a matrimonial website, evolve into marriage, thanks to subtle maneuvering. I stayed close to a friend during the difficult decision to end an uncertain relationship with a loved one in favor of a marriage proposal from a suitable candidate. I was witness to the dynamics triggered by an unplanned pregnancy regarding the unmarried couple concerned and their families. Crucially, talking of love was often the point of departure for addressing other dimensions of life that my interlocutors considered of paramount importance: their anxieties about their conjugal futures, but also their concerns as to how to live a fulfilled life within and beyond marriage, how to combine family and a career, how to pursue their desires without hurting their loved ones. In this sense, the prism of lives and relationships I accessed through these ethnographic encounters provides a glimpse into the desires, hopes, and anxieties of a generation of young women who have lived the consequences of deep social and political changes in Morocco. In the next chapter, I begin to trace how the experience of mass education, delayed marriage, and the search for a professional career have all contributed to the emergence of new gendered selves and aspirations.

2

A Sense of Self

"For us, life is more complicated than that of my mother and grandmother," Hasna said, reflecting on the differences between her everyday experience and that of the previous generations of women in her family. "I don't want to say it was simple for them," she continued. "It was not, but they knew how their lives were supposed to unfold. Today we have more opportunities, but also more doubts. We have to live with these contradictions."

Hasna was twenty-seven when she shared her thoughts in one of our many conversations during my stay in Rabi'a. A bright and sensitive young woman, Hasna is the first girl in her family to pursue a university education. Both her grandmother Naima and her mother, Nura, have never attended school, and both got married early. Naima was married off at twelve and, during her lifetime, was a wife, a mother, and a tireless worker. Nura, who got married at the age of sixteen, takes pride in being the mother of five children. Compared with her illiterate mother and grandmother, Hasna said that she felt she has more opportunities, but she also gave voice to the gendered and existential tensions running deep through her life. Still unmarried and in a precarious job, she wondered whether her desire to fulfill her aspirations to study and have a professional career was worth it. This painful thought made her confused about her innermost desires.

Hasna's experience reflects broader changes that have occurred in al-Azaliyya in the past fifty years, connected with growing female access to education,[1] changing ideals of conjugal and family life, and delayed

1. Public education was introduced in Morocco after independence (1956) and helped narrow the gender gap in education. See "La Femme marocaine en chiffres: tendences d'évolution des caractéristiques démographiques et socio-professionnelles,"

47

marriage.[2] Even though the level of female illiteracy remains high at a regional level, in the past two decades growing access to education in urban areas and the spread of the ideals of the nuclear family have changed how young women like Hasna think about themselves and how they imagine their conjugal futures.[3] Naima and the older generations of women in Rabiʿa described their gendered self as intimately embedded within their birth family and the female worlds in which they carry out a large part of their social lives. For Naima, marriage was a painful fracture in her life as a *bnt*—a term that contextually indicates daughter, girl, virgin, unmarried woman—that marked the social transition to adulthood (D. H. Dwyer 1978; Davis 1983). Naima's daughter Nura could "choose" her prospective husband through secret exchanges, but she was not in love with him initially. She expected love to come after marriage as the marital couple developed mutual trust (*tiqa*), affection (*hanan*), and understanding (*tfahum*). While marriage remains central in the definition of womanhood in central Morocco, Hasna invested the marital bond with new expectations and strove to combine different, and, at times, conflicting, desires and aspirations.

The comparison between Hasna and the previous generations of women in her family traces the emergence of new desires, which reflect broader societal transformations of intimacy and emotional investment from the birth family to the marital bond. However, this generational shift does not delineate a linear passage from "arranged marriage" to "pure love," from family/social constraints to individual freedom in marriage

---

Haut-Commissariat au Plan, https://www.hcp.ma/downloads/ (accessed August 22, 2023).

2. The average age of marriage in Morocco, which was 17.5 for women and 24 for men in 1960, had risen to 25.8 and 31.4 in 2014 (in urban areas the average age of marriage is 26.4 for women and 31.2 for men; RGPH 2014). In the Tadla-Azilal region, the average age of marriage was 28.8 for men and 23.4 for women in 1994 which rose 30.6 for men and 24.3 for women in 2010 (HCP 2019).

3. For a regional overview, see *Monographie Régionale De Tadla Azilal Direction Regionale de Tadla Azilal*, September 2010, Haut-Commissariat au Plan, https://www.hcp.ma/region-drta/docs/Publications/monographie%20regionale%20tadla%20azilal%202010.pdf (accessed September 18, 2023).

choices (Gidden 1992). As I will show, a closer examination of the possi-bilities and existential anxieties that accompany such moves reveals both continuities and ruptures in the ideas of love, marriage, and family ties across generations. Specifically, I concentrate on how Hasna, her mother, Nura, and her grandmother Naima have crafted a sense of self *within* their web of family and affective ties by navigating personal aspirations and social expectations. Looking at their affective worlds as "an area of life where people invest their emotions, their creative energy, and their imaginations" (Carsten 2004, 9), I demonstrate that love and family ties are vital sites where Naima, Nura, and Hasna embody relational modali-ties of femininities, at times enacting desires that defy conventional ideals of family connectivity and male authority. The ways these women situ-ate themselves within and reflect upon the webs of affective and power relationships in which they are intimately involved reveal the centrality of relationality and connectivity in their sense of self (Abu-Lughod 1986; Joseph 1993, 1999). While highlighting continuities in the ways Hasna imagines herself and her affective worlds, I seek to unpack the ambiva-lence running through her sense of self by interrogating her feeling that life is more complicated for her generation than it was for her mother and grandmother. My focus on "intimate selving" (Joseph 1999)—namely, the process of becoming a self within intimate relationships that is trans-formed throughout one's life and is shaped by social and cultural dynam-ics—is combined with close attention to the questions of desire (Joseph 2005; Sehlikoglu 2021), ambivalence (Kondo 1990; Abu Lughod 1990), hope (Moore 2011), and creativity (McNay 2000). Drawing on feminist theorizations, I conceive subjectivity as a site of multiple interlocking dif-ferences (De Lauretis 1990, 116) and concentrate on how my interlocutors "constitute a sense of self through several, often mutually contradictory, positions" (Moore 2007, 17). As Henrietta Moore (2011, 22) argues, while subject positions are produced within the workings of power, difference, and ideologies, "hopes, desires and satisfactions can never be fully cap-tured by forms of regulation." The attention paid to desires, aspirations, hopes, and ambivalences enables a grasp of the complex coexistence of the conflicting desires and self-images inhabiting Hasna's sense of self. I sug-gest that this is connected with ambiguity and multiplicity existing *within* a "single" self (Kondo 1990, 45), but also with the tensions between diverse images of femininity available in contemporary Morocco, which require navigations between, and combinations of, increasingly conflictual female roles and aspirations. By attending to the moral, affective, and imaginative dimensions of the self (Moore 2011), I trace the socially sanctioned paths of self-fulfillment and discipline that shape Hasna's sense of self. I also show how her quest for love opens up a space of self-reflexivity that leads Hasna to rethink herself as a gendered subject in relation to family and society.

Naima: "Once you marry, you become an outsider"

One day in the summer of 2009, Hasna decided it was the right time to introduce me to her grandmother Naima. Following her through the narrow lanes of Rabiʿa, I arrived in front of the two-story house where Naima lived with her children. As Hasna knocked at the iron front door, we heard a voice from inside: "Who is it? (*shkun*)?" "Someone close to you (*qarib*)," Hasna said.[4] Naima's unmarried daughter Hakima came to welcome us. Like the oldest houses in the neighborhood, her house is organized around a central open-pit room—"the center of the house" (*wast d-dar*)—surrounded by four rooms, a small kitchen, and toilet facilities. This housing arrangement reflects the ideal of the extended family. Natural light and fresh air flow through small windows and the internal slit that pierces the walls of the house in the central hall. This slit is called *l-ʿayn d-dar*, "the eye of the house." Around its eye, the house is built like a human body, a space of mediation between inside and outside, human and nonhuman (Pandolfo 1997, 25–26). On the ground floor, Naima lives with her unmarried daughter, while, on the first floor, her son established a separate

---

4. *Qarib* means "near" in physical and geographical terms as well as indicates closeness (*qaraba*) in terms of real or assumed kins. The plural form *qrab* indicates family, friends, and people revolving around the domestic circle. As Dale Eickelman (1981, 93) notes, "Closeness . . . can develop through cooperation with nearby households, mutual herding arrangements, kinship and patronage relations, and other forms of mutual interest."

household after his father died, and "the eye of the house" connects the two flats. In Rabi'a, housing is an ongoing process: houses are extended, lifted, enhanced, or split, mirroring the life trajectories of their inhabitants and the shifting housing arrangements for married couples. In her sitting room, Naima narrated her story, setting her vicissitudes against the backdrop of major historical events in Morocco. Her narrative offers insights into her sense of self and her views on marriage and family ties.

Born in the early 1940s in a rural village in the region of Marrakech, Naima never attended school, and life had been hard for her since childhood. Female work was essential for the survival of farmers' extended families: women woke at dawn, ground the flour, baked bread, cared for livestock, cut the wild grass, and collected wood for the fire, among other tasks. Rolling her eyes, Naima sighed. "When I was six, my daughter, my father died—may God have mercy upon his soul," she said. "My brother and I moved to my maternal relatives' home. Our neighbor, my mother's closest friend, asked for my hand when I was six. My mother accepted." Naima adjusted the big colorful pillow she was lying on and looked into my eyes. "I was so young. I didn't know where to sleep. I slept where I wanted," she said, to note that she was such a little girl.

Naima was expected to have no say in her choice of husband, but whenever her fiancé came to visit her home with her brother, her reaction was harsh: "He'd come to us, and I'd to say to my brother: 'Why have you brought him? What do we want from him?' I carried on telling my brother off, may God bless him! Talking to him was *hshuma* for me, so I didn't speak to him at all. I didn't speak to him until the wedding day (*'ars*)." Beyond the meanings of "shame" and "shameful" (Namaane-Guessous 1991, 7–8), the term *hshuma* evokes a complex set of meanings and emotions comprising both an internal state of shyness, embarrassment, and conduct oriented toward values of propriety, modesty, deference (S. Davis 1983, 23), including the denial of sexuality and lack of interest in love.[5] Naima's avoidance of her fiancé was thus also a gendered embodiment of moral dignity.

---

5. See also Lila Abu Lughod's (1986) discussion of *thsham*.

Like many peasant women of her generation, Naima was married off soon after she reached puberty. "I had my period and a year after I got married," she said, resorting to a common narrative convention (S. Davis 1983, 28). "I didn't want to get married." Naima paused and smiled broadly, then began to laugh, leaning in toward me to touch my hand. She looked into my eye and grinned. "I was scared, my daughter, I didn't have any idea about marriage. Do you understand? I was just twelve, how could I? He was the first one for me, and I was the first one for him." Marriage was and continues to be essential to the social transition from being a *bnt* to a *mr'a* (adult married woman), with the acquisition of the social roles of wife and mother (Dwyer D.H 1978, 61–62; Žvan Elliott 2015). Marriage also transferred a woman's legal control and guardianship (*wali*) from the birth family to the husband (Charrad 2001, 32).

The two families agreed upon the bridewealth (*sdaq*) that the groom (*'aris*) should pay, and the wedding was celebrated. Naima received a dowry (*dhaza*) comprised of traditional Moroccan clothes and ritual gifts (*henna*, sugar loaves, salt, and olive oil). By that time, Naima and her maternal uncles had already moved to al-Azaliyya, whereas her fiancé was working in the Casablanca province. During the first part of the wedding, the *henna* party, female relatives and friends decorate the bride's hands and feet. Naima's marriage followed the communal ceremony called *fatiha*: relatives and neighbors gathered at her home to witness the verbal offer and acceptance of marriage between the two families, in the presence of Islamic scholars reciting the fatiha, the first Sura of the Qur'an. After the guests had been fed, the celebration continued in the groom's place in the Casablanca's province. Finally, the bride (*'arosa*) and the groom were left alone in *laylat l-dokhla* (literally "the night of the entrance"), which alludes to the bride's defloration and the public display of the girl's blood—a powerful demonstration of the bride's virginity on which both the honor of her family and the groom's sexual potency symbolically rest. This also marks the bride's entry into her husband's house. "You become an outsider (*barraniya*) because their [the in-law] home is not like yours," Naima said, giving voice to a widespread female understanding among the women of her generation of marriage as a painful fracture in the female trajectory toward adulthood. Leaving her natal home and the female world that had shaped her life as a *bnt*, the bride enters a new household, where she occupies the lowest position, under the severe supervision of the mother-in-law. Although marriage enabled Naima's bodily and symbolic transformation into a woman and gave her a position in society as a wife and a mother, she never referred to the marital bond as a source of emotional fulfillment.[6] Throughout her life, her birth family has remained a fundamental source of material and emotional support.

"I wanted to go where the people I loved were"

Marriage marked the passage from the bride's natal group to that of her husband's, but, Naima stressed, not to his "origin" (*asl*): "I have an origin. My origin comes from my father—*asl* is such an important thing! . . . It's the same for the bride and the groom. I follow my father, he follows his father."[7] Situating her origin within her father's lineage, Naima affirmed her social identity as distinct from that of her husband (consistently with patrilinearity principles) and emphasized the importance of her birth family over the marital bond.

Even though Naima rooted her origin and social identity in patrilineal kinsmen, she never described them as a source of "intimate selving" (Joseph 1999). After spending a year with her husband, Naima began traveling between her natal village and al-Azaliyya join her maternal uncles and her brother, who remained her main source of love and support over the years. Naima told me the following episode to illustrate her loving bond with her brother: "My husband was away at his natal village and had left me under the protection of my brother-in-law. My uncle Amir

6. During the early years of marriage the marital bond was—and, in certain contexts, still is—considered fragile, but having children, especially males, increased the bride's status, becoming vital sources of support for the future, when she could enjoy greater freedom and independence (Maher 1974; Mernissi 1979; S. Davis 1983; Rassam 1980).

7. A central concept in classic anthropology of the Middle East, *asl* means "root," "origin," "foundation," "noble title," "trunk of a tree" (H. Geertz 1979, 346), and the "blood of origins" in the genealogical sense (Abu Lughod 1986).

arrived to bring me to al-Azaliyya because my brother wanted me with him for his wedding. My brother said, 'I will not celebrate my marriage without my sister!' Do you understand?" Naima asked proudly. "After the wedding," she continued, "I remained with my brother for six months in al-Azaliyya, so my husband sent my brother-in-law to bring me back to my natal village, where he was awaiting me." When her husband returned to his workplace in Casablanca, Naima did not visit him for seven months. She recalled: "His brother came by force and stayed at the *bled*." Listening to her grandmother's self-narrative, Hasna smiled in complicity. "By force (*bzzez*) means that Grandma didn't want to go back to her husband, so he had to send his brother to bring her back to him." Spelling out Naima's words to make me understand, Hasna remarked: "You see? Grandma would spend long periods away from her marital home." In the first years of marriage, mobility was an essential means by which Naima dealt with the stress of a conjugal life far away from her relatives.

"Six months after the king's return," Naima said, "I gave birth to my first daughter in my natal village."[8] Although the political future of Morocco was still unstable, and several political and social forces were involved in a struggle for power (Hibou 2006), the return of Mohammed V marks an epochal event in people's historical imagination. "Two years later, I gave birth to Nura, Hasna's mother," Naima told me. "I had two daughters and my beloved ones were far away, so I said to him, 'I want to go with my uncles to al-Azaliyya.' He stood up and left with my uncle." In a context of dislocation of family ties, Naima succeeded in incorporating her husband into her family web. "I had my uncles and my brother here," she said. "I wanted to go where the people I love were. I've grown up with them since I was young." For Naima, living close to her brother and her maternal relatives was more important than being with her husband. She left her village in the late 1950s. Moving to al-Azaliyya was a meaningful

8. Morocco formally gained its independence from the French Protectorate on March 12, 1956, with the abolition of the Treaty of Fez. Before that, the sultan, Mohammed V, had secured Moroccan independence with the Accord of La Celle-Saint-Cloud (1955) and returned to Morocco on November 16, 1955, from his two-year exile in Madagascar.

event in her life, marked in her self-narrative by a shift from an emphasis on patience to the active affirmation of her desires. Susan Schaefer Davis's (1983) definition of Moroccan women's patience not as passivity but as the capacity to endure and wait until the right moment to take action well captures Naima's way of reckoning with constraints and possibilities in her life.

In Rabi'a, Naima and her husband bought a plot of land, where they built their house, room by room. "Four years after the death of King Mohammed V [February 26, 1961]," Naima said, "I bore my first son. Soon after, many families came over." Newcomers were incorporated into the local community of Rabi'a, and women played a major role in this process by cultivating ties among female neighbors, exchanging visits and services, managing the informal economy, fostering children, and arranging marriages. Even though Naima did not consider working a female duty and expected her husband to provide for the family, she became known as a cook for weddings and celebrations. "I would pay for the electricity and the water," she said, "and I would buy something that I wanted, I'd buy something for my daughters if they wanted it, that's what I used to do." Her work was essential to the income of a poor family, but also a critical aspect of Naima's sense of self. Earning money also enabled her to pay long-distance visits to her relatives without having to beg her husband's permission or plead with him for money. She said: "If I wanted to go to any wedding party, I went without my children. I'd say to him, 'I want to go.' He'd say, 'Go.'" In other words, Naima has built her sense of self on independence—material and emotional—from her husband and on an enduring allegiance to her birth family. The episodes she told about her married life suggest that the relationship between Naima and her husband was imbued with trust, affection, and mutual respect. As an old woman, Naima could take pride in her position as the mother of several children. She was known as a storyteller and a devout Muslim, whose moral qualities made her a respected woman in the community where she lived. As long as Naima was healthy, friends, neighbors, and relatives dropped in and out through the red iron door of her house that was open from dawn to dusk.

Nura: "I wanted seriousness, and then love came"

Sitting on her doorstep, Nura would patiently sieve grain to remove the grit after washing it and then spread it out on a mat on the forecourt of her house to dry in the sun. The wheat comes from the dry land that her husband owns in his natal village in the countryside. Raised in Rabi'a from childhood, Nura belongs to an extended family rooted in the neighborhood since its foundation, whereas her husband Khalid left his family in the countryside at the age of nineteen to search for other sources of income and rented a room in Rabi'a.

Unlike Naima's, Nura's marriage was not arranged by her parents, but neither was it based on love. In her sitting room, recalling the dynamics preceding Khalid's official marriage proposal with her daughters and nieces, Nura laughed and said: "He tried to approach me and I would shout at him abruptly. Shameful approaching me in the street! I'd say to him: 'What do you want? Go your way (*sir f-halk*)!'" Skillfully pouring mint tea into our small glasses from a height of ten inches or more, she went on: "I wanted the seriousness (*l-m'aqul*)." Over time, Khalid's perseverance persuaded Nura of his serious intention. When he was able to provide basic subsistence for a wife, he discreetly approached Nura while she was sieving grain alone and asked for her hand in marriage. "I said welcome (*marhaba*). He went to my father to request my hand. I was sixteen and he was twenty-one." Nura paused and grinned. "I could not stand him, do you understand? But after he asked for my hand, my attitude toward him changed. After marriage love (*l-hobb*) came." Nura's words reveal specific ideas about marriage and conjugal love. Connecting marriage with seriousness instead of investing it with romantic expectations, Nura expressed the idea that love and affection develop over time, as the bond between the marital couple strengthens. The idea that love comes after marriage (*l-hobb tay-ji mn b'ad zawej*) is widespread among old women in al-Azaliyya, although some neighborhood women confided that they have suffered the lack of love in their married life. Nura's denial of interest in love is also part of the way in which she crafts a sense of herself as a respectful and virtuous woman. Her strong personality, recognized by many women in the neighborhood, is the other side of her sense of dignity—and Nura is aware that it helps her win her husband's respect and trust.

Nura's first years of conjugal life were difficult. After their marriage, Khalid rented a room until they could afford to buy a plot of land to build their house, where Nura gave birth to her first daughter, Hasna. Even though Nura lived immersed in her world of family and social relationships, her husband was very jealous and forbade his young wife to leave the house in his absence. Women and girls often claim that a man (*rajul*) should feel protective jealousy (*ghyra*) toward his kinwomen, and this feeling is regarded as a vital dimension of the gendered dynamics of love, honor, and intimate exchanges. "Jealousy" only partially translates *ghyra*'s semantic fields, which evoke an internal feeling that compels an individual to act or react to protect and defend his property, personal honor, or the sexual honor of his female relatives when this is challenged (Nevola 2015, 260). Nura was proud of her husband's jealousy, but did not want it to reduce her freedom of movement within the neighborhood and her web of social relationships. "One day," Nura said, "I went to my mother. I did not want to return home. My mother said, 'You will remain (segregated) at home.' You know? Being divorced was a real shame (*'ayb*)." Since the failure of a marriage is attributed to the woman generally, Hasna commented, being divorced was—and still is—a stigmatizing condition for the divorcee and her family. "My mother advised, 'You have to educate your husband a bit,' so I returned to the marital home and I became clever." Nura began bargaining for conjugal power with her husband, using irony, cleverness, and good humor without igniting open conflicts.[9] Hasna loves listening to Nura's skillful negotiations with her husband. "Tell her about the niqab, mom!" Hasna said, laughing. Nura grinned broadly and began: "When we were strolling in the medina, he wanted me to wear jellaba and niqab (face veil, both of them traditional dress for married women). But, as soon as his back was turned, I'd remove the niqab and say to him, 'You see? My nose is too thin and makes the niqab slip away.'" Hasna commented: "You

9. I refer here to Deniz Kandiyoti's (1988, 286) notion of "patriarchal bargain" to indicate the contextual set of rules regulating gender relations which both genders accommodate, but also contest and renegotiate (albeit women are generally in a weaker position).

see? It was through dialogue with my father that my mother managed to transform his character and soften his jealousy over time."

When Khalid was at work, Nura would spend her time with her female relatives, exchanging regular visits, sharing special dishes, and helping with daily duties. In addition to cultivating family bonds, female friendship and homosociality are critical aspects of her daily life, where she enjoys a large degree of personal autonomy and independence. When Khaled was not working, they would spend time together, as Nura remarked: "He does not go to cafés after a working day, no! He stays at home." Going to cafés with friends after work is an institutionalized form of homosociality in al-Azaliyya, and in Morocco more broadly, that continues after marriage and, at times, competes with conjugal intimacy and family time. Unlike the upper- and middle-class married couples of al-Azaliyya who take part in leisure activities like going to family cafés and restaurants, Nura and Khaled would spend their spare time at home, in the neighborhood, or traveling to the countryside. In the dining room, they would joke and laugh over glasses of mint tea surrounded by their children, relatives, and neighbors. As Hasna told me: "For my parents, love is not that of romantic movies. This is a kind of love you don't speak of, but you can feel it (*dak l-hobb lly ma-tay-tgalsh, walakin tat-hassi bih*)." When I asked her what she meant, she replied: "My father would never say to my mom, 'I love you,' when we are together in the sitting room, but you feel that there is mutual understanding (*tfahum*). You see it from his behavior—he laughs with her, he cares about her, they travel together to the countryside (*bled*)."[10] As Hasna's words emphasize, her parents' love differs from those portrayed in Hollywood movies, but their relationship is imbued with affection, respect, and geniality developed over the years of a good marriage. When a love scene came on television, they would exchange a glance and then lower their eyes, ashamed, before Khalid switched the channel. Within the vertical, intimate relationship between mother and daughter, Hasna had

---

10. The Moroccan term *bled* conveys a set of meanings, such as the country, the countryside, one's natal place. For a discussion of the term, see Geertz (1979) and Rosen (1984).

not only learned how to deal with conjugal and patriarchal power but also, as I will discuss, how to behave as a gendered moral subject.

Mothers and Daughters

There is an intense love between Nura and Hasna, and their relationship is full of care, affection, and good humor. Even though Nura did not attend school, all of her children went to high school or university, and she is particularly proud that Hasna has a university degree. Along with the strong love that bonds Nura and Hasna together, hierarchy and discipline are critical dimensions of their relationship. Even though Nura regards her daughters' education as a priority, she has always required them to contribute to the domestic work and look after their younger siblings. "Since I was six," Hasna recalled, "I learned to master domestic skills such as preparing tea, tidying up or sweeping away the dust that the wind brings inside from the dirt roads. My mother was very strict with me; she would beat me if I didn't help." Hasna's engagement with "kitchen culture" offers an entry point into the quotidian doing (and undoing) of gender within the mother-daughter learning process. Domestic work and food preparation are crucial sites where Nura has passed on to her daughter not only the fundamental knowledge to run a house and a family but also her vision of femininity embedded in everyday engagements with material culture. She is aware that her daughter's daily experience is immeasurably distant from her own in many respects: gender roles and social morals were already changing when Hasna was born in the early 1980s, and more and more girls have been to school and university and wish to work outside the home and the neighborhood. Nevertheless, Nura taught her all the practical skills that, in her view, turn a girl into a capable woman and thrifty housekeeper (*hedga*), qualities that the adult women of Rabi'a appreciate when they are seeking a bride for a son. Passed on from Nura to Hasna, the embodied knowledge related to domestic work, cooking, and baking is rooted in manual dexterity, sapient usages of ingredients, and culinary rituals in which girls in Rabi'a are judged by other women and learn to evaluate themselves. In this sense, "bodily praxis as a mode of knowledge" (Moore 1994, 71) reveals the ways gender imagination is embodied (and called into question) through everyday relations with the material world and spatial practices (Bourdieu 1998, 2000). Hasna's practical engagement with kitchen culture offers critical insights into the performance of female subjectivity, conceived, in Judith Butler's (1993, 1997) sense as the repeated corporal inscriptions, sedimentations, and ritualized practices enacted in accordance with the norms defining femininity and that brings femininity into being.

Among the female duties such as cooking and taking care of the home, baking is invested with gendered moral values and ideals of familiar "togetherness." The several circular loaves Nura and her daughters bake each day to go with the main meals the family gathers to share from a single plate around the table in the living room invoke the moral values of sharing, which, in their view, are part of being a Moroccan family and, in turn, make them a family. Considered to taste different from "the alley bread" (*l-khubs dyal z-zanqa*) available at the neighborhood's grocery store, homemade bread (*l-khubz dyal d-dar*) has specific gendered connotations. Imaginatively woven with the moral quality of the household, baking conjures up the image of caring women and devoted girls who nourish the bodies and souls of their loved ones with their work, time, and creative energies, instead of spending all day out of the home. This intimate relation between the socially constructed ideas of "proper" femininities and the "inside," the home and the neighborhood, emerges powerfully in the expression *bnt d-dar* (literally, "home girl," or "good girl") and in its moral contraposition *bnt z-zanqa*, which translates as "street girl" or "prostitute."

Precisely because of its nurturing and generative qualities, baking conveys the ideal of female domesticity among my interlocutors in Rabi'a—although women and girls greatly enjoy the numerous jokes that ridicule male expectations of female modesty and deference. Cooking and baking are central not only to the imagination and embodiment of normative femininities through which sexualized definitions of womanhood are inscribed into the body but also to the women's sense of self. Nura's and Hasna's everyday engagement with material kitchen culture provides them with culturally sanctioned pathways of self-fulfillment and social recognition, which reveal the interdependence between family members. They find pride and pleasure in cooking and baking for their loved ones.

Even though they are both tiring and time-consuming activities, they enact them as everyday acts of nurturing and sustaining a family, through which they turn a house into a home (hooks 1998). In other words, cooking and baking become central performances of femininity around which Hasna learned to build a sense of self in relation to intimate others. Far from being an unproblematic process, attention paid to kitchen culture also shows how her desire to adhere to the ideal of female domesticity triggered in her deeply ambivalent feelings in which pleasure and recognition interweave with strains. Especially when Hasna was working, domestic chores became a double burden for her. "If a woman works, she always has the burden of domestic work, while a man is not expected to contribute," she would complain. The ambivalence inhabiting Hasna's sense of self evokes the paradoxical character of "subjectivation," a process theorized by Michael Foucault (1975) as the simultaneous becoming of the subject and its subjection and further elaborated by Judith Butler (1993, 15; 1997, 83). In other words, through the everyday emotionally charged engagements with kitchen culture and family ties, Hasna embodies normative femininity that provides both socially sanctioned paths of self-fulfillment and discipline. Concurrently, Hasna's ambivalence becomes socially productive insomuch as it leads her to reflect on the increasingly conflicting gender roles, aspirations, and femininities available to the young women of al-Azaliyya.

Hasna: "I don't need any man"

Hasna is the eldest of four siblings. Unlike her brothers, who would sleep in the living room, she shared a private room with her sister. Although Hasna had little free time for herself during the week, being busy with both her job and domestic chores, her room provided a place for herself, where she could relax, surf the Internet, and talk on the phone with friends. After graduating, she was unemployed for a couple of years, despite trying hard to find a good job. "During this period I started surfing the Internet," she said. "Through the Internet, I could create friendships with people both in Morocco and abroad. Initially, I was very shy. I felt ashamed about talking and sharing my opinion with male strangers." Little by little, the protection of the screen helped her overcome her inhibitions, and she became friends with young Moroccans living in other Arab countries, with whom she shared her thoughts. Like many young people of al-Azaliyya, Hasna had long dreamed of migrating to Italy or Spain, which she envisioned as a paradise, but listening on the internet to the problems faced by young immigrants in Europe or the Gulf led her to change her mind.

In 2008, thanks to a scholarship, Hasna enrolled in a master's degree program. When I met her in 2009, she was working in an office. Although she was underpaid and unhappy with that job, she thought that busying herself was better than staying at home all day. "When you are at home, days are always the same," she explained. "Domestic chores, domestic chores, and that's it. My father doesn't expect me to contribute to the family income, but, for me, it's important to have a job. I can buy something for myself, the house, and my mother and sister." The job was also a means of freedom of mobility, which allowed Hasna to spend time away from tiring domestic routines and the neighborhood, meet people, and learn from new experiences. "I would go to work even on the moon," she often said jokingly.

Hasna's horizon of possibilities differs from that of her illiterate mother and grandmother, but the transformations she experienced brought new tensions into her life. While being educated and economically independent were essential dimensions of her sense of self, getting married was a central concern, too. In urban central Morocco, marriage remains a focal event in male and female social biographies alike. People often say that "marriage accomplishes religion (*zawej ikmml d-din*)," or "it is half of the religion (*zawej ns din*)," and remark about an unmarried woman nearing thirty that "she's missed the bus (*fat 'alyha l-kar*)." When Hasna visited her grandmother, Naima routinely asked her, with loving concern, "When are you going to get married?" Feeling the pressure, she regretted not having married when she was younger and wondered whether it was worth investing so much energy in her university studies, only to find herself unmarried and without a stable job at the age of twenty-seven. Hasna told me: "When I was studying at the university, I received some marriage proposals that I refused because I wanted to complete my university studies first." Hasna's intentional and aspirational putting off of marriage enabled her to pursue her education and search for a career, but then she was sorry to have waited so long and feared the implications of aging out of the marriageable age. Scholars have connected the globally observed delays in marriage and childbearing across the Middle East and beyond to delayed adulthood, with the frustrating condition of waithood, a phenomenon laden with specific gendered consequences (Inhorn and Smith-Hefner 2021). Žvan Elliott (2015) shows not only that it is hard for educated girls in rural southern Morocco to find a respectable and well-paid job in a precarious job market but also that they are depreciated in a context where young age and inexperience are valued in a bride, a condition exposing them to lifelong spinsterhood. Even though in al-Azaliyya, unlike its rural surroundings, female education is not regarded as an obstacle to marriage, delayed marriage creates anxieties in educated adult girls.

Marriage often emerged in Hasna's conversations with her friend Samira (whose story I discuss in chapter 7). "Samira advised me to actively search for a husband instead of waiting," she said. "Some university friends of mine found a husband on matrimonial websites, but I don't want to pay [in order to register] to find a husband, as if I bought one . . ." In a moment of sadness, Hasna said: "I do not need any man. I've always been alone, and I can stay alone for the rest of my life." With these words, Hasna asserted her sense of self as an adult woman independent of her marital status and discussed singlehood as an increasingly thinkable, and even viable, option for her future. Concurrently, she often wondered whether she could ever have a family, a husband, and children: "Are women really happy with their independence? I want to get married, to have a family. I want someone who will take care of me, and wait for me to come home from work, someone I can squabble with. I don't want to be alone." These thoughts brought Hasna pain and suffering, not only because of the social pressures on girls to get married but also because she regarded being a wife and a mother as integral to her desires for, and imagination of, herself in the future.

Being highly educated and unmarried was not the only conflict that Hasna faced. Unlike her mother and grandmother, Hasna described love as a fundamental dimension of life: "As a teenager, I was always fantasizing about love. Of course! Every girl dreams of love and romance, but represses her desires because of family and social control." Unlike her mother, who expected love to come after marriage, Hasna aspired to a love marriage with an educated man with whom she could share ideas, interests, and projects, but she found herself at an impasse. "I do not wish a formal engagement (*khotoba*) without being sure that I'm in love with him," she said. On the other hand, she oscillated between the desire to have a love relationship and the fear that this would lead her to live a se-cret life and lie to her family. "I do not want to date," she said once. "If a man has a serious intention, he should come to ask for my hand. Accord-ing to Islam, an unmarried couple should be engaged [to date]." Aware of the social consequences of breaking a formal engagement, she added: "The problem is that you should be sure about this person. If the girl breaks the engagement one time, it's OK, but if she does so more times, people start gossiping; they say she is not good, she is difficult, et cetera. It's always the woman's fault." Although her sense of uneasiness about family and social control over a woman's body and behavior is explicit, Hasna experienced the affirmation of her desires simultaneously as her right and as a betrayal of her loved ones. "Sometimes, I feel as if I have two heads," she said. The local expressions "having two heads (*juj rios*)" or "one thousand heads (*alf ro'os*)," whereby Hasna gave voice to the conflicting drives that pulled her in different directions, evokes a local theory of the subject conceived of as internally plural, situational, and riven with conflicting drives (Rosen 1984). Etymologically, the notion of identity (*huwiya*) includes the pres-ence of "the other" (*huwa*, the "he"), thus evoking a continuous movement against the immobility of the subject. Inhabited by traces of alterity (Pan-dolfo 1997), the carnal self (*nafs*) is considered to be drawn by multiple desires and instincts that should be dominated and integrated through the development of '*aql*, translatable as "reason" or "rationality" (S. Davis and D. Davis 1989, 6, 47–49). Crucially, Hasna's ambivalence goes beyond the *nafs-'aql* dynamics. Far from being framed as a tension between personal desires and social constraints, her quest for love opens up a space for self-exploration that brings to the fore the competing self-images inhabiting her sense of self: as a dutiful daughter, and as a young, educated woman who wants to control her personal life. This process involves a reflection on herself in relation to her kins and the place she occupies as a woman in the society where she lives.

Brotherly Love and Its Ambiguities

A sense of ambivalence ran deep into Hasna's relations with her brothers as well. In particular, she felt that while being the eldest daughter gave her authority over her brothers, she lost part of her power over them, especially since they came of age, and she often lamented their controlling behavior over her comings and goings. One day, while we were going to the city to run some errands, she recounted that her ten-year-old brother had seen her alone with a young man: "We were sitting on a bench in a public garden, just talking, when I realized he was staring at us." Hasna paused and rolled her eyes, then went on: "When I arrived home, my mother asked me with whom I had been. She knew everything! Do you understand? He had reported to my mom that I was with someone." Hasna's little brother did not inform his father or older brothers, in order to avoid their possible violent reactions. Afterward, Hasna learned from her friend that her brother had approached him, asking why he was alone in the company of his sister. When he replied that he was just a university friend, the little boy did not believe him and reported to his mother what he had seen. Commenting on how Hasna's little brother had proudly faced him, the young man approved his reaction as a socially appropriate expression of masculinity and remarked: "He has *nafs*"—an idiomatic expression indicating one's innate worth and self-respect (Rosen 1984, 34).

This type of love, based on protection, love, and control, which girls experienced within the brotherly bond, is not only central to the reproduction of patriarchal connectivity (Joseph 1994, 2005) but it also often contributes to setting romantic expectations for them around boyfriends and husbands and their ways of assessing their emotional reactions to jealousy and control.[11] Hasna, in contrast, expressed her uneasiness toward

11. I return to this point again in chapters 4 and 7.

her little brother's controlling behavior as a legitimate expression of love, to which she counterpoised equality, respect, and mutual trust as essential dimensions in a love relationship. Calling into question her brothers' role as "guardians of her honor," she commented sarcastically: "You see, my dear, what a patriarchal society is? Even my youngest brother can control me. This made me realize that I have always followed their rules." Following "their rules" meant, for Hasna, accepting male authority over her and her adherence to local gendered ideas of "proper" femininity.

Crucially, Hasna's insights into the intricate ways in which love, power, and protection intersect in brotherly ties stimulated a reflection on the place she occupies in her family. The discovery that she has always followed familial/societal rules made her aware of familial control over her intimate life as part of the broader patriarchal and gender ideologies in Moroccan society. Framing family ties as primary ground for the reproduction of this patriarchal system, Hasna said that women, too, support and contribute to inculcating differential morals and education into their children by using a double standard to evaluate male and female sexual behavior: "My older brother has had many relationships. My mother would like him to get married, but tolerates his relationships as part of a young man's natural needs, whereas she does not want me to be seen with male friends." While Hasna's brothers loitered with friends after school, her mother did not want her to go out unless she had errands to run or university lectures or work to go to. Whenever she saw her daughter preparing to go out with some friends or colleagues, she warned her: "Don't go to the cafés with those people, other people will start gossiping." As Hasna remarked, her mother trusted her but was concerned that the talk of others could cause trouble for her. While I concentrate more squarely on the question of transgression in chapter 5, I wish to remark here that it would be a mistake to represent Hasna's relationship with her brothers only in terms of power and control. For example, she was proud to render various services to her brothers, like cooking their favorite dishes at their request, which she considered a manifestation of care and affection toward them rather than simply a gendered duty. When the boys stayed a long time in the kitchen, she scolded them by asking ironically: "Step out! Are you a woman?" With her spatial activities and utterances, Hasna reiterated the local imagination of masculinity's constitutive connection with "going outside," in the public space, and femininity's connection with the inside, and unreflectively inscribed sexualized oppositions upon social spaces (Bourdieu 1998). Hasna often took the example of her grandmother's loving relationship with her brother to underline the importance of brothers in a woman's life, as they remain, at least in theory, responsible for their sisters throughout life. "In the case of divorce, widowhood, or a woman's conflict with her husband," she said, "brothers have to provide moral and economic support throughout their sisters' life. This is why women get the one-half share in the inheritance of their brothers." Hasna's everyday experience illustrates brothers' and sisters' mutual enmeshment in the ongoing relational shaping of themselves as embodied and gendered selves (Joseph 1994; 1999, 113–40). However, far from being a harmonic dynamic of mutual shaping, it reveals the complex and ambivalent qualities of brotherly love and the ways emerging desires and sense of self led her to call into question gendered modes of love and intimate attachments embedded in family relatedness and connectivity.

Generations of Change

A focus on the ways Naima, Nura, and Hasna craft their sense of self within their family relationships offers insights into the continuities and ruptures that inhabit the affective and social worlds of three generations of women in a poor neighborhood of al-Azaliyya. It evinces the centrality of relationality in their creative making, embodying, and contesting of gendered selves, as well as in shaping their desires and aspirations. As we have seen, each of these women thinks of herself not just as an autonomous subject independently of their loved ones, but as both embedded within and distinct from a web of family relationships, where power and love, care and control, interweave in complex ways (Kondo 1990; Joseph 1994, 1999). For Hasna, as for her mother and grandmother, being part of a family entails a "mutuality of being: persons who are members of one another, who participate intrinsically in each other's existence" (Sahlins 2011, 2). Family ties provide the members with mutual gendered duties and responsibilities, as well as with a place in the world of social relations in which they live.

Under the chronic conditions of financial insecurity that mark women's lives in the poor neighborhoods of al-Azaliyya, the family supplies protection, nurture, reputation, and security. Family members also manage important transitions in people's life trajectories and are imagined as a source of material and emotional support throughout their lives.

While highlighting the embeddedness of the self within their web of family relationships, I have also shown how these women have always negotiated their desires and aspirations by reckoning with the variable sets of unfreedoms and possibilities available in different historical times. Even though Naima upheld the ideal of the husband as the provider, she was proud of her economic contribution to family income and emphasized the independence from her husband this granted her. Being economically independent was part of her moral dignity and sense of self, but it did not mean unlimited freedom. Naima lived her life as a pious Muslim, a devoted wife, and a respected woman in the neighborhood where she lived. Patience and endurance, more than resistance and rebellion against the gendered and social norms of her time, enabled her to survive hardships and to affirm her desires. Her daughter Nura bargained (Kandiyoti 1988) with conjugal power with irony, cleverness, and dialogue to expand her personal space for autonomy vis-à-vis a caring and jealous husband. Even though she imagined a different future unfurling for her daughter, based on education and a career, she transmitted to Hasna the gendered practical skills she considered essential for becoming a wife. The quotidian embodiment of this gendered knowledge passed on across generations provides Hasna with meaningful pathways of self-fulfillment and contributes to shaping her vision of what a woman is and what taking care of intimate others means. Within the vertical relationship between mother and daughter, Hasna has embodied normative modalities of femininity through her practical engagement with kitchen culture. Concurrently, her access to vast "imaginative horizons" (Crapanzano 2004) has enabled her to cultivate new aspirations for her intimate and social life that mark critical ruptures with the previous generations of women in her family. Reflecting on herself as a gendered subject enmeshed in family webs of affections and attachment—and the discipline and gendered domestic habits—Hasna scrutinizes the web of love and control infusing her family ties and interrogates the intimate workings of what she calls "patriarchal society." In particular, Hasna's sense that life is more complicated for her generation exposes how broader socioeconomic changes in Moroccan society have created not only new possibilities in girls' intimate and social lives but also tensions and contradictions that are difficult to handle.

My emphasis on social change notwithstanding, I mean neither to obscure the complexity of the lives of adult women nor to trace a linear trajectory of change. Social change manifests itself in Morocco as a temporally and spatially complex phenomenon involving different regions and social strata in specific ways. Both Naima and Nura came of age in a rapidly changing Moroccan society, but their impoverished background, lack of education, and early marriage prevented them from venturing into unconventional paths. The possibility of chatting with other young men on the Internet, the access to university education, and the search for a professional career were unattainable for them. On the contrary, Hasna grew up in a society where mass education, transnational migration to southern Europe, media technology, and women's work are all a significant part of her everyday life. She enjoys more freedom than Nura and Naima in the definition of her life trajectory, which leads her to question conventional ideas of femininity, and experiences new contradictions and tensions. Having pursued a university education, she has prolonged celibacy, which, together with economic insecurity, engenders existential anxieties about her conjugal future, while her quest for love triggers moral dilemmas because it collides with her family's ideal of femininity, both of which are integral to her sense of self.

Drawing on feminist theorizations of subjectivity as a site of multiple interlocking differences (Moore 1994, 2007; hooks 1981; De Lauretis 1990, 116), I have conceptualized Hasna's gendered self as being shaped simultaneously by several—often mutually contradictory—desires, imaginations, and discourses on femininities contextually available. I have explored modalities of agency and gendered subjectivity that involve patience (S. Davis 1983) and bargaining (Kandiyoti 1988) as tactical reckonings with patriarchal connectivity (Joseph 1993). As new desires and existential tensions have emerged in the rapidly changing setting of al-Azaliyya, I have also paid attention to how Hasna reflects on the complexity of her life and seeks to inhabit such complexity in unanticipated ways. Young women like Hasna seek to keep together competing desires, aspirations, and gendered imaginations to craft themselves and their affective worlds. Crucially, Hasna's quest for love, with the tensions it triggers, initiates a self-reflective process that interrogates the societal norms shaping intimate dimensions of her life. So far I have concentrated on schooling and professional aspirations as major triggers for change in Hasna's experience, but these dynamics also interweave with new imaginations of intimate life, subjectivities, and desires promoted by the "Islamic awakening." And it is precisely to the variety of ways in which young women engage with a revivalist vision of Islam to reimagine themselves and their intimate worlds that the next chapter is dedicated.

3

Reforming Desires

"God is the Greatest . . . (*Allahu akbar*)": the *mu'adhdhin*'s call to prayer echoed powerfully in Hasna's home. For a moment, everything paused. Hasna stopped separating the small pellets of the couscous steaming in a *couscoussière* over the meat boiling in the vegetable broth. Her mother turned off the Al Jazeera news broadcast she was watching. "God is the greatest," she and Hasna both whispered in soft voices. It was Friday, the holy day of worship for Muslims, and a flow of believers was heading to the neighborhood mosque. Hasna returned to the couscous that her family would gather to share from a colorful communal dish after the Friday prayer. Once finished, Hasna and her mother performed ablutions and, after fixing their veils, prayed in the sitting room. On the other side of al-Azaliyya, Ilham, my host's younger daughter in hay el-Mounia, lifted her hands off the sewing machine and turned the TV volume down, leaving voiceless on the screen the protagonists of the Turkish soap (*musalsala*) accompanying the rhythm of her work in her sister's dressmaking shop. She closed the shop shutters and climbed up to her home for lunch. Unlike government offices, private workplaces, modern stores, and supermarkets that stay open, most of the small shops of al-Azaliyya, including Ilham's, would remain closed after the Friday sermon or reopen in the late afternoon. Like Hasna, Ilham attended the mosque only on special occasions but would regularly pray at home. Friday afternoons were moments of rest, which Ilham would spend praying and reading the Qur'an. Friday was also special because she could watch *Star Academy*, the popular pan-Arab reality show where talented young people from various Arab countries compete as dancers, actors, singers, and other performers.

71

The two vignettes that begin this chapter draw attention to the complex coexistence of worldly and religious horizons in the everyday lives of the young women of al-Azaliyya. The rhythm of Ilham's working days, as well as Hasna's domestic routine, were shaped by *both* religion and television. The mosque and the satellite were central to the ways in which my interlocutors reimagined themselves as consciously Muslim. Using the mosque (*jam'a*) and the satellite (*l-parabol*) as two ethnographic entry points into young women's practical, imaginative, and affective engagements with revivalist Islam, I trace in this chapter the religious subjectivities emerging against the backdrop of the increased societal influence of the Islamic revival in al-Azaliyya. A focus on young women's discourses and practices around the mosque and the satellite reveals how they resorted to both worldly and religious vocabularies and imaginations to rethink their intimate and moral worlds. Discussing the impact of young Moroccans' exposure to global entertainment and TV cultures on their intimate and social worlds in the 1980s and 1990s, scholars have argued that globalized media consumption enabled young Moroccans to cultivate new orientations and expectations that challenged traditional values regarding sexuality, marriage, and gender dynamics (S. Davis and D. Davis 1989, 115–17, 1995; Ossman 1994; Bennani-Chraïbi 1994). In particular, Susan Schaefer Davis and Douglas Davis borrow Fatema Mernissi's image (1993, cit. in S. Davis and D. Davis 1995a)—"the mosque and the satellite"—to capture the encounter between "traditional" and Islamic cultural heritage, symbolized by the mosque, with the Western technologies and cultural products accessed via satellite television. As these authors (1995, 578–79) note: "Young people . . . seemed acutely aware of the contradictions between traditional and modern ways—between the mosque and the satellite." Compared with the situation described by these authors, the multifarious ways in which my interlocutors engaged with the mosque and the satellite, far from reflecting an opposition between "traditional" and "modern" ways, reveal the extent to which what is "modern" (*'asry*) and what is "traditional" (*taqlidy*) have been reimagined in the past few decades. In al-Azaliyya, "modernness"—conceived in Lara Deeb's (2006, 4) terms as "the state of being modern as 'modern' is understood in a particular context"—was no longer associated uniquely with the West. On the contrary, the search for an Islamic modernness has become a fundamental goal of certain strands of revivalist movements in Morocco and beyond. Central to the revivalist project, the reform of selves, desires, and sociabilities has contributed to the emergence of new imaginations of social, intimate, and political life.

Many women and girls in al-Azaliyya have engaged with an Islamic modernness by donning the veil, praying regularly, changing their dress styles and sociability, trying to learn more about Islam, or attending mosque lessons. Whether or not they prayed regularly, most young women I knew described the increased attendance of the mosque by women, including girls, as a recent phenomenon, one that reflects the renewed importance of religion in people's everyday lives. This change toward what my interlocutors described as conscious and informed ways of being Muslim was imagined and narrated as a break with the past, when people were "far from their religion," as they would claim. Concurrently, most watched a vast array of televised romances, soap operas and programs, including *Star Academy*. Against the backdrop of the liberalization of TV broadcasting promoted by Mohammed VI and the massive spread of satellite dishes in al-Azaliyya over the past fifteen years, new TV channels have contributed to reshaping young women's imaginations in unexpected ways.[1] Hollywood and Egyptian movies and Turkish soaps have brought powerful romantic expectations into the intimate and conjugal lives of young women and their mothers. Far from imagining satellite television simply as the counterpart of the mosque, however, my interlocutors

1. Mohammed VI's accession to the throne in 1999 contributed to important changes in the telecommunication sectors. Through the High Commission for Audiovisual Communication, the new king established in 2002 a legal framework for the liberalization of radio and TV in Morocco, culminating in the Audiovisual Communication Law (2004), which ended the state's monopoly and thus the number of radio stations and national television channels has increased significantly (Hibou and Tozy 2002). In the climate of political openness and freedom of speech promoted by Mohammed VI, television programs on 2M began addressing the issues of poverty, corruption, human rights violations, and government ineffectiveness, allowing ordinary people to speak into the microphone and express their views.

evoked it as a source of religious knowledge and authority. Through new religious channels and charismatic preachers' invitation to piety, satellite television has brought into young women's lives a renewed sense of, and a desire for, morality.

Attending to the variety of ways in which young women engaged with both the satellite and the mosque, my aim in this chapter is not only to take religion and the everyday in the same conceptual frame but also to trace how they provide grounds for self-making with which my interlocutors craft modern, moral, joyful subjectivities. In so doing, I do not set Islamic piety and normativity against the so-called everyday Islam, conceptualized as an opposition between neoorthodox practices and creative resistance to religious norms (Fadil and Fernando 2015, 65). Building on Deeb's (2015, 95) insight that Islam and the everyday should be thought about together, as two mutually constitutive aspects of people's lives, I show how young women creatively resorted to both religious and worldly vocabularies, ideas, and imaginations, as coexisting grounds of self-making and reflexivity. Looking at their becoming consciously Muslim, I begin by following my interlocutors into the weekly lessons at the mosque-reading group in Rabi'a. I examine how the neighborhood preacher involved women and girls inside and outside the mosque to bring them closer to what she presented as an authentic vision of Islam. Specifically, I concentrate on the teachings aiming at an "Islamization" of ideas and practices regarding marital love, sexuality, and family ties. Then I shift the ethnographic gaze from the mosque to the satellite to bring into focus how TV broadcasts were evoked in everyday life situations to reflect on changes in social and intimate life.

Finally, I move on to consider the variety of religious sensibilities, desires, and sartorial practices displayed by young women who did not adhere to the vision of Islamic femininity promoted by the participants in the mosque movement in Rabi'a, nor did they share the same ideas of love, marriage, and conjugality. While considering themselves religious, young women like Hasna and others regarded the neoorthodox interpretation of Islam promoted by the preacher as too strict. Considering themselves still young, they did not feel ready to change their modes of sociality, nor were they willing to cover their body from head to toe. Rather, they blended fashion and modesty in their style of dress and combined longing for both romance and piety in their media practices, thereby materializing the coexistence of religious and worldly desires in crafting new gendered selves. As I argue, their everyday practices cannot be framed—nor are understood by my interlocutors themselves—in terms of "deviance" from an "authentic" Islam, but instead reflect different understandings of what it means to be a young Muslim woman in contemporary Morocco. For young women like Hasna and the others we will encounter in this book, both televised romance and piety, along with fashion and modesty, are integral elements of their sense of self and intimate desires.

Consciously Muslim

Wearing a long loose robe, her head covered by a sober dark *khimar* (a long veil that extends over the torso), Saliha, a sixteen-year-old high school student, would go to the home of her close friend Hayat, a few blocks away, to rehearse some Qur'anic verses for their recitation course at the mosque in Rabi'a. Sitting together in the living room, the two friends listened to each other reciting the Qur'an and quoting the hadith (deeds and sayings of the Prophet Muhammad). They also chatted and laughed in an intimate atmosphere of deep conversation and amusement.

Saliha lived with her family in Rabi'a. She would often invite me for tea at her home or visit Naima's unmarried daughter Hakima to rehearse Qur'anic verses for the mosque lessons. Sitting in her living room at a table set for tea with jam, homemade bread, and dates, Saliha told me that three of her five siblings live abroad: one in Spain and two in America. "My eldest brother was the first to migrate to America," she said, "and then my sister followed him and married there." Saliha paused to take a sip of mint tea. "In America," she said, "he started attending the mosque and meeting Muslims from all over the world." In such a multicultural environment, her brother learned about what she called "correct Islam (*Islam sahih*)." I asked: "What do you mean by 'correct Islam'?" She replied: "Migrants abroad come to know Islam better than people in Morocco do because, especially in the past, religious practices were blended with local traditions and superstitions." Saliha's vision of "true Islam" evokes what Olivier Roy (2004) describes as "deterritorialized Islam": Islam purified from local tradition. Religious satellite broadcasts also contributed to a correct vision of Islam, as she said: "Today the situation has changed because women study and attend Qur'anic lessons, and even illiterate people can learn about Islam through satellite broadcasts." In addition to her brother's influence on her discovery of "true Islam," Saliha's religious path began during high school, thanks to her friend Hayat. "I went through a personal crisis," she said. "I felt a deep distance from my parents and peers, who were interested only in dating and having fun. Hayat invited me to pray regularly to find peace in my heart, so we started praying together at school." Saliha fixed her hijab and murmured: "You know? Sometimes you get along better with a friend than with your relatives." Saliha emphasized the distance between her vision of Islam and that of her father, whom she described as a conservative (*muhafid*) and traditional man (*taqalidy*). In becoming consciously Muslim, Saliha's faith finds elaboration through a revivalist vocabulary centered on the idea of "correct/true" (*sahih*/*haqiq*) Islam. This idea resonates with what Deeb (2006, 20), in her discussion of the Shi'i community in Lebanon, defines as "authentication": a move away from "tradition" toward an "authentic" understanding of Islam. Crucially, this process acquires a specific generational connotation as Saliha's discussion of the veil elicits. "I started wearing it at thirteen because my father made pressing demands on me, although he did not force me (*mashy bzzez*)," she made it clear. "Initially," she went on, "I did not want to veil (*ma kntsh baghiya*)! I was only thirteen. I did not know (*ma kntsh 'arfa*) the real meaning of the hijab, which I regarded as a traditional practice. Thanks to Hayat, I became aware of its religious meaning." Describing her decision to wear the hijab as an inner move from social/family pressure to the deliberate adherence to Islam, Saliha resorted to Islamic piety to mark a generational distinction and to affirm a sense of self beyond the embedded one.

Saliha's move from "traditional" to "true" Islam reflects a global gap, noted across different Muslim contexts and the diaspora, between parents and their children's correct Islamic practices (Rozario 2011; Menin 2011; Liberatore 2017). Islamic learning enabled Saliha to understand not only that God's will comes above male family instructions but also that she has her soul, for which she is responsible and on which can act deliberately.

Since then, Saliha has devoted herself to pious entertainment, changing her overall dress style and avoiding physical proximity with boys, including handshaking. Contrasting her lifestyle with that of her peers, she said: "Many teenagers want to follow Western fashions and lifestyles. They listen to love songs and rap music, which is full of swear words. But this is contrary to Islam because music has the power to affect human emotions!" Saliha abhorred rock and folk music (*sha'bi*) and preferred listening to sacred music, sometimes when it had no instruments. "I know my schoolmates regarded my view as 'too strict,' but you see? I am a people person. I love laughing, joking, and talking with others, but within the limits set by Islam." With her friend Hayat, Saliha would watch religious satellite broadcasts and search for information on Islamic websites, the Internet, and Facebook; they also attended the weekly lessons of Qur'anic recitation at the neighborhood mosque. These lessons, which I discuss in the following sections, provided women and girls with "correct" Islamic practice and, as we will see, encouraged them to aspire to reform their intimate and social worlds.

The Neighborhood Mosque Lessons

The mosque lessons (*dars*, pl. *darus*) Saliha, Hayat, and Hakima attend in Rabi'a started in 2010, as had been the case in other neighborhoods since the 1990s, and are part of the broader networks of mosques, reading groups, religious associations, and book markets animating the Islamic revival in al-Azaliyya. Wishing to deepen their knowledge of Islam, a heterogeneous group of twenty-five to thirty women and girls would gather in the mosque on Sundays at 2 p.m. to memorize the Qur'an and study the Sunna (the authoritative tradition of the Prophet Muhammad) under the guidance of Sumiya, an unmarried woman in her late twenties who works as a secretary. Many attendants are illiterate or have a low level of education, but there are also a few high school students and some more educated women. Whereas the majority wear the veil and jellaba, a few others wear a *khimar* and the face veil (niqab), covering their body from head to toe. Sumiya does not have any formal training but attended mosque lessons for several years in various districts in al-Azaliyya and is also part of a religious association in al-Azaliyya connected with the Islamist Parti de la Justice et du Développement (PJD). As Sumiya explained to me: "I promoted the creation of the reading group because I wished my neighborhood had one, too."

During the weekly lessons she delivered in the neighborhood mosque, Sumiya would call the attendees to prayer, invite them to recite the Qur'an, correct their pronunciation, and encourage them to improve. In the second part of the lesson, she would read some verses from the Qur'an, explaining their meanings in the Moroccan dialect so all the women could understand. The women listened to her and asked questions while the children ran around after each other and clambered onto their mothers' laps. Always smiling and speaking in a gentle way, Sumiya would link her explanations with the hadith of the Prophet and make extensive reference to popular culture and ordinary people's lives to demonstrate that Islam is a religion for everyone. Sumiya's teachings reflect the PJD's idea of an ethical civic society within an Islamic frame of reference and its emphasis on personal ethics in the formation of a community of virtuous citizens (Zaghal 2005). At the same time, she established clear boundaries between what is forbidden and what is permitted. Let me consider the question of the hijab. During a lesson, Sumiya said: "A woman should not veil because she feels obliged (*mashy bzzez*) or is searching for social approval, but rather because she wants to feel closer to God." Meanwhile, she presented veiling and dressing modestly as essential duties for Muslim women and drew a clear distinction between what she called the "true veil" (*hijab haqiqi*) and the "modern veil" (*hijab 'asry*), meaning a combination of the veil and tight-fitting clothes she associated with vanity and self-beautification. She clarified: "Islam requires the complete covering of the body, the arms and feet, with loose garments that cover the female body."

Central to Sumiya's preaching, the emphasis on personal ethics and piety contributes to delineating her vision of Islamic femininity. While the "pious self" has been examined brilliantly by Saba Mahmood (2001, 2005) and the scholars inspired by her landmark work, in this chapter I dwell on a less explored aspect of the Islamic revival: how piety is played out in women's intimate and marital relationships. Sumiya defined the family as the "bricks of society" and the foundation of the community of

Muslims (*umma*). "Good family ties," she said in a lesson devoted to this topic, "need unity and dialogue between the marital couple." After telling the group about the fundamental value of marriage in Islam, Sumiya added: "Today, family ties are weakening, and the divorce rate is increasing because our society is far from Islam." Similar statements, which I heard in different contexts, reflect and shape a sense of the present as a time of spiritual crisis that requires ethical reform. Women and girls listened carefully, nodding in agreement. "Islamic law and the Sunna," Sumiya went on, "regulate every aspect of marriage, starting with the selection of a spouse, which should involve not solely two individuals but also the family and the community. Boys and girls can get to know each other—this is *ta'aruf*—in the presence of a third party." Suddenly Sumiya's tone became serious: "The marital bond is weak when Islamic principles are not applied and when people care too much about wealth and appearance. Today, many families accept a marriage proposal tempted by the offer of a substantial sum of money [as a dowry for their daughter] without asking for information about the candidate and his family. Then problems arise." For Sumiya, people's focus on material aspects rather than the more essential factors is detrimental to the marriage. "Don't look at the visa or money," she advised, "but at the man's religious ideas (*afkar d-diniya*), his morality (*akhlaq*), his behavior (*tsarrufat*), and personality (*shakhsiya*)."

The care of conjugality and sexual intimacy is another critical aspect of Sumiya's teachings. Sumiya did not expect love between the married couple to precede marriage but understood that it happens, as young people have many opportunities to get to know each other. Addressing the unmarried attendees, she said: "Many young people get infatuated and commit sins, but if you felt there is pure love (*l-hobb nqi*) between you, you should speak to your parents and get engaged. Marriage prevents the young from engaging in illicit relationships, so widespread in our Moroccan society." In other words, Sumiya did not disapprove of premarital love a priori but instead condemned the illicit affairs it can lead to. Whereas she depicted premarital love as potentially dangerous, marital love and sexual harmony occupied a central place in her teachings. She insisted that married women should nourish love, dialogue, and mutual understanding by following the example of the Prophet. Smiling broadly, Sumiya addressed the adult women by mentioning a key figure in popular tele-vised culture: "I know you women like Mohannad, but you should know that the Prophet was a loving and caring husband!" Sumiya's evocation of the Turkish soap *Nour* (In Turkish, *Gümüş*) and its charming protago-nist Mohannad (starring Kıvanç Tatlıtuğ), made women and girls smile and laugh. Aired on MBC in 2008 in the Syrian dialect and subsequently dubbed in the Moroccan dialect on 2M, *Nour* was a very successful pro-gram that tells the story of Mohannad, a wealthy man forced to marry his cousin Nour, a poor village woman. Initially a submissive wife, Nour succeeds in establishing herself professionally and making her husband return her love. With the support of Mohannad, she runs a business and becomes economically independent (Jabbour 2017, 145–64). The relation-ship between Nour and her husband evolves into one based on romantic love between equals, which Mohannad displays in many ways, from gifts to verbal declarations of love.

When I asked Hasna about *Nour*, she said: "This soap created many problems. Wives started complaining about their husbands, and husbands became jealous of their wife's infatuation with Mohannan." In diverse Muslim contexts, *Nour* was depicted as a trigger for marital breakdown and a source of moral panic (Salamandra 2012). In Morocco, *Nour* was blamed for promoting "individual liberty, women's emancipation and au-dacity" (Skouri 2015, 359), and experts debated whether dubbing it in the Moroccan dialect enhanced its emotional effects and the deep identifica-tion it elicited (Miller 2012). Whereas public debates focused on *Nour*'s dangerous power to (re)shape women's conjugal expectations, Hasna high-lighted that this soap not simply aroused new desires but made them reflect on their married lives and express their frustrations with their husbands: "This soap offered a vision of conjugal love distant from the experience of many married women in Rabi'a. Do you know? In Morocco, husbands are not romantic with their wives. Often women suffer in marriage as they feel their husbands do not express their love by bringing gifts or saying, 'I love you.' Many men think they are not real men if they show love to their wives." In Hasna's view, this soap, more than igniting conflicts, encouraged the emergence of existing tensions connected to certain strands of mascu-linity and their everyday enactments in marital relations. Hasna paused and then added smiling, "In my view, love is essential (*l'amour rah shy haja daroriya*) to living together and having good communication (*tawasol*)."

Aware of the influence of *Nour* on neighborhood women and girls, Sumiya did not condemn it as immoral in her teaching but juxtaposed the figure of Mohannad with that of the Prophet and his romantic attitude toward his wife 'Aisha. In so doing, she offered a persuasive narrative in which the romantic imaginations and visions of intimate lives disseminated by Mexican and Turkish soaps are contrasted with the example of the Prophet and the correct practice of Islam as the solution, even to intimate tensions. Sumiya's engagement with popular culture enticed the attendees and instilled in them what she considered an "authentically" Islamic vision of conjugality. Let me report another example of Sumiya's endeavor to Islamize conjugal love. Criticizing those women who try to manipulate their husbands through magic (*siher*) to make them love and desire them sexually, she said: "There is an Islamic way to deal with your husband, and the Sunna provides important guidance. Don't go to the sorceress (*shuwwefa*)! Just rely on halal magic"—a term she used to refer to the practices that encourage conjugal intimacy and successful companionable marriage. "You women," Sumiya said, "are responsible for creating a climate of dialogue and mutual understanding within their marital homes." She offered some tips: "Don't be aggressive with your husbands when they come back home, talking about the problems with the children or money, because they have also worked all day and are tired. Be patient and discuss family problems at the right time." Touching on intimate dimensions of women's married and sexual lives, Sumiya advised them to take special care of themselves and their bodies so that their husbands would continue to desire them sexually instead of wishing to engage in extramarital affairs. Smiling broadly, she said: "When you women go to wedding parties, you are well dressed and perfumed, but you do not take the same care of your appearance for the sake of your marriage! When your husband comes home, you present yourself in pajamas after doing the housework!" Once again, her utterances made women laugh and smile because most could identify themselves with this scenario. Then, moving to intimate dimensions of married life, Sumiya said: "I know sexual intercourse can be a source of tensions, as men are more willing to have sex than their wives are, but sexuality should not be a taboo topic between a husband and his wife. If you don't feel like having sex, you should explain to your husband that you are tired instead of simply turning your back to him."

Speaking directly to the daily concerns of women and young women in Rabi'a, Sumiya defines an "authentically" Islamic interpretation of love, conjugality, and intimacy that marks a move away from tradition. Such an "Islamic way" diverges from the allegedly traditional discourses emphasizing female shyness in sexual life (see chapter 2) and the emancipatory visions of women's autonomy in marriage proposed by the Turkish soap. In the following sections, I discuss Sumiya's efforts to Islamize marriage by moving outside her official preaching at the mosque.

Islamizing Marriage

Sumiya tried to bring neighborhood women and girls closer to God by creating teaching moments during informal gatherings and wedding celebrations. I realized this when Saliha told me that there would be no lesson at the mosque because Sumiya had to perform religious music at a wedding celebration. When we arrived at the wedding and sat in a room where our hostesses served a meal, I asked Sumiya jokingly: "Is there no class today?" She answered, smiling: "We will do the lesson here!" I assumed that she was kidding, but when we went to the terrace crowded with women and girls sitting on the carpets, I realized that she was about to turn the wedding into an occasion in which she could deliver her teachings. After taking her place at one side of the room with the other women, Sumiya captured the attention of the wedding guests. "My sisters, welcome to this wedding!" she exclaimed. "This wedding is different from those with the band playing folk music and *shikhat* (the sensuous female singers and dancers) because we will celebrate the marriage with God." Sumiya then assured the participants that they would have fun by dancing, singing, and enjoying the party in the presence of God: "We meet in the presence of Allah and have fun because there is everything in Islam."

Sumiya's premises marked a sharp difference from the wedding celebrations I have observed over the years in both urban and rural contexts in the Tadla. Variously reflecting the spouses' families' wealth, social class, regional origin, and religious sensibility, these weddings included a variety of profane and sacred rituals, where locally defined "traditional" (*taqlidy*) and "modern" (*'asry*) elements mingle in complex ways. For most of the women and girls I knew, weddings are exciting, fun moments where unmarried women enjoy the possibility of beautifying themselves, dancing, interacting with unrelated young men, and, perhaps, meeting a potential husband. Most of my interlocutors appreciated especially those spectacular events, which are often celebrated in a rented lounge, lasting the entire night, during which the bride changes up to seven times into colorful dresses, including a Western white wedding dress (*la robe*) and an Indian sari, inspired by Hollywood and Bollywood movies, respectively, and special Moroccan garments. Although these dresses are rented, such weddings are expensive because of the presence of a band (*l-group*) playing folk music, the entertainment provided by the *shikhat* (sing. *shikha*, a female leader), and the rented venues and the catering for numerous guests.[2] This type of ceremony—marked by, for example, the ostentation of wealth, the presence of modern musicians playing licentious love songs, the men and women dancing together—was precisely what Sumiya condemned. As she explained: "Islamic wedding parties are simple, but simplicity does not entail a lack of fun! We'll have fun in Islamic ways!" Far from inculcating an atmosphere of austerity, Sumiya sought to orient fun toward a spiritual purpose (Bayat 2007; Nieuwkerk 2008; Harb and Deeb 2013) and proposed a joyful Islam. Having fun in "Islamic ways" entailed replacing folk music with religious music and organizing separate gatherings for women and men. As Zakia Salime (2016, 56) notes, "Until the 1980s, it was uncommon to see marriages celebrated with religious songs composed and sung by women for a woman's public. These newly reinvented women-only spaces and new ethics of sociability were articulated as the 'Islamic way.'"

2. *Shikhat* are sensual female professional performers who dance and sing for different audiences and at different types of private and public celebrations, from weddings and circumcisions to saints' festivals, among other festivities. Because of their sensual performances and interaction with unrelated men, *shikhat* are considered "loose" and "free" women; for a discussion of *shikhat*, see Kapchan (1996, chap. 7).

Sumiya and her group played the drums and sang religious songs to celebrate divine magnificence. After each song, a PJD activist would tell religious stories and comment on the importance of dialogue, respect, understanding, and mutual obligations between spouses. Let me consider one religious story (*qissa diniya*) told by an activist quoting Imam Sadiq: before leaving on a journey, a man ordered his wife not to leave the house in his absence. Since the woman's father was sick, she asked the Prophet for permission to visit him. The Prophet replied that she should obey her husband and stay at home. When her father's condition worsened, the woman asked the Prophet again for permission to visit her father, but the answer was the same as before. When her father eventually died, the woman's husband was still on a journey, so she asked the Prophet for permission to attend her father's funeral, but again this was refused. Once the father was buried, the Prophet informed the woman that, because of her obedience, Allah had forgiven her father's sins and her own. This story, which emphasizes the priority of the marital bond on the birth family and the wife's unconditional obedience to her husband, offers a different picture from the one we often get in studies of women's prayer and Islamic education circles, where the knowledge is argued as liberatory. While these studies emphasize the empowering qualities of Islamic piety and show how young women can challenge family male authority via appeal to "proper Islamic knowledge" or to "the higher authority of Islam or God" over their male family (Rozario 2011; Huq 2008), this story legitimizes very hierarchical relationships between husband and wife. A similar vision of marital relations contrasts with the cultural repertoires to which the older generations of women I met have long resorted to balancing uneven power relations between the married couple. Older women often connected their predicaments to the vulnerable position a bride occupies in the in-laws' household, the uneven power relations between the sexes, and the tensions between marital bonds and their birth family—all questions addressed in the classic anthropological literature in North Africa and the Middle East. In contrast, Sumiya framed such tensions, including sexual, in terms of misapplications of Islamic principles and, in affirming an authentically Islamic vision of conjugality, dismissed as "un-Islamic" alternative discourses to which generations of women in al-Azaliyya have long resorted to contain and challenge male authority on them.

Televised Romances and Passionate Preachers

During the wedding celebration, I learned that Naima's daughter Hakima, too, was part of Sumiya's group. Hakima, aged thirty-seven at the time, could only attend primary school, but, despite her poor education, she was intellectually curious and resourceful. She was a henna artist and a singer in marriage ceremonies before a prolonged illness put her life upside down. In this tragic moment of her life, Sumiya helped Hakima by taking her closer to religion. In the late 1990s, when they began to attend the mosque reading groups in various neighborhoods of al-Azaliyya, Hakima dismissed her fashionable clothes and makeup and put on a loose, simply decorated jellaba and a sober veil. Hakima was critical of her female kins' passion for romantic movies and soaps, admonishing that the devil (*shaytan*) was operating within them. Discussing both Western and Middle Eastern "impious" entertainment and cultural productions, Hakima said: "Television is negative because if young people watch a girl on television with her belly uncovered, everyone will want to go around with a bare belly." Hakima's concern that such programs stir a dangerous blend of aesthetic fruition and practicality (Taussig 1991) evokes the operative force of television—in other words, what television as a specific medium is thought to do by acting upon the viewer. While I agree with Hakima's ideas about the power of identification that visual and bodily engagement with the reality of the filmic stories wields on people, how young women interpreted, selected, and appropriated creatively competing televised invitations revealed more complex dynamics than she suggested (Abu Lughod 2005; Kottak 2016). My interlocutors would resort to mass-mediated stories to reflect upon the changing intimate and moral life in al-Azaliyya, as I begin to show through Hakima's and her niece Hasna's discussion of the successful Mexican soap opera *Guadalupe.*

Produced in Mexico (1994–95) and dubbed into Modern Standard Arabic during the mid-1990s, the TV series *Guadalupe: The Secret of Our*

Lives, starring Edith Gonzales, tells the troubled love story of Guadalupe and Alfredo, marked by the history of hatred and revenge between their respective families. After her father's death, Guadalupe lives with her impoverished mother until she marries Alfredo. Alfredo marries Guadalupe as part of his revenge before falling in love with her. Hasna said that Guadalupe was so successful and influential that, even in their waking lives, adolescents "absorbed" their heroine physically by mimicking her physical movements and style. Pointing out the emotional aspect of their involvement in this troubled romance, she added that never has a soap so enthralled Morocco's people—a common perception among my young interlocutors. "At the time," Hasna said, "I was in the early years of high school, and everybody was dating (*kul shy kano kay-sahbo*)." Hasna's nostalgia perhaps reflects the coming of age of a generation of girls who experienced growing access to education and gender-mixed sociality. Commenting sarcastically on her aunt's fervent religiosity whenever she invited us to stop watching romantic movies and TV serials, Hasna told me that Hakima was herself a passionate viewer of films and soap operas, particularly this one: "My aunt, like most people, would have never missed an episode of *Guadalupe*!" When I asked Hakima about this Mexican soap, I realized that her memory of it was associated with a bygone past of loose morality from which she had moved away. Depicting the past as a time of ignorance, Hakima said: "We would call shameful (*hshuma*) what diverged from our customs (*'adat*) without really knowing our religion. Even though something was shameful according to religion, people found it normal. We didn't know. But when we started watching religious satellite channels, we became aware (*wa'y*)." In becoming aware, the perception of morality shifted, as Hakima said, since people began to distinguish what is forbidden (*haram*) according to Islam and what is shameful (*hshuma*) according to social norms. Becoming consciously Muslim also engenders the sense of a split in the timeline, a temporal rupture infusing the present with new spiritual meanings and transcendent hopes.

Satellite television, however, is not only experienced as a reversed moral world or as a potential source of moral disorder but also as integral to how many young women I met narrated their engagement with Islam. Some of them, indeed, evoked the influence of satellite TV channels and, in particular, the new communicative style of charismatic televised preachers in stirring their involvement in Islam. The proliferation of sources of religious knowledge via CDs and cassettes for the recitation of the Qur'an or sermons and book since the 1970s and, more recently, the rapid development of religious satellite channels and other forms of mass mediation have all contributed to reconfiguring people's understandings and experiences of Islam (Eickelman and Anderson 1999; Schulz 2006; Hirschkind 2006; Moll 2012). This emerged in my conversations with Hasna and her friend Lina as they compared Islamic knowledge transmission in the Fridays' religious programs on national television with the enticing style of preaching of 'Amr Khaled. Like Hasna, Lina was a university-educated young woman aged twenty-six when we first met. The two friends often participated together in public competitions to become schoolteachers. In their experience, Islamic schoolteachers were conservative people unable to address topics related to students' everyday concerns. "National religious programs," Hasna said, "transmitted teachings far away from the problems people face daily. In contrast, 'Amr Khaled was able to motivate people to draw closer to religion. The way he speaks, the topics he discusses are engaging." Emphasizing the emotional dimension of her involvement in 'Amr Khaled's lessons, Lina added: "The way he recounted the life of the Prophet was so moving. Listening to 'Amr Khaled reciting the Qur'an or recounting the life of the Prophet, many people have felt moved to tears!" A university graduate in economics without any formal religious training, Amr Khaled delivered TV teaching successfully by touching on topics such as personal piety and family ties, the uses of the Internet and leisure, premarital romance, and dating. As with Sumiya's "pedagogy of persuasion" (Mahmood 2005), 'Amr Khaled's style of preaching promoted a nonpolitical message focused on personal salvation and piety as well as set out neat boundaries between what is permitted and what is unacceptable to "real Muslims"—for example, premarital sex and non-Islamic forms of entertainment such as drinking alcohol, clubbing, or using drugs (Moll 2010, 2012; Rock 2010).

The dynamics of intense emotional identification with other people's experiences, which his style reproduces in his viewers, are comparable to the melodramatic effects of soap operas in triggering a deep involvement with the protagonists' experiences. Such emotional identification has practical and productive effects, as Lina suggested: "It was watching his televised lessons that I realized how Islam is relevant to my life." Lina's words reveal the influence of religious satellite programs in deepening her understanding of Islamic ideas and practices. Similarly, Hasna emphasized how her involvement with Amr Khaled's teachings stimulated her to deepen her knowledge of the Prophet's life. She could learn more about love and marriage in Islam by surfing Islamic websites. During casual conversations, Hasna would tell me how the Prophet related to others or behaved in particular circumstances, or the intensity of the love he nourished for his wife 'Aisha. "'Aisha, after eating some meat off a bone," she said, quoting from hadiths collected in the Sunan an-Nasai, "used to pass the bone to the Prophet, who would place his mouth in the same place where hers had been. Likewise, when she offered him a cup of water, he would place his lips at the same place where she had drunk." For Hasna, the relationship between 'Aisha and the Prophet, learned through Islamic booklets, religious broadcasts, and websites, reveals the fundamental role of love in the Islamic view of conjugal life.

While Lina and Hasna loved watching 'Amr Khaled, their media practices were not limited to religious channels. Unlike Hakima and Saliha, who regarded televised romance and piety—and fashion and modesty—as incompatible, they would move eclectically from pious to worldly forms of entertainment, switching from Turkish soap operas to all-news satellite channels like Al Jazeera, the American movies on MBC, and Rotana Cinema. They did not consider watching romantic movies and soaps as deviations from Islam but simply as a time of leisure and diversion in their daily routines that coexist with their search for piety.

Hasna and Lina put on the veil in their mid-twenties, followed by many female relatives and friends in Rabi'a. "When we were adolescents, only a few girls in the town were wearing the veil," Hasna said. "You know? We were horrified at the idea!" she added laughing. "Old women wore the traditional Moroccan dress: jellaba and niqab. Women would wear the veil only after marrying, but girls would wear the miniskirt (*minijupe*)." Hasna paused before adding: "My father did not allow me to wear it, however!"

Thinking of that time, she went on: "Only very religious girls would wear the veil. Girls used to put the veil on and off contextually, for example, to go home after hammam [public steam baths] or to take the Islamic studies exams." She remarked that, especially during the hot summer days, she would think about wearing the veil: "In this heat, I would suffocate." Before deciding to don it, young women like Hasna perceived the veil as an unbearable burden, the materialization of very religious girls' piety and older women's practice. During my fieldwork, in contrast, they described it as a religious obligation, a way of feeling closer to God, a conscious and intentional choice, an object of fashion and beautification, or a combination of the above. Both Hasna and Lina would dress modestly, choosing garments that covered their body shape but wished to appear fashionable and elegant for a promenade in the town or a meeting with friends. They respected the vision of Sumiya, whom they have known since childhood as a real tomboy. However, they considered themselves too young to cover their bodies with wide clothes and dismiss their light makeup. Similarly, they did not regard dating as necessarily against religion, as Lina said: "You should meet a guy and get to know each other before engagement! It's not forbidden. But you should not meet alone in isolated places. We Muslims believe that there is *shaytan* [Satan] between the boy and the girl leading them to temptations and committing sins." Lina imagined dating as a way of getting to know each other before a formal engagement, which could be compatible with Islam as long as the physical distance is respected (I return to this in chapter 7). "Of course," she added, "it should not last long! Just the time to understand if the guy is serious and if you are compatible." Instead of resorting to abstract Islamic normativity, Hasna and Lina searched for ways of combining competing desires according to Islamic pillars. Next, I continue to explore the coexistence of different media worlds within my interlocutors' everyday life by returning to the story of Ilham.

An Ethical Sense of Beauty

Just like Hasna and Lina, after she graduated Ilham participated in numerous state entrance examinations to become a teacher in a state school, but she never succeeded because of, in her view, the widespread corruption and her lack of reliable social connections (*waseta*). In the meantime, she took a vocational course to help her older sister in her dressmaking shop. Ilham and her sister were gifted "modern dressmakers" (*khayata 'asriya*) who tailored both modern versions of traditional Moroccan dress and Western-style clothes like skirts, blouses, and coats. As we have seen, television accompanied the tempo of Ilham's activities, shaping her daytime; she especially liked Turkish soaps, which she watched while sewing clothes for her customers. Television was also a frequent reference in women's discussions of the models that clients want, and modest Turkish dresses (like long, elegant buttoned overcoats) figured prominently in the shop window. The customers would bring along their fabrics, bought in the medina, and a drawing of the dress they had admired in their favorite soaps or women's magazines such as *Femmes du Maroc*, requiring modest rearrangements of the original models. While the multifaceted Islamic fashion taking shape through women's and girls' everyday sartorial practices in al-Azaliyya is part of a global phenomenon (Moors 2007; Tarlo 2010; Tarlo and Moors 2013) irreducible to their engagements with satellite television, television, too, contributes to shaping my interlocutors' ethical sense of beauty.

Apart from working, shopping and running errands in the medina occasionally punctuated Ilham's daytime, offering rare opportunities for us to be alone and exchange ideas without her family. Unlike Hasna and Lina, who often discussed the topics of love and marriage, Ilham condemned the girls who engage in premarital romance. Whenever I tried to address the topic of love, she remarked severely: "Love [before marriage] is forbidden (haram) in Islam. Unlike in Europe, in Muslim countries, marriage is the only sanctioned union between unrelated women and men." When I asked Ilham whether she wanted to get married, she would reply simply by sighing: "*In sha llah*" (if God wills), thereby expressing her religious feeling and dislocating her agency in her future marriage onto greater powers. "Which characteristics are you looking for in a future husband?" I asked her once. She replied in a severe tone: "I am not searching for anything. I will be content with what God wants for me. I just want him to be religious."

Given Ilham's stern religious feelings, her attraction to Turkish soaps, and even more to *Star Academy*, puzzled me initially. The reality show broadcasted activities such as dancing and singing in public that Ilham considered immoral and from which she kept a moral distance—not to mention the idea that unmarried men and women could cohabit under the same roof and have love affairs. *Star Academy*, launched by the Lebanese satellite channel LBC (Lebanese Broadcasting Corporation) in 2003, had unprecedented success throughout North Africa and the Middle East and was routinely accompanied by debates about its (im)morality (Kraidy 2009b). During her lunch break, Ilham also watched the daily broadcast of the everyday life of the mixed group of unmarried male and female students whose adventures were followed by several cameras twenty-four hours a day. Over time, however, I came to realize that Ilham's fascination with *Star Academy* triggered in her complex dynamics of identification and disidentification. As a flight from reality and a mediated time-space for diversion, TV programs like *Star Academy* and romantic soaps filled her daily routines with exciting experiences that she did not want to live in her "real" life.

Ilham's fervent religious feelings and her media practices deserve our attention for the insights they offer into one of the many articulations of seemingly conflicting desires that inhabit the sense of self and imagination of young women in al-Azaliyya. Unlike Hakima, who discussed (satellite) television as a medium with specific intrinsic qualities, dangerously able to act upon people, Ilham did not think that religious feelings could be affected by her worldly, even "impious" media contents. On the contrary, she selectively appropriated and used televised images as a source of inspiration for her work and her self-styling. She liked Turkish fashion, which she considered a mixture of glamour and modesty. However, Ilham did not earn a real salary, as she would give a large part of the money earned to their parents. Nor did she have access to the glamorous headscarves and modest clothing available in expensive chain stores like the Turkish *Tekbir* (literally, "God is great") that has become increasingly popular in the big cities of Morocco (Guessous 2011, 217). When she had some spare time from shop work and housework, she sewed clothes for herself, taking inspiration from the models she admired on television or in women's magazines. She was proud of the elegant long, light-green Turkish over-coats, slightly narrowed along the waistline, that she had embellished with simple buttons and embroidered pockets. By sewing together imaginative materials and textures of the worlds not accessible to her in reality, Ilham created her pathways into them, interweaving religious piety, consumer-ist desires, and Islamic fashion instead of experiencing them as mutually contradictory. Like Ilham, most young women I knew could not afford to buy expensive clothes from the European and Middle Eastern chain stores in the Moroccan megalopolis, but they loved shopping for the cheaper, secondhand versions available in the weekly markets.

Through the creative mixtures of pious and fashionable elements, young women have shaped new Muslim fashion in al-Azaliyya. "Iqra on top, Rotana Cinema below (*l-fuq Iqra', l-taht Rotana Cinema*)" is the tele-vised image some Moroccan youths used to evoke the strident coexistence of apparently antithetical worlds in the self-styling of their female peers. Founded in 1998, Iqra is the first modern Salafi-oriented satellite channel that explicitly aims to promote a "conservative re-Islamization focused on individual ethical behavior" (Galal 2012, 20) and a modern Muslim life. Advertised by the controversial Lebanese pop star Hayfa Wahbi, Rotana Cinema was launched in 2005 to complement the vast array of Rotana channels for music videos, entertainment programs, and concerts. With this reference, Moroccan youths would ironically indicate those girls who match headscarves of brightly colored thick material with tight-fitting jeans to self-style as "fashionably modest" (Jones 2010). While this mock-ing image does not do justice to the aesthetic orientations that motivate young women, it gestures toward some of the new religious subjectivities and sartorial practices emerging against the backdrop of the increasing societal influence of the Islamic revival in Morocco. Far from being just a matter of surfaces, young women's sartorial practices reveal their under-standings of what is ethical and what is beauty. Intimately connected with the questions of agency and choice (Moors 2003, 52), and with evolving ideas of being both modern and religious, they uncover girls' endeavors to inhabit different worlds.

Inhabiting Different Worlds

Tracing the slipping of new religious horizons in the everyday lives of young women in al-Azaliyya, I have explored the different ways they engage in the ethical reform of subjectivity, sociability, and intimacy on the wave of the revivalist call to Islam. Since the 2000s, this phenomenon, which started in the 1980s (Salime 2016), has been not limited to Islamist circles, but is deeply embedded in my interlocutors' everyday worlds. Using the mosque and the satellite as ethnographic entry points into young women's ways of grappling with revivalist Islam, I have traced their changing perceptions of religion, conjugality, and modernity. Far from reflecting a neat opposition between West and East—and between "modern" and "traditional" ways—they have become both central to this process. Compared with the mid-1990s, when Susan and Douglas Davis tried to capture the encounter of modern and traditional ways, this shift reveals critical transformations in the evolving meanings of "modernness" against the backdrop of the growth of mass higher education, the increased influence of Saudi-financed Islamic training, and the developing of Islamic media (Eickelman 1992; Howe 2005; Spadola 2014). Starting with the mosque, I have emphasized the extent to which the mosque reading group in Rabi'a has opened up critical spaces of Islamic sociality, where women and girls have embodied new ethical and aesthetical practices and forged authoritative models of "Islamic femininity." Like Saliha and Hayat, they have developed a friendship from sharing the same spiritual path and have crafted joyful ways of being consciously Muslim. Following Saliha, Hayat, and Hakima into the social life of the course in Qur'anic recitation in Rabi'a, I have traced the ways religious activists like Sumiya promoted the ethical reform of women's desires and intimacies as one ground for promoting the Islamization of Moroccan society. As happens in other contexts (Piela 2011; Liberatore 2016), young women's engagement with Islamic piety enabled them not only to craft a sense of self beyond the embedded one but also to rethink gender roles and imagine an Islamic avenue to marriage. Concurrently, the path promoted by religious activists like Sumiya puts forward a normative definition of the female body, Islamic femininity, and conjugal relations that dismisses as "inauthentic" alternative ways of living Islam (Marsden 2005).

The powerful narrative proposed by Sumiya, which presents Islam as the solution to intimate and societal tensions, encounters and competes with the vast array of romantic imaginations disseminated by satellite television. Offering different images of modern gendered selves and intimate lives, satellite television provides imaginative resources through which my interlocutors reflect upon themselves and their affective worlds; it also provides the vocabularies by which they elaborate the changes they experience in their everyday life. In addition to romantic comedies, movies, and soap operas, religious channels and charismatic preachers have come to populate their homes, stirring the desire to deepen their knowledge of Islam. Precisely because satellite penetrates young women's homes with worldly and pious invitations simultaneously, satellite television emerges both as a new source of knowledge and authority and as a reversed moral world, a flight from reality and an essential part of its construction (Abu Lughod 2004). Whereas some pious women and girls condemn satellite television as "impious" formats of entertainment such as movies, soap operas, and reality TV programs as potentially dangerous, most girls I knew switched between religious and mundane cultural products. The media practices of Hasna, Lina, and Ilham bring into focus modes of engaging with the Islamic revival that blends fashion and modesty, and piety and romance. For most young women in this book, being religious and veiled does not preclude the desire to be beautiful, nor to experience premarital love and dating in an "Islamic way" (I point to which I return later in this book). Far from dismissing this blending as "inauthentic" or "un-Islamic," both televised romance and piety—and both fashion and modesty—emerge as variously coconstituted elements of my interlocutors' sense of self.

The coexistence of both worldly and religious horizons in their daily lives invites us to move beyond a sharp opposition between piety and the everyday that underlies recent debates (Fadil and Fernando 2015) and to focus instead on their various—and, at times, unexpected—intertwinings. The simultaneity of competing desires and aspirations in the sartorial and mediated practices (both religious and profane) explored in this chapter emerges even more powerfully in young women's quest for love.

While I have focused here on the emergence of new religious subjectivities and desires with a particular emphasis on ethics and aesthetics, in the following chapters I continue to discuss how the desire for piety and romance interweaves. Before I do, let me conclude this chapter by highlighting that my emphasis on "both/and" does not downplay the ambivalences and contradictions (Schielke 2009) surrounding young women's desire to combine competing desires and aspirations. As we have seen, the need to scrutinize and redraw the boundaries of bodily behavior and clothing that are considered acceptable according to Islam illuminates the complex, and sometimes uneasy, coexistence of consumerist desires, search for piety, and quest for romantic love. Their practices, however, invite us to see these young women as gendered subjects who creatively inhabit several distinct grounds of self-making and multiple subjectivation processes in their everyday lives. As a direct continuation of this reflection, I show in the following chapter how television and the mass-mediated stories it conveys are also central in the ways young women grapple with the dramatic transformations affecting their social and intimate lives. Tracing the coexistence of religious and worldly horizons in the romantic life of Ghizlan, I show that soap operas, by creating a deep emotional identification with the protagonists of the story, offer powerful metanarratives through which she can "emplot" the tensions running deep through her life. More broadly, in chapter 4, we will see how competing visions of modernness intersect with the ideas of love that are invoked by Ghizlan in her reflections on changing forms of intimate and social life in Morocco.

4

The Unpredictability of Love

"Without satellite television I would feel lost!" Ghizlan would exclaim while we were watching various TV programs in her room, ranging from news on Al Jazeera to Hollywood romantic movies and her favorite Egyptian soaps. Ghizlan was a university-educated, unmarried woman in her mid-thirties when I met her. She worked in a bank and, every evening before bed, she would choose her clothes and accessories for the next day, carefully matching her shoes and handbag with brightly colored veils. When she was a little girl, she dreamed of having a car, an office, and a good job. Unlike her classmates who flirted with boys, she was a teenager devoted to her studies. Recalling that period, she said: "I didn't experience adolescence (*murahaqa*) like the other girls, I was serious. The girls would hang around and have boyfriends, while I studied, day and night. I had to be the first one to make my parents happy." Ghizlan's parents wanted the girls to be educated, like the boys, and to build their future.

Originally from a rural village in the Tadla Plain, they moved to al-Azaliyya when her father became a junior administrator and settled in a rented house in hay el-Mounia, as part of the inward migration of civil servants and schoolteachers during the 1960s and 1970s. When Ghizlan's father rose to a managerial position, they relocated to a two-story villa in a new neighborhood where Ghizlan occupied an independent apartment on the second floor. Unlike her father, who could obtain a diploma despite his humble origins, her mother 'Aisha attended school only until she reached puberty. Although this was common practice among peasant families, she never forgave her parents for withdrawing her. The school was a long way from home, and they were afraid that something might happen to her on the way, but they did not regard education as essential to a girl's upbringing.

'Aisha was married off at fifteen to a man aged twenty-two. She was not consulted about her prospective marriage, nor did any contact occur between her and the groom before the wedding day. "They did not ask your opinion," she said. "The families agreed, and that's it. They told me, 'You are not going to meet him till the night of the wedding.'" 'Aisha paused and sighed. "Every girl would go mad with crying, 'Poor me!' At the age of thirteen or fourteen, the girl would go to her mother-in-law and do housework all day." 'Aisha's recollection resonates with the narratives of the older generations of village women, who depict marriage as a painful fracture in the life of a girl. However, it also reveals her dreams of trespass (Mernissi 1994). She told me that she was afraid of marriage but also curious about her future husband, whom she saw at a distance, riding his motorbike. More than marriage, she made clear, it was the image of herself on the motorbike that occupied her fantasy as a girl. In 'Aisha's recollection, the motorbike evoked the dream of freedom and adventure in a girl who had never left her home village. Unfortunately, she explained, things turned out differently from her expectations: "I just wanted the motorbike. I liked the motorbike! I wanted it! When I got married, he sold the motorbike to pay for the wedding. The motorbike had gone and what remained for me was the tiredness, my mother-in-law, the washing to do, the mosque . . . there is no God but God."

After the wedding, 'Aisha moved to her in-laws' home, where she worked in the fields and did all the housework, as a young bride was expected to do. During the first years of marriage, her life was hard. When she moved to al-Azaliyya, she left behind the work in the field and in the rural household, but was busy with childbearing and raising children without the help of her female kin. After forty years of conjugal life, the marital bond between 'Aisha and her husband is filled with affection and mutual respect. However, she said, "This love does not appear. It remains inside of me." She does not declare her love to her husband, nor does her husband declare his to her, because it would be shameful (*hshuma*), she explained, but his gestures give voice to his feelings.

'Aisha has spent her life taking care of her five children and devoted her spare time to tailoring and embroidery. Since her children have grown up, she has started attending the lessons in Qur'anic recitation at the neighborhood mosque. While cooking and cleaning, she often listened to the cassette of *Surat al Baqara* that she was trying to memorize for her final examination. Thinking over her experience, she said: "Every mother hopes her daughter is better than she is. She wants her daughter to be well dressed, educated, and independent of her husband, with her own money in her pocket. I want her to work . . . I don't want her to carry on crying! Because we cried so much, and what scared us in our father we feared in our husband." Linking female education and economic independence with the hope of a better life, 'Aisha's words not only evoke gendered aspirations intimately connected with images of the "modern life" (*ma'ysha 'asriya*) experienced and displayed in urban Morocco but also reveal her hope for different relationships between men and women, husband and wife. While Ghizlan took after her mother with her sensitivity and patience, she is also feisty and determined. She imagines marriage as a project based on love and choice that she hopes to pursue along with the search for self-realization and a professional career. Thus, at first sight, the comparison between Ghizlan and her mother might appear as a rapid shift from a vision of marriage as an inescapable destiny to an ideal of married life as a site of emotional fulfillment and a choice based on love. However, as we will see, this shift is far from being linear and unproblematic. Notwithstanding its promise of a happy conclusion, the dream of love engenders ambivalence and unexpected outcomes in Ghizlan's life.

Following how the unexpected manifests itself in Ghizlan's self-narrative, I trace in this chapter the ways she shifts between the worldly and the religious horizons in order to recompose the unfulfilled promises of love and to reflect on broader societal changes in Morocco. I show how, alongside the vocabulary of freedom and choice infusing her romantic dreams, Ghizlan invokes the Islamic idea of "destiny"—intended as a person's divinely preordained future—to make sense of and reckon with the unpredictability of intimate relationships. Much debated in classic Islamic thought (Watt 1948; De Cillis 2014), destiny is a fundamental dimension shaping religious and social life in Morocco (Eickelman 1976,

125–28; Crapanzano 2014; Menin 2015, 2016, 2020; Elliot 2016) and beyond.[1] People in the Tadla often evoke destiny to discuss future events, as well as to rationalize experiences of misfortune and failure as part of a divine design. The notion of destiny enables Ghizlan to make sense of unforeseen and painful twists in her intimate life as well as voices broader anxieties and disenchantment with the rapid pace of modernization in Morocco. At a historical time when the ethical reform of sensibility is at stake, Ghizlan's quest for individual freedom and autonomy in marital choice does not simply collide with the ideals of social connectivity and the ethics of the subject cultivated as Moroccan customs and traditions (*'adat wa t-taqalid*); it also competes with the "politico-theological imagination" (Pandolfo 2007) that has profoundly reformed religious subjectivities and intimate desires and has interrogated the meanings of being "modern" in al-Azaliyya.

Ghizlan's story shows how strands of Islamic revivalism are able to smooth over the contradictions and anxieties inhabiting everyday life (Schielke 2009). Crucially, her reliance on the Islamic vocabulary and imagination of destiny interrogates the very possibilities of human freedom and choice in a world in which human agency, desire, and intentionality encounter worldly and transcendental powers. Central to Ghizlan's narrative is the experience of "being acted upon" by broader powers, human, social, divine, a notion that I borrow from Amira Mittermaier's (2011, 2012) work on dream visions. Tracing how people grapple with the forces of the "Elsewhere" in their dreaming and waking lives, Mittermaier shifts the theoretical focus of her analysis beyond questions of intentionality and deliberate action to focus instead on the experience of "being acted upon" by visible and invisible forces. Powerfully positioning divine transcendental agency in the texture of mundane events, Ghizlan's experience invites us to dwell on the unresolved tensions between "acting" and "being acted upon" as constitutive of the experience of love and of life itself. Creatively inhabiting Islamic theologies of destiny to discuss her intimate life,

---

1. Recent anthropological works on notions of divine predestination and human free will within and beyond the MENA region include, for example, Nevola (2018); Schielke (2015); Gaibazzi and Gardini (2015); and D'Angelo (2019).

Ghizlan's quest for love foregrounds an understanding of freedom and choice that directs our attention to what transcends human capacity to shape oneself and one's complex life. It impels us to problematize the idea of "freedom" as an absence of limits and to reimagine it as the condition for acting within the limits set by worldly and transcendental powers.

Unfilled Romance

On a lazy Saturday afternoon, while waiting for Ghizlan to finish putting on her makeup to go for a stroll in the town, I switched on the television in her room and saw that *Titanic* was being broadcast on the satellite channel Fox Movies. One of the most successful romantic Hollywood movies of all time, *Titanic* tells the love story of Rose, a girl engaged to a rich aristocrat, and Jack, a poor but charming young man, during the *Titanic*'s tragic transatlantic passage. The naivete of my question of whether she had ever seen the film became clear when she replied that she had watched it several times: both on television and big screens at cafés, with friends. She came to sit by me on her sofa and confessed that she had never managed to hold back her tears when Rose wakes up after the collision of the *Titanic* with the iceberg and realizes that Jack is clinging lifeless to the wooden panel that saved her, surrounded by the icy waves of the Atlantic Ocean.

While *Titanic* embodies a powerful image of romantic love among my female interlocutors in al-Azaliyya, Ghizlan reminded me that the historical depth of love in Morocco and in Arab worlds more broadly is irreducible to the influence of Western literacy tradition or the recent Hollywood or Bollywood film industry. She emphasized these long-standing literary and poetic traditions and their extremely rich vocabularies by mentioning romantic tales, similar to Shakespeare's *Romeo and Juliet*, that tell of the tragic story of two lovers thwarted by their families, such as *'Antar and 'Abla* and *Jamil and Buthayna*. She recited by heart some verses from the popular story of *Layla and Qays*, which she had learned in elementary school. The story goes that Layla and Qays/Majnun belonged to two neighboring clans and fell in love, but her family opposed their union. Qays would compose poems for Layla and become possessed by love like a madman (*majnun*). Being unconsummated, the love between Layla and

Qays remains eternal and pure. These tales belong to the 'udhri genre and epitomize the ideal of chaste love, which was further elaborated in Sufi traditions and the repertoire of love poetry (Allen 2000, 102–9). Sufis have devoted close attention to the various states of mind and the agonies and delights connected with passionate love ('ishq), conceived as a mystical and sensual pathway toward God (Webner 2017).

Glizlan also recounted the popular Tamazight legend of *Isli and Tislit*. Isli and Tislit belonged to two different tribal groups, and, because of the opposition of their families, they left their villages in the High Atlas Mountains and went to Imilchil, where, in desperation, they cried themselves to death. According to the legend, their tears formed two lakes. Like the tragic love story of the 'udhri tradition, that of Isli and Tislit reveals the extent to which the trope of unfulfilled romance is rooted in the popular imagination.[2] In these classic tales, the protagonists' love defies the rules of their society and ends tragically, in madness, anguish, or death, thereby becoming a potent reminder of the dangers of passionate love and the predominance of society over the dyad. Of course, there are other traditions of love and passion, which Ghizlan never mentioned in our conversations, perhaps because—as we will see as her narrative unfolds—these tragic tales of unfilled romance resonated with her own experience. While the topic of tragic love runs deep in Moroccan society, Ghizlan belongs to a generation that has experienced the complex intertwining between classic romantic imaginations and other love stories conveyed by Western and non-Western movies and soaps. As a teenager in the 1990s, Ghizlan loved watching Indian, American, and Egyptian movies and TV series on national television, which, in her view, provided good models to her generation. "There were love stories, but they were serious," she commented. "Our generation mainly watched Indian movies, and the majority were romantic movies. There was nothing bad about it. There was a boy who

2. Other poetic traditions on love and passion have shaped popular imagination in Morocco, such as the genre called *malhun*, which developed in the fifteenth century. *Malhun* expresses feelings of passionate and extreme love, including the libertine and erotic registers that continue to inform the vocabulary of love in Morocco (Miller and Cheikh 2010). Significantly, Ghislan focused only on the classic tales of unfulfilled romance.

loved a girl, and he would sing and dance. It was a romantic story, not like today. Have you seen what the singers look like? There's Haifa, the Lebanese singer. Nowadays, satellite television is full of such things!"[3] Contrasting her experience with the current situation, Ghizlan emphasized the extent to which satellite television has reshaped the dynamics of intimate relationships and inflected young people's romantic imaginations. Recalling her adolescence, she expressed nostalgia for the time when premarital love was "pure." As I will discuss, however, beyond signifying sincere sentiments between a girl and a boy and serious intentions to build a life together, "pure love" evokes an idealized past and a sense of anxiety vis-à-vis the present.

Pure Love

Ghizlan told me that when she was an adolescent, boys and girls had few opportunities to meet outside the school because of parental and social supervision. Worried that something might happen to her, her mother instilled in her the fear of boys, advising her about the dangers of following them in isolated and empty places. When she was an adolescent, she said, the relationships between lovers were romantic. "If a boy wanted to communicate with a girl, he would put a love letter (*risala*) in her textbook or deliver romantic messages through the discreet mediation of a trustworthy person or a little child . . . It was romantic indeed, and that love was pure!" Ghizlan exclaimed. Kept hidden from the parents and the public gaze, premarital romances were cultivated discreetly in the gender-mixed school and the neighborhood. Couples arranged secret meetings at the street corner or a few blocks away from their home for fear that parents or siblings might see them; they exchanged words of love, but were shy and respectful. "If the boy was in love with a girl, he loved her truly. The majority of my female friends who were in a relationship got married to

3. Haifa Wehbe is a Lebanese pop star and actress who is extremely popular in Arab countries, but is also criticized for her provocative and sensual video clips and performances.

their boyfriends," Ghizlan said to emphasize the purity of such romances. This idyllic picture of the past when love bonds were based on "pure love" is contrasted with what Ghizlan described as the present-day commodification of love relationships whose goal is a hedonistic pleasure instead of marriage. She said: "There are no more sentiments from heart to heart (*de coeur vers le coeur*), it has become body to body (*le corp vers le corp*). There isn't the ideal of marriage." For Ghizlan, there is no seriousness or respect in contemporary relationships: boys and girls jump from one relationship to another without thinking of marriage. In particular, she connected this change to the role of satellite television, which, in her view, has reshaped intimate dynamics among young people. For example, she claimed that the pervasive presence of seductive singers and actresses on television has a negative influence on boys: "When a boy sees a naked girl, what does he look at? Her brain? . . . Television always gives you models, whether negative or positive. Our generation had good models."

In addition to emphasizing the implication of satellite television on youths' romantic imagination, Ghizlan also suggested that different media of personal communication (in this case, love letters and mobile phones) generate radically different types of relationships and gendered dynamics. She thought that the uncontrolled proliferation of mobile phones and the Internet has contributed to the "corruption" of love. She said: "Today, you find the girl who has so many affairs and a hundred phone numbers on her mobile." While I discuss the role of digital technologies in the intimate lives of young women in al-Azaliyya in chapter 7, here I wish to problematize Ghizlan's reflection on the corrupting effects of satellite television and digital technologies on people's intimate lives. Ghizlan's sense of nostalgia for an idealized past and its lost purity, I suggest, is not just a way of talking about the past; it reflects her disenchantment with the Western-inspired model of modernity and her present engagement with revivalist imagination. Discussing the implications of rapid transformations in people's lives and their sense of selfhood, Ghizlan argued that the Arabization of public education from the late 1970s and several political and social events in the past few decades in Morocco and the Middle East have led Moroccans away from Western-inspired models of progress and encouraged the rediscovery of their religious identity.[4] "My father's generation grew up in the dawn of independence and was formed within French culture, which was considered the model of civilization par excellence," she said. "Today, Moroccans want to return to their own culture."

For Ghizlan, the liberalization of national television and the arrival of satellite dishes have played a role in these processes by allowing Moroccans to get broader access to news and learn more about Islam. At the same time, she argued, some entertainment programs, movies, and music video clips available on satellite television have disseminated superficial messages among young people. She also claimed that globalization had intensified the crisis that the family is undergoing in Morocco: the contemporary lifestyle takes parents away from home all day so that supervising their children has become increasingly difficult, especially since digital technologies have intruded into daily life. She said: "Nowadays you can talk at home on your mobile. With the mobile phone you can text about anything to anyone and you receive a message back, then the Internet . . . now everything has got into our homes." Making people directly addressable, mobile phones and the Internet undermine parental control.

Ghizlan's reflection on the commodification of intimate relationships and the loss of values characterizing contemporary Moroccan society captures a broader sense of anxiety about the social and intimate effects of globalized modernity, which finds elaboration through a revivalist vocabulary. In particular, it evokes the charismatic figure of Sheikh Abdessalam Yassine, his moral concern about Western cultural influence, his critique of modernity, and his invitation to cultivate spirituality and reject empty rationalism and materialism. Sheikh Yassine (1928–2012), the founder of the Justice and Spirituality movement (al-'adl wa al-ihsan) is considered the most prominent voice against the Western-inspired model of modernity; he denounces its disruptive effects and condemns the corruption of

---

4. In 1977, King Hassan II (1961–99) promoted the Arabization of state education in order to undermine the basis of critical thinking which had influenced generations of left-wing political activists over the previous few decades (Vermeren 2006, 75).

the Westernized elites that rule Morocco.[5] In *Winning the Modern World for Islam* (2000, 24), Yassine argues that, since colonial times, Western hegemony has produced "spiritual dispossession, the flattering of one's being, the disfiguration of the soul." Only by submitting to God's will and Islamic principles, he avers, can Muslims counter the "spiritual murder" (64) perpetrated by the secularist ideas that celebrate the individual as self-made and autonomous, blind to what goes beyond worldly reality. In particular, Yassine (2003) calls believers to cultivate spirituality to become receptive to divine revelations and the realm of *al-ghayb*, a crucial Islamic concept that refers to the "Unseen," the invisible world imperceptible to human beings and the divine mystery (Bubandt, Rytter, and Suhr 2017).[6] Crucially, as I will discuss, Ghizlan evokes the idea of destiny to make sense of misfortunes, but also to point to her limited capacity to direct the course of events in the face of greater powers. While she imagines love as a pure and elective union between two individuals, Ghizlan experiences it as a dangerous adventure along the thin lines between human agency and destiny, personal desires and social constraints.

Destined Love

One evening, while I was helping Ghizlan peel vegetables in the kitchen to prepare dinner, we started talking about love and the deep emotions connected with being in love (in French, *être amoureuse*; in darija,

---

5. According to Driss Maghraoui (2009, 109–28), the polarization of the religious and the secular infusing Yassine's prophetic message is the major recent twist in the long-standing debates around Moroccan modernity. Unlike the twentieth-century Salafi reformists who aspired to modernize Islam and prove its compatibility with modern sciences through its purification from traditional practices, Yassine aspires to Islamize modernity.

6. According to Yassine (2003, xi), "the Muslim mind" is threatened by the secular, materialistic mind, "a mind preoccupied with worldly affairs and veiled from the realities of the *ghayb* [the Unseen, divine mystery], so long as it does not learn from Revelation and does not perceive the light of Revelation."

mughrama). As the seat of feelings, Ghizlan explained, "the heart beats (*l-qalb tay-drab*), and one feels excited and cheerful." Unlike a general attraction, she added, love entails deep emotional commitment and involvement. "Liking someone is not the same as being in love," she said. "Love is a different thing. You feel something special in the heart, and your mind keeps working as if you were dreaming, but you are awake (*ybqa rask khddam bhal kat-hlmy w nty fayqa*)."

On the other hand, Ghizlan added that love relationships are complicated, in Morocco and all Arab countries alike, because they seldom lead to marriage. Although this contradicts her previous statements that most of her friends got married to the men they were in love with, it reflects the opinion of the majority of my young interlocutors. Moving away from the poetic language of emotion toward more pragmatic considerations regarding marriage, Ghizlan said: "According to Islam, marriage is a project (*zwej huwa mshro'*) that both of you should desire. You should know the person you are marrying, see him, talk to him, discuss things, but you shouldn't let too much time go by, as love diminishes (*l-hobb kay-nqs*)." Noticing that I looked puzzled about her theory that love diminishes over time, Ghizlan took a piece of paper and drew a flame on it: "Love is like a fire (*bhal l-'afiya*). In the beginning, it burns brightly. Then it dies out." She paused, looking into my eyes, and then went on: "At first, you're lost in the thought of him. You think about what he told you, what he did. When he calls you, your heart thuds and when he doesn't you suffer so much. Then the flame dies out, and you become like relatives." Challenging the wisdom that warns against illusory infatuations and the dangers of love, Ghizlan suggested that, given the transience of love, the important decision about marriage should be taken when the flame of passion is still burning intensely, arguably because it is in this very moment that people dare to struggle for love. Notwithstanding the importance that Ghizlan accorded to love and choice in marriage decisions, she also stressed that the outcome of a relationship is not simply a matter of love or individual will. It is, rather, connected with al-*qada' wa l-qadar*: God's absolute decree (*qada'*) and the destiny (*qadar*) written for each person long before their soul is infused into their body (Glassé and Smith 2003).

The contentious relationship between predestination and free will (*ikhtiyar*) has long captured the attention of numerous Islamic theologians, philosophers, and mystics, raising compelling questions on the nature of divine and human will (Watt 1948; Belo 2006; De Cillis 2014, 1–18). Qur'anic passages support both ideas of divine omnipotence and human free action, and different theological-philosophical schools have elaborated radically varying answers to the question of human participation in destiny.[7] The mainstream Sunni tradition was influenced by the Ash'arite view, which combines divine predestination and human free will, based on the idea that God conferred on human beings the power to act and responsibility for their action (Belo 2006; de Cillis 2014).[8] The complex coexistence of destiny and free will is present in commonsense knowledge in central Morocco, where major events in people's lives, including marriage, are believed to be written since the beginning of times. Far from setting destiny and human free will in opposition, the widespread belief that people attain in life what God has preordained is combined with an insistence on freedom and responsibility for individual actions, which will be answered for on Judgment Day. Intrigued by the way in which Ghizlan shifted from a worldly horizon of passion and choice to a mystical one in which personal agency meets powers that transcend human control and rational understanding, I asked her to clarify the connections between love and destiny. In response, she went back to her piece of paper: "Maybe you love Jack and then meet Michael. You thought of marrying Jack, but eventually you get married to Michael." Since Ghizlan's example seemed to contradict her previous statements about the importance of freedom and passion in marital choice, I pressed her to explain further how destiny may affect such intimate decisions. She replied: "Destiny

---

7. The Qadarite, for example, affirmed divine human free will over divine predetermination; the Mu'tazila, in contrast, upheld a rationalist theory of human free will. The problem of compatibility remained central for the prominent medieval Islamic thinkers Ibn al 'Arabi, Avicenna, and al-Ghazali (De Cillis 2014, 10–16; Watt 1948).

8. Al-Ash'ari (AD 936) and his school, the Ash'arite, emphasized the coexistence of divine predestination and human free will and responsibility.

means whether or not something is written for us. God knows every-thing—the day you will come to life, what will happen to you when you'll get married, and to whom."

Shifting her focus from God's power to decree to the incommensu-rability of human and divine knowledge, Ghizlan's words suggest that seemingly contingent events may be part of a divine design and purpose beyond human understanding. To understand her viewpoint on the rela-tions between predestination and free will, I asked: "What is the role of free will? Put in these terms, is everything fated to be?" She replied firmly: "No. The two angels who alight on your shoulders write everything you do—the good and bad actions. There is room for responsibility and choice, but there are things that we cannot decide." In answering my questions, Ghizlan resorted to established sets of theological arguments about the practical experience of acting freely to fulfill one's destiny. However, I felt there was something deeply personal in her reflection on love and destiny, something I began to figure out when I stayed overnight at her home, and she recounted to me a sad story about something that had happened to her almost ten years earlier.

When she was twenty-four, Ghizlan received some text messages on her mobile, sent by mistake from someone she did not know, and, per-suaded that the message was important, she let the stranger know that she was not the person he was seeking. They started talking, and then they realized that they both lived in al-Azaliyya—which Ghizlan described as a coincidence (sodfa)—and decided to meet in a café. "Hearing his voice, I imagined he was fat, but he was slim and cute, three years older than me," she recalled, smiling. After their first meeting, they started dat-ing regularly, and their accidental meeting led to love. "We would meet in cafés and public places a bit far away—where my parents didn't go. I kept it hidden from other people. We would meet every day." After three years together, they decided to marry. Ghizlan informed her parents that a man would come to ask for her hand, and they prepared sweets to greet their guest. To her astonishment, no one came knocking at the door that day. Just a few days later, Ghizlan's sweetheart told her that he had not come because he found out that he had serious heart problems and had to undergo an operation without any guarantee of survival. Aware of the complexity that surrounds the passage from love to marriage, Ghizlan did not trust him and jumped to the conclusion that he had changed his mind about their marriage without having the courage to face her. Deeply hurt by his behavior, she decided to break off their relationship and avoid any contact with him. A few months later, Ghizlan learned that her beloved had passed away. She went through a period of profound suffering. "I was so shocked that after that I didn't date anyone else, in case that story might repeat itself," she said. "It's hard to let someone enter your heart."

Despite her despair over the loss of her beloved, Ghizlan gradually recovered herself and fell in love with another man. The failure of this second love story triggered a profound crisis that reconfigured her relationship with the divine. Retrospectively, Ghizlan recast the tragic failure of her love stories in terms of destiny. Her engagement with the Islamic theology of *qada' wa l-qadar* (divine decree and predestination) provides a convincing explanatory theory for her experiences of failure and misfortune (Schielke 2015; Nevola 2018). Perhaps most importantly, Ghizlan's deeper inquiry into her emotional state, her confusion and her desire to understand what God wills for her life furnished her with tools of resilience and trust that go beyond rational explanation. Islamic ideas that God has a purpose for His creatures, and that thus human beings should rely on Him not only provided her with emotional healing but also enabled her to develop intimate reflection on the unpredictability of intimate relationships.[9] This deeper understanding of life comes from leaning into her faith and a more adult orientation to the world, where things are not just "God's will" or "my own choice," but a rounded, woven tapestry of both aspects. Coming to this place of accepting complexity, un-knowing, and that several things can all be true at once is a major achievement of adulthood that Ghizlan reached through a painful process. It is precisely through loving and coming to terms with the failure of love that Ghizlan has grown up and grown spiritually. As we will see, Ghizlan's understanding of the

---

9. Discussing the Islamic concept of *tawakkul* (reliance on God), Sherine Hamdy (2009, 176) argues: "It is not interpreted as a passive form of fatalism that negates human agency but is in fact a disposition whose achievement requires active and persistent work on the self."

fragility of the human agency under God's will does not lead her to deny the possibility of choice and responsibility. On the contrary, the idea of divine predestination opens a reflection on the questions of choice and responsibility via-à-vis the mundane powers shaping the love dynamics. To do this, let me first trace how Ghizlan narrated her second love story.

The Love of the "Arab Man"

Two years after the death of her beloved one, one of Ghizlan's maternal relatives visited her family with her son Ahmed, to whom Ghizlan had been emotionally attached since childhood. Ahmed had left the village of his birth in the Atlas Mountains to study in Casablanca and then had found a job in Tangier, so they had not seen each other for ten years. When they met again, an intense feeling blossomed: "I don't know if it was love or what . . . neither of us said a word. I felt something and he, too—as you look into each other's eyes, the fire is burning." Suddenly Ghizlan's tone became serious: "You can't change what is written (*ma 'andksh ma-t-bddly had shy lly maktub*). . . . Even if I love you and you love me, when God wants something for you . . . there is nothing you can do. Since then, I have believed in God." Anticipating the tragic ending of their relationship, Ghizlan's words stress the limits of human freedom and choice in the face of greater powers. This insight, as we will see, radically transformed her relationship with God by making her aware of the need for divine guidance.

After meeting in al-Azaliyya, Ahmed and Ghizlan kept in touch via mobile phone and the Internet until his mother became ill. Since his father was working far away, and Ahmed had no sisters or female relatives nearby, he asked Ghizlan to help care for his mother. "We were one family, one house," Ghizlan said, to explain that the ties between the two families legitimized Ahmed's call for help. Recalling the time spent together, she smiled, and her eyes became dreamy. She said: "I spent such a wonderful week! Outings, sweet words, beautiful conversations . . . I loved him, I was crazy about him, [and he said] 'I love you, I'm crazy about you.' If he just saw someone turning to me, he shouted at him. . . . At that time we were still beautiful, without the veil. You go out, and he doesn't want you to, you feel that the man is jealous of you. . . . If you want to go out, he says 'No, I'll come with you.' . . . The love of the Arab man . . . I spent a week as if I had set foot in paradise."

Listening to her words, I was surprised that an independent and feisty young woman like Ghizlan was attracted to such a seemingly control-ling man, expressing his love through jealousy and control. Noting my puzzlement, she tried to explain to me what she called "the love of the Arab man": "Because you're not Moroccan, you don't know what the Arab man is like." More than just a remark on my outsider-ness, Ghizlan's com-ment was a genuine attempt to teach me something about love dynamics in Morocco that she assumed were different in Europe. In chapter 1, I discussed *ghyra*, or the "protective jealousy" of a man toward his women relatives, in the context of marital and brotherly relationships, arguing that many young women regard *ghyra* as central to the dynamics of love, protection, and honor. Similarly, Ghizlan described sentiments and public expressions of *ghyra* as essential aspects of men's love and gendered per-formances of masculinity. "I don't care too much when a man says, 'I love you.' But if you feel that he is jealous of you (*tay-ghyr 'alik, l-ghyra, la jalou-sie*), if someone phones you, he wants to know who he is and doesn't want you to go around naked [meaning not covered properly], and take care of you and if you need anything he supplies it, then you feel he loves you." Ghizlan also added that a woman feels relaxed with a man who keeps his word and is resolute: "We girls want a man with these characteristics. Even if we say we don't, we like the determined men!" In other words, Ghizlan associates a man's "true" love with expressions of jealousy, which entails control and protection, emerging, as we have seen in chapter 2, from the constellations of family ties and affection as well as everyday acts of car-ing, taking care, and providing for necessities (Naguib 2015).

Ghizlan returned to her story, saying that, after her flawless week with Ahmed, his mother was hospitalized and eventually died. After this shocking event, Ghizlan continued to keep in touch with her boyfriend through texts and calls for a year until Ahmed's father also died. In these sad circumstances, Ghizlan and her family visited Ahmed's home, and, on arrival, she discovered that he had married another woman. She said she wanted to cry and scream, but her parents did not know about their relationship, so she kept silent until she became ill with a fever. "My parents weren't aware of Ahmed's marriage because they had not been in touch since the death of his mother. It was a *fatiha* ceremony [not registered officially], and it wasn't celebrated with a [more public] banquet." Ahmed's wife was a neighbor who would help his mother with her domestic chores and continued to clean the house and cook for Ahmed and his father after his mother's death. Since it was not acceptable for an unrelated young woman to drop in and out of the home of two men, Ahmed's father forced his son to marry her. At this point, Ghizlan's tone became serious: "I told you—you love me, I love you, but marriage is something else."

Shifting her narrative from destiny to hardship, Ghizlan gave voice to a critique of the mundane powers that constrain people's choices and actions. She explained that, despite the sentiments that bind two lovers, love and marriage follow different logics in Moroccan society—a common idea among my young interlocutors that I discuss further in chapter 6. Some families support a love marriage, and the couples often succeed in marriage by making their love match seem to be arranged. When marriage is at stake, however, pragmatic considerations regarding family respectability and social class and deference to parental authority may weigh more heavily than love. In her retrospective gaze on past events, Ghizlan "emplotted" (Bruner 1987) the tragic epilogue of her love story through the language of kinship and destiny to highlight the social and transcendental powers shaping the limits and possibilities of human action and choice. Nevertheless, she demanded responsibility and called for agency as a moral imperative, to which Ahmed failed to respond. Expressing her disappointment with his silence and misbehavior, she said: "I still haven't forgotten. He is a betrayer (*ghddar*), it shouldn't have happened! . . . We were tied together by blood." Her words emphasize that, even though Ahmed did not have the power to make a choice, and she could understand that he did not dare to challenge his father's will, he should have never betrayed her love by hiding his marriage with another woman.

Ghizlan explained that this second misfortune in her affective life made her deeply aware of her need to "follow the right pathway" and put on the veil, which she described as the starting point for cultivating spirituality. In a sense, veil and faith become a protection for her, small barriers against untrustworthy men, her weaknesses, and the pull of desire. As will become clear in the next sections, Ghizlan's submission to God's will and the competing desires and aspirations that inhabit her sense of self seem irreducible to the individual ethics of the "pious subject" theorized by Saba Mahmood (2001, 2005). Together with her spiritual aspirations to cultivate a "pious self," she continued to pursue her quest for love, making both piety and romance two constitutive dimensions of her being a young Muslim woman.

Women Who Outstrip Men

Moving between worldly and religious vocabularies, Ghizlan reflected upon the tensions between the sexes with respect to changing gendered subjectivities and life expectations. For instance, she said that God made women from Adam's rib, which lies near the heart; hence they are more tender than men. "Men, however, do not want women who are also capable, as they do not accept that women can be better than them or more educated," she commented. "Even in foreplay," she went on, "men want to keep women underneath—they don't let them on top." Crucially, Ghizlan resorted to religious vocabulary to criticize the gendered dynamics of power in love relationships and express her uneasiness about the constraints surrounding female sexuality. In her opinion, men's sexual desire is inflamed as they cast their gaze on the female body. "Of course, women think of sex, too. Men think of sex every five minutes and—perhaps they are ashamed to admit it—but women think of it, too!" She added: "For me, virginity is not essential, but you may have problems. Generally, men don't accept a woman who is not a virgin. That's a risk, as you never know how your liaison will end. For you [Europeans] it's different. It's hard, don't you think? When there is no freedom, it's hard." Ghizlan's words suggest that sex and love are problematic because parents can object to a love marriage, but many young men do not accept women who are not virgins or who have a higher social position or a strong personality. Like other young women in al-Azaliyya, Ghizlan described virginity as a social expectation more than a personal value and complained about the constraints in girls' sexuality. In other contexts—or even in the same breath—she mobilized religious arguments on virginity to distinguish between essentialized categories of "Muslims" and "Westerners" and stressed that the latter are lacking in values because they are far away from religion, although I had the impression that such arguments served Ghizlan to position herself in a politically charged polarization between Islam and the West more than to talk of sex. On another occasion, Ghizlan discussed sexuality in the light of the contradictions brought into young women's lives by higher education and changing life aspirations.

She said: "I feel that I want to have sex (*je veux faire l'amour*), but I don't. I control myself but it's hard to restrain myself. I can do it, but the man can't control himself easily. That's why religion says that we should marry young, why so? . . . If you delay marriage until thirty, it gets harder and harder! But you study first—studying has delayed my marriage. I can't marry someone who tells me, 'No,' as I've suffered for studying, I was the best student in my class."

Ghizlan's words capture the tensions that mark the intimate lives of many young women who have postponed marriage to seek a professional career and have passed the age regarded as appropriate for a girl to marry. Whereas in European biologized discourses on sexuality, hormonal dynamics make thirty-year-old people less enslaved to their passions than a fifteen-year-old, Ghizlan emphasized that delayed marriage makes sexual passions difficult to control. Reversing traditional visions depicting girls and women as having a powerful, if not uncontrolled, sexual appetite (Rassam 1980; Dwyer 1978, 151; Mernissi 2002), Ghizlan described male sexual desire as stronger than female—although she did not deny her sexual desire and her strife to restrain it. Since young people are burdened with a strong sexual desire that renders them "hot" (*skhun*), as desire is like heat in the body, early marriage is the "Islamic solution" to prevent *fasad* (prostitution, degradation, corruption, moral depravity) caused by the delay of marriage, she explained, because regular sexual activity enables men to "cool down" (*tbard*). In other words, for Ghizlan, marriage at an early age, which allows for the fulfillment of sexual and emotional necessities, contains social disorder. At the same time, she also pointed to the tensions that early marriage would have created in her life: it would have thwarted her lifelong dreams of a career, she said. Moreover, Ghizlan believed that marriage and family life are very important, but she could not accept a man who would restrict her freedom. Crucially, Ghizlan resorts to a revivalist vocabulary to frame the tensions triggered by the socioeconomic transformations in women's lives, but a revivalist project neither entirely resolves her conflicts nor completely fulfills her aspirations. The Egyptian soap *Na'am, Mazelto Anisa* (Yes, I'm Not Married Yet), which Ghizlan watched daily, provided another discourse on women's difficulties in crafting their affective lives in worlds of changing gendered possibilities. Watching this soap with Ghizlan and listening to her comments on the incidents in the life of the protagonist, I realized that it offered a meaningful frame with which she could emplot and make sense of her experience. Broadcast on Nile Television Network, it tells the story of an educated woman who works as a teacher and lives alone in a flat. Despite her cultured and bourgeois surroundings, she suffers from pressure to marry from her family and peers. Although Ghizlan made it clear that her family did not press her to marry, she identified this TV story with her predicament, thereby reframing it as a broader phenomenon that involves educated and independent women. In her view, this soap addressed the uneasy condition of those women who have pursued their aspirations and then find it difficult to find a husband who lives up to their expectations. "In my view," Ghizlan said, "a woman should not marry for fear of being considered a spinster (*bayra*)"—a difficult condition in the context where she lives. She received some marriage proposals that she refused because they set unacceptable conditions, such as quitting her job and her friends, replacing her fashionable attire with loose-fitting Moroccan jellaba, or living with the groom's family in the countryside.

When I had this conversation with Ghizlan, she had been in a relationship with Abdelhedi for three years. A graduate in agriculture nearing his forties, Abdelhedi worked in the family's agribusiness firm. During the weekends, they often went together to nice cafés and restaurants away from al-Azaliyya. When I spent time with them, Abdelhedi and Ghizlan were always joking with each other. A good understanding and complicity between the two were palpable from the glances and words they exchanged, even though Ghizlan often complained that he did not call her as frequently as he used to at the beginning. Their relationship was not disclosed to her parents, as Ghizlan adopted the "Don't ask, don't tell policy" (Ozyegin 2015, 7), although, she said, they could imagine it. She told me that they would like to marry in the future, and they often talked about it, but, instead of calling for a quick marriage, as she did at the beginning of our conversation, she now admitted that she had become suspicious about men and their love.

> There's love between us, but all of them took something away from me because it isn't *l'amour fatal* [fatal love.] I love him, but there is always a part of my brain that says I don't give you a hundred percent, I give you ninety percent or eighty percent. Always this part of my brain keeps saying "He's lying" as *j'ai perdue toute la confiance à l'homme* [I've lost my trust in men]. I tell myself, "Maybe I love him, maybe I'll give him my heart," but another thing may separate us, as it separated me from the first and the second ones. Now one part loves and the other stays away, as if you were on a dark street and your brain is awake, that's what I feel.

Her words voiced her inner conflict, between her desire to love and the fear of suffering again. The unpredictability of intimate relationships urged Ghizlan to subordinate her feelings to rationality because, as popular wisdom suggests, passionate love makes people vulnerable. Ghizlan's previous reflections on love and passion gave way to more pragmatic considerations about the importance of economic stability, independence, and equality in a marital bond. She said: "Day by day, you begin to understand life, not the dream world but real life, because when you are thirty, life is real, while before you looked at *la vie imaginaire* [the imaginary life]—we eat potatoes and sleep serenely. Now you don't think so any longer. A man has to be serious, with his work and his money, and you with yours, the same level." Imagining her ideal husband, Ghizlan underlines the importance of belonging to the same level and, like her mother, of economic independence from a partner. While Ghizlan's shift toward a more pragmatic understanding of love partly reflects her disillusionment with the pure love she idealized during girlhood, her idea that love alone is not enough to have a happy life reveals a change of perspective resulting from her nearing adulthood and from her deeper understanding of "real life." As much as her evolving relationship with her faith and questions of destiny, Ghizlan's growing up becomes a movement toward a more mature adult understanding of life and love. In 2015, Ghizlan announced her marriage to her boyfriend not as a pragmatic compromise but as a good, sensible match where trust and companionship grew over time.

Bounded Freedom

Ghizlan's story reveals the complex expectations and disillusionments surrounding the lived experience of romantic love in the rapidly changing socioeconomic setting of al-Azaliyya. Unlike the classic tales of chaste love that ends in madness, anguish, or death, the modern ideal of married life based on love and choice promises personal fulfillment and a happy ending. However, when she slips into the dream of modern love, she encounters the powers and constraints that compel her to reflect on the limits of the human capacity to control the course of events. As Ghizlan's disenchantment grows with what she describes as a Western-inspired vision of modernity, she engages with a revivalist imagination and vocabulary to articulate the tragic incidents that fragmented her intimate world. She resorts to the Islamic idea of destiny to make sense of her failed loves as transformative events that made her aware of the fragility of human agency and the need for God's guidance. Like the search for romantic love, though, the Islamic revival conveys a "grand narrative" (Schielke 2015) laden with compelling promises that avoid both ambivalence and the conflicting values that permeate everyday lives. While Ghizlan embraces piety, other unresolved tensions in her life find elaboration through the mass-mediated stories conveyed by TV serials and soaps.

The richness and lived texture of Ghizlan's story testifies to the complexities and doubts inhabiting her sense of self. My argument, however, is not only about these complexities and doubts (Schielke 2010). Close attention to multiplicities and contradictions has long been at the core of feminist theorizations on subjectivity and agency, which have, in turn, contributed to the dismemberment of coherent visions of subjects and to the expansion of the notion of agency so as to include imaginative dimensions, desires, and unconscious motivations (McNay 1990; Kondo 1990; Moore 1994, 2007, 2011). My argument in this chapter has been that Ghizlan's story further enriches anthropological theorizations on Muslim subjectivities by bringing into focus the constitutive coexistence of pious and worldly horizons in the ways in which she crafts herself and her intimate life. Alternating the language of choice and freedom with that of destiny, Ghizlan foregrounds the unresolved tensions between acting and being acted upon that shape the experience of love in central Morocco. Her attempts to reckon with the unpredictability of intimate relationships give voice to the fundamental human condition of being confronted by forces and powers that are beyond personal control and even understanding. Concurrently, through the language of love, Ghizlan reflects on the space left open by worldly and transcendental powers. Underlying Ghizlan's intimate quest is an existential reflection on the very possibilities for individual freedom of choice in a world of greater powers. Her evocation of destiny goes far beyond indicating a divinely predestined future, and it does not simply point to a powerful explanatory theory of failure; it also relates to events and situations that are experienced as inevitable, including various dimensions of intimate and social life that cannot be chosen, controlled, or struggled against, but must be accepted, lived with, and worked through. By locating the vicissitudes of human life at the intersection of worldly and transcendental powers and rationalities, Ghizlan's story draws attention to modalities of agency and (inter)subjectivity that are submitted to God's will but are not centered upon intentionality, will, and desire. Although, as I have shown, these are all critical dimensions of her actions and thoughts, her story insistently points to what transcends people's capacity to shape themselves and their complex lives. Whereas Ghizlan says, rightly, that there are dimensions of life that cannot be decided, I have also traced the manifold ways in which her lived experience of being acted upon interweaves with and calls for agency and responsibility.

Ultimately, Ghislan's reflection brings into focus an idea of freedom *from* religious/cultural/political constraints that diverge from what authors have identified with mainstream liberal and feminist traditions. Notably, Mahmood (2001, 2005) problematizes the universality of the desire for "freedom" assumed a priori in much liberal and feminist thinking.

While Mahmood (2005, 170–73) briefly discusses Islamic destiny, the paradigm of ethical self-cultivation she presents leaves little room for exploring an alternative understanding of freedom within the piety movement. James Laidlaw (2013), inspired by Foucault's late work, explores the paths of ethical self-fashioning in Jainism as practices of freedom, thus making the possibilities of human freedom central to his ethnographic and theoretical inquiry. From different perspectives, both Joel Robbins (2007, 2012) and Jarret Zigon (2009, 263) maintain that ethics and ethical life also involve conscious moments of choice and freedom—the latter is intended both in terms of how the norms are inhabited and desired for and of how these are reimagined. However, as Claudio Sopranzetti notes (2016, 72), these authors' reflections on freedom have largely remained at the analytical level, without exploring its multiple ethnographic manifestations.

Drawing on the unresolved paradox of acting and being acted upon in Islamic theologies of destiny, Ghizlan's quest for love powerfully brings to the fore an emic perspective on freedom that dislocates and invites us to rethink some of the very questions we are accustomed to asking about subjectivity, agency, and ethics. It enriches current debates by interrogating the human capacity to act freely and make choices in situations shaped by transcendental forces, human powers, and material contingencies. As an unpredictable encounter with human and divine alterity, Ghizlan's quest for love becomes a learning ground, on which she encounters the experience of limits as core dimensions of human life, choice, and freedom. Her creative inhabitation of the limits of being foregrounds an understanding of "freedom" as the possibility to act *within* the limits set by God, rather than the capacity to overcome them. In this sense, free will unfurls itself on the motile ground opened up at the intersection of mundane and transcendental powers. The complex relation between acting and being acted upon reveals a relational space where God's omnipotence both manifests itself and finds its limits in the possibility of human free will and ethical responsibility for one's actions. This does not imply a self-possessed subject, since human freedom is granted by God as evidence of His magnanimity; it is precisely in the unresolved tensions between acting and being acted upon that the possibility of human freedom resides. This intrinsically relational perspective recognizes the complex texture of human and nonhuman agencies, relationships, forces, and powers about which people make choices, to exercise their freedom and strive to give their lives the desired direction. Premarital love is a privileged site from which to observe the encounter of the manifold powers and intentionalities involved in its actualization. As a direct continuation of this theoretical discussion, in the next chapters I continue to discuss the local ideas of love, choice, and freedom emerging through the search for fun and transgression.

5

Fun, Freedom, and Transgression

"I was fifteen when I first ventured into a man-only café (*mqahwa*) with a female friend. I was so curious to know what happened inside because it was strictly forbidden for us—the girls—to go into men's traditional coffeehouses. Once inside, I saw my cousin with his friends. I sneaked out in order not to be seen . . ." Sanaa laughed, thinking back to the risk that her cousin might catch her. "Doing forbidden things is the greatest fun!" she said with a smirk. Interweaving fun and transgression in her recollection, Sanaa evoked the mixture of pleasure and danger pervading the experience of penetrating such a "forbidden male place," where men old and young would gather to watch football matches, read newspapers, smoke cigarettes, and chat with their friends over a coffee. An exuberant young woman in her early twenties, Sanaa shared that memory with me as an example of her always having enjoyed breaking the rules.

I first met Sanaa in the dressmaker shop of my hostesses, Leyla and Ilham, in hay el-Mounia about a month after I arrived in al-Azaliyya in 2009. Sanaa lived with her family in the new part of the neighborhood and, occasionally, she would pass by Layla's shop to greet the two sisters. "Come in, my sister, and sit down (*dokhly khuty, ajy tglsy*)," Leyla would say. Following the conventional rules of polite conversations, Layla inquired about her health, then asked, hoping that Sanaa would help me in my research topic on migration, "You know young people of the 'outside' [migrants], don't you?" "A lot," Sanaa replied. "Take her with you," Leyla said peremptorily. From then on, I began taking part in Sanaa's leisure activities, following her and her friends to cafés, swimming pools, and private parties. Sanaa did not like modest clothes and preferred wearing tight jeans and fancy T-shirts. She said she was not a *bnt d-dar* ("home girl," "good girl"); she liked going out and having fun more than staying at home. Compared with Leyla and Ilham, who offered me a normative view of the rules in Morocco, Sanaa's outspokenness and irreverent behavior puzzled me initially. Whenever I asked her questions about what, according to local norms and gendered moralities, is considered "appropriate" or "improper," she would answer: "It depends . . . (*'ala hsab*)," thereby calling into question my attempts to find a "fixed moral order"—a coherent set of ideas and practices—in the dynamics of life in al-Azaliyya.

Concentrating on Sanaa's experience, I explore in this chapter the constitutive role of transgression in the gendered politics of fun, love, and sexuality in al-Azaliyya. A few scholars have devoted attention to youth, fun, and sexuality against the backdrop of neoliberal globalization and emerging leisure economies in Morocco and the Middle East more broadly (Bennani-Chraibi 1995; Hegazy 2007; Harrara and Bayat 2010; Bakass and Ferrand 2013; Ben Moussa 2019; Cheikh 2020a, 2020b), including new geographies of "Islamic" leisure and consumption (Nieuwkerk 2008; Herding 2013, 119; Deeb and Harb 2014). In her work on youth cultures in Morocco, Mériam Cheikh (2020a, 2020b) examines the experiences of "the girls who get out" (*l-bnat lly kay-kharjo*) in Tangier—namely, working-class girls who engaged in sex in return for money. Moving her analysis beyond the simplistic association of "getting out" with prostitution, Cheikh contextualizes the variety of practices enacted by girls—including dating, having fun, and entering into love relationships—within broader patterns of gender-mixing, fun, and experiences of freedom and transgression that mark the emergence of youth cultures in urban Morocco. Girls' practices, which are central to crafting the self and developing a sense of freedom, affect their reputation by making them vulnerable in the context of delayed marriage and economic uncertainty. Importantly, Cheikh invites us to consider girls' fun and love practices as "a lighthouse in the dark that casts a concrete light on the current change" instead of a "revelation of the ongoing deviance" (2020b, 435).

Following Cheikh's insights, I situate young people's search for fun, freedom, and transgression as expressions of an emerging youth culture in urban central Morocco. I foreground the "set of presumptions about self, society and life" (Bayat 2007, 455) it conveys, while interrogating the relations between gendered selves and norms by focusing on the questions of silence and secrecy. As we will see, Sanaa described having fun and getting out as constitutive dimensions of her youthfulness. Her yearnings bring into focus desires that call into question conventional modalities of femininity and respectability in al-Azaliyya and trace the emergence of new gendered selves and subjectivations. Crucially, Sanaa's search for fun is not limited to the overt infringement of the norms, but includes silence and secret practices through which she creatively navigates the tensions between what she describes as "the life of the family and society" and the "hidden life."

Using Sanaa's experience as an ethnographic starting point, I trace the dynamics of revealing and concealing through which young women seek to fulfill competing desires of conformity and desires that defy family and societal expectations. In a context like al-Azaliyya, where the perception of public morality is intimately related to people's gazes, conformity is an important dimension of the construction of respectable gendered selves. Generally, parents worry about gossip (*kelma n-nass*) and do not allow their daughters to enjoy the same freedom of movement as their brothers. Whereas boys spend much time outside of the home, the degree of freedom of movement that girls enjoy depends on their parents' ideas and inclinations. While Sanaa's family granted her considerable freedom, most girls I knew were not allowed to stand around without a purpose. Even though girls' leisure time was more disciplined and supervised than their male peers, they enacted various tricks and secrecy practices to circumvent familial and social control over their intimate lives and leisure activities.

A focus on the interplay of public conformity and discreet infringements of the norms reveals refined "etiquettes of transgression" through which social norms and gendered moralities are both contested and complied with. I conceive of discreet transgressions, silence, and secrecy as gendered social practices that allow for specific modalities of *inhabiting* the norm (Mahmood 2005) and of reckoning with its malleability. As long as it remains secret, the transgression of norms opens fundamental spaces for freedom and agency, especially when it comes to the desire for premarital love and sex (Carey 2010; Ozyegin 2015; Malmström 2016). Open transgressions position a girl as a "bad girl," in the sense of "women who defy patriarchies," whose "badness was attributed to them by sexist and male-dominated society that has attempted to define, limit, and control women" (Miller and Bardsley 2005, 1). As in other Muslim contexts (Chappatte 2014; El Aji 2017, 19–20; Chaudat and Lachheb 2018, 18–19), what is compromising in people's eyes is not the mere infringement of the norm, which often coexists with public conformity, but the fact that it contravenes the local "etiquettes of transgression" by making visible what is supposed to remain hidden. Highlighting the plasticity of the norms, my intention in this chapter is not only to complicate the relations between norm and transgression but also to trace how the societal boundaries of proper femininity and female respectability are redrawn, played out, and creatively inhabited through transgressions both open and secret. Following Sanaa around the places where she liked to spend her free time and meeting the people she spent it with, in what follows I begin to trace the gendered cultural ideals orienting public life in al-Azaliyya and their commonplace transgression.

Killing Time and Having Fun

When Sanaa was not working regularly and had more free time, she enjoyed watching her favorite Turkish and Egyptian TV serials, entertainment programs, and music channels like MTV. Attuned to global youth culture and local fashion, Sanaa would regularly go to Nabyl's hairdresser shop in her neighborhood to have her hair styled and her eyebrows and nails done. Omnipresent everywhere, a picture of the king appears on a wall of Nabyl's salon, but most of the surfaces are covered with images of Western and Middle Eastern actresses, and there are many fashion magazines and catalogs for customers to scour for style ideas. In central Morocco, there is an ancient beauty culture in which women and girls take care of themselves and their appearance; for example, they visit hammam (public steam bath), rim their eyes with eye-blackener, use natural products for scrubbing and moisturizing their skin and for dyeing their hair with henna, perfume themselves with rosewater, and depilate their body with homemade caramel creams. In contrast, Susan Ossman (2002) notes that regularly attending beauty parlors and hairdressing salons regularly is a way of embodying global images of beauty, a practice that conveys specific ideas of social class, modernity, and urbanity. Sanaa's leisure and beauty practices are shaped by her class status, but, like the majority of my acquaintances, they creatively combine both allegedly traditional and modern beauty cultures. For example, she attended both hammam and hairdressing salons. She would go to the gym regularly to do Middle Eastern dancing and practice yoga. More than watching television or doing sport, what she liked most was spending time in youth cafés, hanging around and having fun with her gender-mixed group of friends because, as she claimed, it helped her "to lift her mood" (*nbddl l-ju'a*).

The ways of spending leisure time and the people one meets and the places where one goes are variously defined by gender, class, social position, and consumption practices. While Sanaa's experience of fun takes shape within a young culture crossing social class (Cheikh 2020a), it also molds and is molded by leisure activities and heterosociality that she associates with being a modern, educated, and middle-class young woman. There were economic differences among her group of friends, but they all shared a similar cultural background and the global imagination. On afternoons, they would meet on the first floor of a café outside the neighborhood, where they chat, laugh, and enjoy watching football matches and music video clips on the maxiscreen. The first floors of the modern cafés are places where lovers can meet on a date away from other people's gaze, and where Sanaa and her best friend, Amal, were free to smoke cigarettes (smoking in public in al-Azaliyya being unacceptable for women). Amal lived in hay el-Mounia with her family, and the two girls had known each other since primary school. As with other types of goods, cigarettes were shared in the name of the egalitarian spirit that bonds friends together; when it was time to leave, the young men, in turn, would pick up the bill and pay for the others. During the winter, when every day seemed the same, spending every afternoon in a café was boring, and, in Sanaa's view, escaping routine was difficult in a city with a limited range of leisure and entertainment activities.

Compared with cosmopolitan Tangier and the other big Moroccan cities, young people in al-Azaliyya have far fewer opportunities to meet with friends and have fun beyond the local spaces of youth socialization available in the town such as snack bars, youth cafés, and public gardens. For example, Sanaa would complain that al-Azaliyya is lacking places where the young can go; the only cinema in the town, where, as a child, she used to go with her family to watch Disney cartoons and American movies, had been closed. Because she loved dancing, she lamented the lack of discotheques or clubs: "In Rabat or Casablanca, there are many nightclubs and discotheques. Here, the only place where one could dance are the bars of the hotels, but these are frequented mainly by prostitutes." To kill time, Sanaa and her friends often went to Khaled's flat to watch a movie, have lunch, or improvise a party. The son of two civil servants, Khaled had spent a few years in Italy and made his living running a small supermarket established with the money he earned abroad. Living alone and nearing his mid-thirties, Khaled was considered a *zufry*: a single man thought to be leading a wild life without the responsibility that marriage and a family entail. Sneaking in and out of Khaled's flat, Sanaa and Amal were careful to avoid the gaze of the omnipresent gossipers, greatly enjoying the sense of transgression that was part of the fun.

When the winter is over, there are more things for young people to do in al-Azaliyya, like promenading in the gardens or organizing a day trip out of town. On hot summer days, Sanaa and her friends used to go to the big hotels' swimming pools a few kilometers away. Unlike the cheapest public swimming pool, which Sanaa described as "dirty" and "crowded with boys," the ones at the hotels are quiet and bordered with flower gardens. Middle-class families with children and migrants back in Morocco for the summer holidays go there to escape the hot weather and enjoy the relaxed atmosphere. Veiled women sit comfortably under the shade of beach umbrellas, while young women in bikinis—or partially covered with tight-fitting shorts and a tank top—sip refreshments or swim in the pool. Dressed in a colorful bikini, Sanaa's sensual water games and physical proximity with her boyfriend were far from going unnoticed. She was aware that her behavior made people talk about her, but she said she did not want to feel conditioned by what people say because, in her view, going to cafés or the swimming pool with her mixed-sex group should be regarded as ordinary activities for girls, not exceptional. "Were we in Rabat or Casablanca, this would be normal, but, here, the majority of people have a narrow-minded mentality (*'aqliyya masduda*), apart from the elites who live like you in Europe," she said to affirm her right to have fun. Sanaa associated the possibilities of fun and open-mindedness with the elites in the big cities and the "outside," which she took as homogeneous categories instead of considering internal differences. Once she returned to hay el-Mounia, she was careful to conceal some of her activities, such as smoking and spending evenings with her gender-mixed group of friends, from her family and neighbors. Aware that rumors run quickly from word of mouth in her neighborhood, her friends would park their cars a few blocks from her home after an evening out to avoid being seen in their company. Sanaa's imagination of fun and transgression is shaped by the global youth culture that she accessed through satellite television and music, as well as by her vision of upper-class youth cultures in the Moroccan megalopolis. Moreover, the palpable presence of "the outside" expanded further her horizon of imagination and shaped her idea of what an eventful life looks like. It is against this wide range of cultural references that Sanaa reflects on the limits and possibilities present in al-Azaliyya.

Summer Nights and Daydreams of Elsewhere

During summer evenings, when the main avenues of al-Azaliyya are crowded until late, Sanaa's parents allowed her to stay out until 11 p.m. with her female friends in the medina or the neighborhood. After telling her parents that she would be with "the girls" (*l-bnat*), she joined her group of friends in the cafés instead, driving up into the Middle Atlas Mountains when a car was available. Driving up the mountain in the night, listening to loud music and singing her favorite songs, Sanaa felt full of a sense of freedom and lightheartedness. "I feel good! You feel good?" she would ask me, moving to the rhythm of James Brown's famous song. Under the starry sky, Sanaa and her friends sat chatting in the quiet of the mountains, singing, laughing, and smoking hashish, and inevitably jokes and topics of conversation intruded from the "outside."

A powerful dimension of the youth culture in al-Azaliyya, "the outside" entered their conversations while helping to shape their imaginations of a better life (Capello 2009; Vacchiano 2022; Elliot 2021). Many young men depicted migration as essential to build a future in a context where conventional trajectories of upward social mobility are increasingly inaccessible (Menin 2016; Vacchiano 2022). The future often means "building *durof*" (Juntunen 2002)—namely, the socioeconomic conditions they need if they are to fulfill their gendered duties and to participate as adult men in the social and economic worlds. Only a few migrants succeed in establishing themselves as an "adult man" (*rajul*) by investing "the outside money" (*l-flus dyal brra*) in the family, a marriage, or a local business, and some others squander their earnings in ephemeral forms of consumption and vulgar display of wealth (McMurray 2001; Salih 2003). For Sanaa and her friends, the dream of migrating to Italy or Spain does not evoke the achievement of social adulthood in terms of "building *durof*," but in terms of making money and enjoying an eventful life. Some of Sanaa's friends grew up, like her, in families where, at their age, their parents entered jobs with lifelong benefits in the public sector as schoolteachers and civil servants. They, by contrast, belong to a generation who face unemployment, and the money they earn does not suffice to lead a comfortable middle-class life, which, in my young interlocutors' terms, means having a good job, owning a modern apartment, going to restaurants, sending their kids to private school, owning a car, or traveling. Unlike her parents' generation, who benefited from the postcolonial state policy of public education, Sanaa was skeptical about the value of education in her society. Apart from the prestigious private institutions in Morocco or abroad, to which her family could not afford to send her, she considered studying at the state university to be a waste of time in a society where corruption (*l-fasad l-idary*) and bribery (*rshwa*) are widespread, and personal connections (*waseta*) matter more than formal education. Skeptical of state education and desirous of economic independence, Sanaa obtained a diploma as a computer technician in a private school, but she could only find temporary jobs. The lure of the outside and its materialization in the dream of migration foreground the tensions between, on the one hand, her longing for globalized consumerism and, on the other hand, the narrowing of the social and economic opportunities available to the aspiring lower-middle class and middle classes under market liberalization (Cohen 2003, 2004;

Newcomb 2017). In this sense, the lure of the outside reveals the changing situation and generational shifts in what is aspire-able.

Conceived as the chance to live an eventful and exciting life, the longing for the outside acquired specifically gendered connotations for Sanaa and Amal, who imagined migration as the opportunity to "see how you live in Europe" and to experience "total freedom," as they call the possibility to enjoy life as they wish without moral reproach and social consequences. Aware of the power that returning migrants exert when they tell stories about the outside, Leyla would play with her friends' imaginations. Leyla comes from hay el-Mounia, and she and Sanaa and Amal have known each other since girlhood. After she migrated to Italy following her brothers a few years earlier, in the summer of 2009, she came back driving her Italian-plated car. New cars are expensive in Morocco and denote affluence, being associated with the local middle and upper classes and the outside. Looking like a celebrity, with her fake Dolce & Gabbana sunglasses, Valentino handbag, and pretentious manners, Leyla told Sanaa and Amal about the new fashions and the exciting life she leads in Italy. Clearly (at least to me) lying, Leyla claimed that she worked as the manager of a brand shop in Italy and earned a lot of money. Leyla's narratives contributed to shaping the girls' imagination of the possibilities intrinsic to the "outside," while, at the same time, remolding their sense of locality. Comparing their everyday lives with the cosmopolitan and globalized culture, of which Sanaa and her friends aspired to be part, made al-Azaliyya look like a boring small town and made them feel stuck at the margins of the global stage in which the riches and the successful migrants (in their mind, at least) can partake. In his work on would-be Egyptian emigrants, Samuli Schielke (2008, 2015) notes that the expectations of a better life infusing their dreams of emigration make them impatient and discontented, pervaded by a sense of boredom (*malal*). For Schielke (2015, 33), "boredom is an objective state of monotony, but being bored requires the capacity to aim for more and to become aware that there is an alternative to the monotony." As Daniel Mains (2017, 39) writes with respect of urban Ethiopian young men: "Boredom is not only the sensation of having too much time; it is also the sense that the passage of time and day-to-day experience are not meaningful because they do not conform to expectations of progress." In his book on the urban Nepali middle class, Mark Liechty (2020) shows how young people are so overrun by dreams and desires of "elsewhere" accessed through consumption ton of global cultural products that they imagine themselves as hardly alive, cut off from the "real life" of New York and London that they watch on television. Similarly, Sanaa's and her friends' sense of boredom reflects the unfulfilled ground of aspirations and expectations surrounding their dream of leading an eventful life, which they connect with the outside and the lifestyle of upper-class youth in the Moroccan megalopolis, against which they compare the own everyday experiences. Other friends of Sanaa tried to demystify Sanaa's image of the outside by describing the difficulties they had to face abroad. After arriving in Italy and Spain, these young men realized that making money honestly was harder than they had expected, and they had found not a land of opportunities but of unskilled jobs and racism. While achieving economic independence was central to Sanaa's desire to migrate, the chance to enjoy "real freedom" also played a crucial role. When I asked her what she meant by "total freedom," she answered: "I want to tell you how I want to live my life. I want to be free (*horra*), I want to go out, and I want to have a relationship with the man I love, and go to the café with him. I want to travel, to go foreign countries, and to go to the mountains. I want to have fun. I want this life, do you understand?" Sanaa was convinced that, in order to live the life she wanted to live, she needed either money or documents to travel to the outside.

Hidden Lives

Sanaa's irreverent behavior did not go unnoticed, and at times it created tensions with some family members, including her older brother, who associated her longing for fun with disregard for family values. A religiously committed married man in his mid-thirties, he judged her display of indifference to social norms as a form of individualism and disrespect for family connectedness contrary to Islamic values. "You want to behave like a *gawriya*, but you are Arab and Muslim," he often blamed her for what he interpreted as the corrupting influence of Western culture and media consumption. Her mother, a poorly educated and devoted woman who attended women's afternoon religious gatherings in homes, would defend Sanaa, stressing that inner motivations are more important than strictly religious practices and physical appearance. However, when they were alone, she pleaded with Sanaa to cover her shoulders and legs—pleas that Sanaa usually resisted by asserting her right to dress as she chose or insisting that the weather was too hot. When discussing her brother's pressure on her to "dress decently," she claimed that things were different in the past. "When I was a little girl," she said, "unmarried young women would wear the miniskirt, and in my parents' time, in the 1970s, *hippyism* was the trend. There was a hippie culture in Morocco." She also argued that the hijab is not part of traditional dress in Morocco, and that mainly adult women would wear the veil: "My mother donned the *zif* [Moroccan headscarf] only after her marriage, as it was common practice at that time."

Sanaa's words need context. She is right when she claims that women's style of dress was different in the past. As Zakia Salime (2016) points out, in the 1970s the jellaba and the *zif* were mainly confined to the older generation of women; only by the mid-1980s did new Islamic dress codes and "imported fashion" spread in Morocco on the wave of the increasing societal influence of Islamic revival. A hippie culture did exist in Morocco, but the phenomenon was limited to some left-wing student circles and foreign tourists, and, certainly, sexual freedom was not the trend. In invoking this past, Sanaa not only expressed her disappointment with her brother's severe judgment of her behavior but also dislocated "neoorthodox" modes of religiosity that, in her view, have become hegemonic in her town, as extrinsic to Morocco's cultural and religious traditions. She complained that the social control of young women's bodies and sexual behavior has increased in recent years. She said: "Some female neighbors and relatives who have started attending the mosque lessons or religious associations insisted that I should veil. They say, 'You should veil to become pure internally (*nqiya f-l-dkhl*).' I don't think purity has to do with a piece of cloth." Sanaa's words resonate with the narratives that circulate within progressive and feminist circles described by Nadia Guessous (2011, 2020), some of which have been central in the discussions surrounding the Mudawwana reform in 2004. Similarly, the women I met in al-Azaliyya who defined themselves as "secular" (entailing a separation between the religious and the political spheres) or "feminist" evoked the past to express their discontent with what they perceived as the severe tone of public morality and the increased societal influence of Islamist movements. They interpreted the ethical reform of intimate and social lives undertaken by Islamic activists, like the ones we met in chapter 3, as a dangerous political project that threatens women's freedoms and the gender equality for which they campaign. Like Sanaa, they regarded the spread of the hijab as a new phenomenon that does not belong to "Moroccan tradition," but rather is imported from Saudi Arabia via religious satellite programs and by emigrants.

Sanaa did not describe herself as a feminist or secular person, and, although she is not a strictly practicing Muslim, she considered herself religious; she respected some of the fundamental pillars of Islam, such as fasting during Ramadan and avoiding alcohol. She thought that not veiling was a way of being coherent with her ideas and practices since, in her view, the choice of veiling and dressing modestly also entails changing one's bodily behavior and sociality. She said, "I will tell you something—I do not want to wear a veil. If I had the veil, I could not sit in cafés, swim in a bikini, or have male friends." Sanaa considered herself an educated and independent girl who knew about life and hence did not intend to accept any compromises, nor did she care about appearing to be a "good girl" in other people's eyes. In her view, not all veiled girls are animated by the desire to be internally pure, and some use the veil in order to display an image of themselves as good girls or, perhaps, to find a husband. While casting doubts on those veiled girls who go to cafés and have a boyfriend, she also made clear: "I don't want to say these girls are hypocrites (sing. *munafiq*). I believe the cause is the social hypocrisy (*l-nifaq l-ijtima'ay*) that exists in Morocco." In other words, Sanaa associated the gap between the pious look and worldly practices of some veiled young women with social hypocrisy that imposes on these girls the imperative to lead a double life in order to keep up appearances in public and pursue less socially approved desires discreetly. Beyond the veil, Sanaa felt that the majority of young women, including herself, must lie and keep certain things secret. So as to make me understand, she said: "Look, I will tell you how our society is. Now the problem we have in Moroccan society is that we are an Islamic state, we are Arabs, but despite that, we have the European culture in our brains (*'andna f-dmaghna taqafa wropiya*)." Perhaps evoking Morocco's history of intimate and highly ambivalent relations with European—and, in particular, French—culture by the time of the Protectorate, or perhaps thinking of the influence of global televised cultural products on her generation, Sanaa thought that *both* the East (*l-sharq*) and the West (*l-gharb*) are critical sources of identity for young Moroccans. In her opinion, this dual belonging triggers deep contradictions in young women's sense of self. "Especially the young woman who studies," Sanaa explained, "who desires a different life, and so she starts having two lives (*juj dyal l-hayat*), the hidden life (*l-hayat mkhabbiya*) she wants to live—she goes out, she has a boyfriend and travels with him, she works, and then she lives the life we live here, the life of family and society (*l-hayat dyal l-'ay'la w dyal l-mujtama'*)." Referring to the first type of life she had described, Sanaa said: "This is the life I want (*ana l-hayat lly baghyaha*), but often a family cannot bear this life, and hence it remains hidden to the family and society." Of course, not all of the educated young women I knew transgressed social and religious norms. Sanaa's reflections, however, foreground key gendered tensions running through the lives of young women in al-Azaliyya. Learning to live a hidden life is an essential way of reckoning with and navigating competing desires and self-images. The coexistence of a hidden life with a public one ("the life of family and society") is made possible by refined "etiquettes of transgression" based on silence and secrecy practices. Learning to master such etiquettes of transgression opens crucial spaces for enacting desires that cannot be voiced publicly, and this becomes particularly important when it comes to the questions of premarital sex and intimacy. Concurrently, having to keep together two different lives and self-images often creates a sense of fragmentation in my interlocutors, as they have to hide aspects of their life from the people they love.

Silences and Secrets

"If a girl has a boyfriend and has sex with him, she would say she hasn't. Why? Because she is scared," Sanaa said during one of our conversations about premarital sex, promptly adding: "If a girl has a relationship with her boyfriend that lasts five or ten years, can you believe that they haven't had sex? If you believe it, I will think you are mad!" With her words, Sanaa pointed to the gap between the fact that premarital intimacy—with or without vaginal penetration—is widespread (Bakass and Ferrand 2013; Boufraioua 2017; El Aji 2018) and the overwhelming taboos surrounding sexuality (Nagi 2017) in Moroccan society. In her groundbreaking work on young women's intimate lives in Casablanca in the 1980s, Moroccan sociologist Soumaya Naamane-Guessous (1991) connects the unspeakability of sex to the local idea of *hshuma* (discussed in chapter 2) that surrounds invocations of sexuality and renders it unspeakable. For Naamane-Guessous, silence and shame are deeply ingrained in the power relations that substantiate the domination of women's bodies and work to produce their submission to sexual norms. While Naamane-Guessous's insights capture important dynamics surrounding premarital sex and intimacy in central Morocco, my young interlocutors' experiences and thoughts complicate the relations between sexual secrecy and gendered norms.

By discussing the fears associated with premarital sex, Sanaa points to societal control of young women's bodies. As gossip makes public what is supposed to remain secret, it potentially endangers their reputations (*sumʻa*). However, Sanaa's words also gesture toward girls' strategic use of silence to protect themselves from the threat of gossip and the loss of respectability, thereby shedding light on the agentive potential of silence.[1] Highlighting the situational meaning of silence, Roisin Ryan-Flood and Rosalind Gill (2010, xvi) note that "sometimes silence can be a tool of oppression. . . . Sometimes silence is a strategic response to oppression; one that allows subjects to persist in their own way; one that acknowledges that, under certain circumstances, speech might not be empowering, let alone sensible." Moving beyond the repression/resistance opposition, silence and secrecy can be productively situated within the broader politics of (un)sayability in Moroccan society.[2] From this perspective, silence and

1. For an overview of recent anthropological (re)discovery of silence and ethnographic explorations of silence/power/knowledge relations, see Cartovata and Pilotto (2021).

2. I return to this crucial point in chapter 6, where, following my interlocutors' reflections, I connect the dynamics of secrecy/silence to Taussig's (1999) famous elaboration of "public secrets."

secrecy are not only about the gendered embodiment of shame and shyness that reproduces the patriarchal power but can also be legitimate modalities for negotiating gendered dynamics in contexts of uneven power relations. Sociologist Gul Ozyegin (2015, 72) makes a similar point in her exploration of young women's intimate lives in Turkey when she argues that sexual secrecy enhances their freedom to navigate their clandestine lives. As Maria Malmström (2016) shows in her ethnography on young Egyptian women, "the secret self" has agentive and manipulative potentials as long as transgressive actions remain unknown. This resonates with Sanaa's discussion of the tensions between what she calls the "life of family and society" and a "hidden life." Indeed, some young women in al-Azaliyya use silence (*l-skut*) and secrecy (*l-sirriya*) to deal with competing—and, at times, conflicting—gendered moralities and desires. However, this does not mean that they are free of moral conflicts as sexual secrecy often generates ambivalence and guilt (Cheikh 2009; Ozyegin 2015, 73).

In Morocco, the vocabulary surrounding the loss of virginity evokes male violence and female passivity: *khsarha* ("he ruined her"), *sarahha* ("he pulled it"), and *tqabbha* ("he drilled her"). In commonsense knowledge, the girl and her family are held responsible for her virginal status. The moral conflicts and the ambivalence emerging from the experience of sexual transgression and concealment are not triggered only by the tensions between the self and societal norms as opposed, abstract entities but also by the deeply affective and relational dimensions of family connectivity, by desires of belonging and recognition. This affective dimension emerges powerfully in Sanaa's reflections: "The majority of young women keep this life secret because a mother cannot bear to know that her daughter would travel and have sex with a man who is not her husband. You always have to lie to the people you love." With her words, Sanaa suggests that young women's decisions about revealing and displaying are marked not just by fear and social pressure but also by deep concern with the sensibility of the people they love. Despite her outspokenness, Sanaa, too, relied on silence to live the life she wanted to live. However, as Annerienke Fioole (2021) notes, far from establishing a rigid opposition between public and secret spheres of life, unmarried couples in Morocco create space for intimacy through mutual discretion in which friends and relatives can be involved contextually. For example, Sanaa carefully avoided mentioning her love relationship to her father, while she would speak overtly of her boyfriend with her mother, including her into a "conglomerate of confidents" (Fioole 2021, 136)—in other words, "people supposed to be 'in the know.'" Her mother would like to see her daughter married soon, to silence possible gossip, but Sanaa considered herself too young to be married and preferred to enjoy her freedom.

In Sanaa's story, as well as in Najat's romantic vicissitudes discussed in the introduction, mothers know about their daughters' love relationships. They express deep concern for their daughter's reputation and virginal status as they are aware that the lack of virginity may make them vulnerable to her husband and in-laws. This is because the ideal of the virgin bride is widely affirmed in central Morocco, and because mothers fear that the lack of virginity might position their daughter in uneven relations with the family she marries into. The tensions between the ideals and the practices surrounding female sexuality are palpable in the phenomenon of hymen repair surgery, which powerfully reveals both the transgression of the norms and the way unmarried women seek to embody the conventional ideal of the pure bride (El Aji 2018; Wynn 2016; Wynn and Hassanein 2017; Ozyegin 2015; Malmström 2016). Both long-term and temporary hymenoplasty are expensive procedures outlawed under Moroccan law and performed secretly. Sanaa cast doubt on the efficacy of such methods: "Maybe the operation enables one to pass the virginity test, but I don't think a man can really believe it." Whereas some scholars interpret hymenoplasty as a "covert form of resistance" (Ahmadi 2016, 223), a strategy to render "women's sexual histories illegible to observers" (Wynn 2016, 557), Sanaa described it as an example of the hypocrisy of society, while adding: "Perhaps the problem we have is not just virginity itself. It also depends on the family, whether their thinking is modern ('asry), traditional (taqlidy) or conservative (muhafid). Then it depends on the man and his mentality. Regarding nonvirgin girls, if they marry and find someone modern and understanding, otherwise they can have problems with their families and with themselves."

Disguising the bride's virginal status, however, is far from being a new phenomenon, and generations of women have long collectively cooperated to restore virginity artificially on the eve of the wedding by relying on the "traditional methods" for the public display of the bride's blood (S. Davis 1983; Mernissi 1982; Namaane-Guessous 1991, 191–92). In real-life situations, the way in which virginity—and the lack of it—is handled depends on the attitudes of the individuals and families involved. In some cases, the question of virginity is dealt with between husband and wife; for example, some married couples go to a hotel or on a honeymoon after the marriage contract is signed to keep the question of the bride's virginity a private matter. In other cases, the lack of virginity might be a problem, casting shame on the girl and her family. Occasionally, female gossip and secrets uncover a much more complex reality than the official statements suggest. For example, one piece of gossip circulated among Sanaa's female friends that a high school friend of theirs got married to a man with whom she did not have a relationship. When the husband discovered that she was not a virgin (*bekra*, or *'uzuba*), she threatened that if he dared to make it public, she would say "he was not a man" (meaning he was unable to manage intercourse). Imagined and shared as "the 'truth' behind the 'truth'" (Stewart and Strathern 2004, 39) in informal circles of friends, girls' gossip can convey here a discourse on female slyness and crafty defiance of the sexual norms that undermine and play with the conventional visions of the virginal spouse.

The Shifting Boundaries of Intimacy

Sanaa and other girls discussed sex by using a range of terms, like the Arabic expression *'alaqa jinsiya* (sexual relations), or more colloquial expressions such as *dir sex* (to do sex/to have sex) and their equivalents in French (*faire l'amour* and *relation sexuelle*) or those that euphemize sex—for instance, *n'as m'a shy wahed* (to sleep with someone). The ways in which they speak about their sexual encounters, however, are irreducible to the dichotomy opposing chastity versus the loss of virginity, revealing instead a range of intimacy practices that do not necessarily entail penetrative intercourse. Some of my female interlocutors only had mere flirtations, often mediated by digital technologies (to be discussed further in chapter 7) and refused sexual intimacy with their fiancés, afraid that they might not marry them precisely because they were not able to resist their advances. For example, Hasna considered keeping her virginity until marriage an integral aspect of her gendered self and often discussed even kissing in terms of *fasad* (prostitution). Others disclosed that they had kissed their boyfriend, touched his intimate parts, or engaged in other sexual practices that leave the hymen intact, such as rubbing the penis between the thighs without penetration or partial penetration. Scholars also document anal intercourse across Muslim countries as a sexual practice that enables girls to experience intimacy without losing their virginity.[3] Even though none of my interlocutors has ever admitted they experienced it, some mentioned anal sex in conversations on the contradiction of imposing virginity on girls or in the context of girls who have sex for money but want to keep their hymen intact.

Generally, my female interlocutors recognize that some young men do not want to know about a girl's previous sexual life, but think that these are the minority. Sometimes they lament that boys "just play at love" (*ghyr kay-la'abo b l-hobb*) and seek it "to pass time" (*bash kay-dwzo l-wqt*), in certain cases even making bets with their male friends on their ability to conquer a girl; when they gain what they want, some girls claimed, they lose interest in and respect for her and look for another girl to play with. Consequently, girls try to be "tough" (*qasha*) in order to remain respected and keep a boy's interest (Menin 2018). While Sanaa agreed that trust (*tiqa*) can be difficult to build, she also said of this reasoning: "Could you ever know if you will stay together with a man forever? Can you trust a man one hundred percent?"—suggesting that fear that a relationship would end should not make a young woman restrain her sexual desire (*shahwa*). Overtly affirming girls' right to sexual pleasure beyond marriage, Sanaa did not describe sex in terms of transgression or as "male trickery"—sex given on the promise of marriage—but rather as a source of pleasure that women can pursue for its own sake. She looked into my eyes and said: "Listen! Virginity is something very important in our society, but,

---

3. S. Davis and D. Davis (1989, 120) and Bakass and Ferrand (2013) describe similar dynamics. See also Foster (2002, 98–110) for a comparative perspective on Tunisia, and Sadeghi (2010, 273–90) and Mahdavi (2009) on Iran.

between boys and girls, there is attraction. Islam recognizes that women too feel pleasure in sexual relationships." Expressing her viewpoint on sex, Sanaa did not mobilize the language of human rights, nor did she frame her claims as feminist, but she evoked the fundamental place of sexuality and sexual pleasure in Islam (Bouhdiba 1975). Going against the grain of public discourse and morality in al-Azaliyya, Sanaa added: "For me, a man and a woman should not necessarily be married [to have sex]. Perhaps not the first month, but after six months, physical intimacy is something natural in a couple." She paused and made clear: "I speak in this way because I am modern and educated, but people with a small mentality would say this is a shame. It is not like for you. On the outside, this is considered normal." With her words and acts, Sanaa connected the act of speaking of premarital sex with female education, independence, and open mindedness, thus making it a powerful performance of her being modern.

Like Sanaa, her friend Hafida described sex as a key dimension of love. A single woman in her early thirties, Hafida runs her small business in a rented clothes shop in hay el-Mounia. One day, sitting in her shop when it was empty of customers, we began conversing about premarital relationships. Hafida said: "Can a woman live without love? If there isn't love in life, there is nothing!" When I asked her what she meant by "love," she replied: "Love is having a good relationship, mutual understanding, a satisfactory sexual life (*l-hayat l-jinsiya*)—this is love, and this is rare." As her narrative unfolded, I worked out that Hafida, like Ghizlan, had a tragic love story to tell: when she was twenty, she started a relationship with a young man that lasted for five years. They wanted to marry, but his mother opposed their marriage. "She was very jealous and did not intend to share her son's love with another woman," Hafida explained. Ever since, this has prevented her from loving another man. "You know," she said, "most men want to have authority (*sulta*) over a woman. *La liberté* . . . Now I can talk and laugh, but when you have a love relationship . . . a man can tell me, 'Don't go there! Don't talk with your friends!' I cannot bear it! This is the problem." Despite feeling that she was missing something in her emotional and sexual life, Hafida claimed singlehood—which is for her both an unintentional and intentional circumstance—as a viable alternative to a marriage with a controlling man who might constrain the independence that she has gained through her work. "I want a life partner," Hafida added. "I don't want someone who controls me. Now I control myself. I have my money, I live alone, I go wherever I want, I talk with whomever I want." While Hafida's status as an unmarried woman ambiguously positioned her as a *bnt* in the liminal space of unachieved adulthood, she practiced adultness beyond marriage thanks to the freedom and economic independence she has achieved with her work.

As with Hafida, some young women with different social backgrounds expressed disillusionment about marriage and hoped to be economically independent to take control of their lives; a few also claimed that they wanted to stay single. Some young men, too, expressed disenchantment with marriage. Among them, there is Nabyl. One day, when I accompanied Sanaa to Nabyl's to have her eyebrows plucked, we found his shop empty, which allowed us to start a conversation about love and marriage. A single man in his mid-thirties, Nabyl is both Sanaa's hairdresser and her friend. Nabyl countered common assumptions about marriage and the widespread discourse depicting having children as a (social and religious) duty, and importantly, as what makes life worth living. He complained that, in most cases, marriage is not based on a free choice, but is, rather, a social obligation: "In Morocco, you must marry, have children, have a family, otherwise you are not considered a person, an individual (*fard*)." Nabyl expressed his disappointment in the dominant idea of personhood in central Morocco as subsumed in familial and social ties, deeply enmeshed in webs of obligations and gendered duties that, in his view, leave little room for choice and self-determination. He also opened the possibility of thinking of manliness (*rajuliya*) beyond marriage and fatherhood.

Tracing the emergence of novel masculinities across North Africa and the Middle East, scholars discuss how men facing infertility imagine and practice manliness beyond fatherhood (Inhorn 2012; Inhorn and Naguib 2018; Isidoros and Inhorn 2022). Nabyl went a step further in defining singlehood and childlessness as socially legitimate and even desirable options for a man. "Oftentimes," he said, "you marry a person you don't know intimately. Maybe she is a good girl, the one your parents liked, but you don't have sexual chemistry or you don't get on well with her. Couples should be free to live together before marriage and see if they can have a life together. In al-Azaliyya," he added, "living together is impossible for unmarried couples because people are narrow-minded and would judge it scandalous, not to mention homosexual couples living together."

Nabyl's comment on gay couples' predicament requires context. As in all Muslim countries, homosexuality in Morocco is considered contrary to Islam and criminalized by state law,[4] but homoeroticism does exist.[5] While only "reception" is culturally devalued as passive/*zamel* (Dialmy 2019), same-sex practices do not always result in fixed gender identities, nor do they necessarily undermine a man's respectability and masculinity (Dialmy 2000; Rebucini 2013). Only in the past two decades has the term "gay" (as well as "lesbian," "transgender," and the like) emerged as a specific gendered identity in Morocco (Dialmy 2019). On the other hand, the rise of the LGBTQ+ movement in Morocco, the activism of intellectuals like Moroccan writer Abdellah Taïa, and the campaigns for the depenalization of homosexuality have been paralleled by the "birth of homophobia in Morocco," which "expresses an Islamic and an Islamist refusal of homosexuality as a normalized and legal identity" associated to Western culture (Dialmy 2019, 258). According to Abdessamad Dialmy, same-sex practices are less tolerated today, and the risk of collective homophobic violence is real. Nabyl's words thus refer precisely to the emerging debates on individual freedoms and sexual rights in Morocco, as well as to growing homophobia.

After we left Nabyl's shop, on our way back home Sanaa said that, in a small town like al-Azaliyya, it is difficult for unmarried couples to cohabit, but, in Casablanca, her older brother lived with his fiancé, now his wife, as boyfriend and girlfriend (*msahbiyn*). "The problem is that

---

4. Article 489 of Morocco's Penal Code defines homosexuality as "an indecent act or act against nature" and punishes it with from six months to three years in prison and a fine of two hundred to one thousand dirham.

5. While a focus on homosexuality is beyond the scope of this book, it worth noting that some scholars trace the confinement of sex to heterosexual marriage as a relatively recent norm that emerged as a result of colonial encounters and the modernist project of the heteronormalization of sexualities beginning in late nineteenth-century Iran (Najmabadi 2005; Babayan and Najmabadi 2008; Afary 2009).

when my parents went on a visit, he must pretend he shared the apartment with a male friend," she added, laughing. The fragments of conversations shared in everyday life situations with Sanaa and her friends show that new gendered subjectivities have emerged in recent decades, and new desires are given voice in the (semi)public spaces of socialization and friendship relationships. Sanaa, Nabyl, and Hafida were not the only people who openly contested the central role of marriage in the definition of social adulthood in central Morocco. They also claimed alternative ways of being gendered selves and searched for intimate connections beyond socially prescribed pathways.

Embodying "Badness"

Framing the complex interplay of revealing and concealing that shapes the contours of transgression as a social and gendered practice, I have argued that transgression in al-Azaliyya does not lay merely in the act of breaking the norms but in contravening it publicly, as keeping the smooth public face is considered a vital aspect of respectable and moral selves. Philippe Chaudat and Monia Lachheb (2018, 17–27) make a similar point when they argue that transgression is not necessarily an index, or a "revelation" (Cheikh 2020b, 435), of deviance but a constant and structural dimension in North African societies. Transgression, they maintain, is tolerated by the religious and political powers that be as long as it remains secret and does not overtly call into question the social and moral orders. Sexual transgression embodied in the visibility of an out-of-wedlock pregnancy poses challenge to the social, religious, and political order due to the oxymoron it represents in a context where legitimate filiation and descent are permitted only within marriage. As long as it remains secret, the sexual transgression does not necessarily undermine the girl's sexual honor (*sharaf*) and reputation (*sum'a*), especially when the intact hymen is preserved. As we have seen, the loss of virginity can be disguised or repaired in various ways, or can be managed privately between the marital couple, whereas an out-of-wedlock pregnancy can be hardly dissimulated. Before the 2004 Mudawwana reform, the state had less control over family ties, and both marriage and out-of-wedlock pregnancy could be simply registered later (Fioole 2020). In contemporary al-Azaliyya, unless marriage is arranged to cover potential scandals, such pregnancies cast a shadow on the girl's moral conduct.

Crucially, single motherhood is far from being a new phenomenon in Morocco, and, in the past, its potential to trigger scandal was accommodated through cover-up strategies.[6] Amal Bousba and Abderrahim Anbi (2017) note that, starting from the 1980s, the decrease of traditional mechanisms to integrate/invisibilize unwed mothers and their children, in tandem with the lack of institutional support in a rapidly changing socioeconomic scenery, has contributed to the visibility, and stigmatization, of single motherhood.

Notwithstanding the increased visibility of the phenomenon in the past few decades, thanks to the efforts of organizations providing support and campaigning for full citizenship rights,[7] unwed mothers (in French, *mères célibataires*) and their children face affective, social, economic, and legal discrimination (Namaane-Guessous, Guessous 2011, 13; Capelli 2021; Bousbaa 2022).[8] I could observe some of the consequences of unintended pregnancy when Sanaa's friend Amal discovered she was expecting. Although Amal did not face economic and legal discrimination, her pregnancy positioned her as a "bad girl" (*khayba*) in the eye of society. The notion of "bad girls"—conceived here as "women whose transgressive behaviors and perspectives challenge societal norms in the Arab world" (Yaqub 2017, 3)—helps me unravel the socially constructed boundaries

---

6. For example, I was told that, especially in the past, people used to explain an unwed girl's pregnancy with the claim that she incidentally got in contact with sperm in hammam. Bousbaa and Anbi (2017, 55) describe such beliefs as "licit protection mechanisms" used until the 1980s to maintain social cohesion.

7. Children born out of wedlock are called "bastards" (*wuld haram*) and do not have legal recognition (see note 8).

8. According to Article 490 of the Moroccan Penal Code, single mothers are punishable with imprisonment of a month to a year for *zina*. Similarly, the father is punishable for *zina*, without having any obligation toward the child afterward. The reformed Mudawwana introduces provisions for the recognition of paternity (e.g., if the couple can prove that conception occurred during formal engagement); it also allows the mother to resort to DNA analysis (Bousbaa and Anbi 2017, 56).

between "proper" and "improper" femininities, and the gender and sexual ideologies underlying them.

Like Sanaa, Amal had a relationship for a few years but did not plan her pregnancy, nor was her boyfriend enthusiastic about becoming a father, at least initially. Amal and her boyfriend tried to collect the money to terminate the pregnancy without letting their family know about it. Although abortion is illegal in Morocco, it is performed clandestinely under the payment of one thousand to ten thousand dirham (Gruénais 2017).[9] The couple could not afford the operation and had to face their parents. Amal's mother, who was supportive, spoke to Amal's father, who stopped speaking to her. Amal's boyfriend's father firmly opposed their marriage by casting doubts on her respectability and his son's paternity of the child. Her boyfriend's father's opposition profoundly affected their relationship, and her boyfriend became cold and distant. Amal said: "There was real love between us. Everything was good . . . we loved each other. I was used to doing everything with him. I could not live without him. Now our relationship has changed due to these problems. He does not look like the type of person I met at the beginning." Amal lamented that her boyfriend would phone her day and night and was always available for her; they spent their spare time together, while now she had to phone him to talk or to arrange a meeting with him. She said: "He's given me very little [money] since I got pregnant . . . but what I want to say is, what kind of love is this? A person who really loves you stays by you. If you have problems, he stays with you, he talks with you. He knows I have a problem and he does not want to have anything to do with me . . . when I was all right, I didn't have any problems, he loved me, but this is not love! He can go to a *teleboutique* with two dirham and phone me, but he doesn't."

In Amal's eyes, her boyfriend's misbehavior denoted his lack of sincere love toward her. She thought that as long as she was economically

9. According to the Moroccan Penal Code, unless in the case of a woman whose health is in danger or who has been raped (Art. 453), abortion is illegal, and those physicians who perform clandestine operations risk up to five years imprisonment and a fine of two hundred to five hundred dirham (Art. 449), and the woman risks six to twenty-four months in jail (Art. 454).

independent, he enjoyed keeping her company, but when she got pregnant, he distanced himself and escaped his responsibility. On the other hand, she tried to make sense of his misbehavior by speculating that he did not want to compromise his reputation in "men's society" by meeting her in public. In her view, his friends meddled in the affair and insinuated that she was an "easy girl." She said, "His friends say to him, 'Is it true, this marriage? What have you done? We saw Amal is pregnant. It's not you who did it.' This is the question he does not want to be asked, do you understand? This is why he does not try to meet me now outside because my belly is growing. I don't want to meet him and go around. I want him to come and visit me and see what I need, to phone me and ask: 'How are you? How is the baby? Do you need anything?' Because this is not only my child, do you understand?"

With Amal, Sanaa often reflected on the gendered power dynamics between unmarried couples. So far, indeed, the two girls had experienced egalitarian relationships with their boyfriends, but the difficult situation Amal was facing made them feel more concretely the gendered inequalities in their society. Sanaa, too, thought that Amal's boyfriend was not behaving responsibly toward her and the baby. "You see?" she would ask. "As long as you are independent . . . but when you have problems . . . but this is not *l'amour*. You see, the girl becomes pregnant (*hamla*) and the guy runs away from her (*kay-harb 'aliha*)." Many friends distanced themselves from Amal, while Sanaa stayed by her in this difficult moment of her life.

As I felt particularly touched and disoriented by Amal's story, I discussed it with Hasna (they did not know each other), because I wished to grasp her stance on the situation and more generally on the delicate question of out-of-wedlock pregnancy. Despite the difference between the two girls, Hasna did not express moral judgment of Amal's sexual conduct, as I expected, but rather empathized with her. Contextually, she recounted to me the story of a neighborhood boy: "The guy fell in love with a girl from another neighborhood and they started a relationship. After a few years, she became pregnant, and marriage was quickly arranged by the two families." However, Hasna said, marriage did not prevent tensions between the bride and her groom's sisters from emerging during the year in which the couple lived in his family's home, and eventually the couple decided to move to a rented apartment in another neighborhood. Hasna explained that tensions were aroused because, "for people, a nonvirgin bride loses her value (*qima*), as if the man did her a favor by marrying her." Contrasting the behavior of Amal's boyfriend to that of the neighborhood guy, Hasna remarked that the latter never cast a shadow over his girlfriend's morality. While the responsibility for an unintended pregnancy generally falls on girls, the story she told me challenges commonsense ideas of female respectability and male honor in central Morocco. Unlike Amal's boyfriend, the guy took up his responsibility toward his girlfriend and, after marriage, did not hesitate to leave his family's home when he realized that the atmosphere was unbearable for her.

Amal and her boyfriend married eventually, but they did not celebrate their wedding. This lack of publicity generated discontent and rumor among Amal's entourage. She often had to defend herself against her relatives' criticism and disapproval. It was not just the lack of public celebrations that Amal had to explain, but the fact that she did not live with her husband—she remained at her parents' home during her pregnancy. She always claimed that they were seeking a modern apartment to start their married life, but lacked the money and time to rent and furnish it, so she preferred to stay at home with the help of her mother. When we were alone, however, she often complained that her husband's family did not want her at home; on the other hand, she emphasized that she did not want to live with people who would look down on her. Amal's mother told me that she was willing to host the couple in their home. When I visited Amal in 2013, however, she and her baby were still living with her parents. I could not grasp Amal's situation and wondered if divorce might be a possibility in the end, especially since her mother asked me if I could find a visa for her daughter to emigrate to Italy. Sanaa, too, wanted to emigrate.

Inhabiting the Malleability of the Norms

Tracing how young women navigate the gendered cultural ideals orienting public life in al-Azaliyya, I have foregrounded in this chapter the central place of transgression in the local dynamics of fun, love, and sex.

Specifically, I have explored both hidden and open transgressions, not merely as modalities of challenging the norms, but as gendered social practices (Hardon and Posel 2012; Ryan-Flood and Gill 2010) through which young women creatively inhabit the tensions between what Sanaa calls "the life of the family and the society" and the "hidden life." Sanaa's idea of the hidden life, with the refined "etiquettes of transgression" sustaining it, recalls Gul Ozyegin's (2015) notion of façade as the collective and collaborative acts in which previous generations, too, had invested in the pursuit of resistance, repudiation, and individual agency on the one hand and conformity, connectivity, continuity on the other. The secrecy practices and discreet transgressions described here enable the young women of al-Azaliyya to fulfill competing desires and self-images in situations requiring different enactments of the gendered selves.

Far from understanding open and hidden transgressions romantically as a form of resistance (Abu-Lughod 1990), I have argued that mastering the local etiquettes of transgression can be framed more productively as a distinctive way of inhabiting the malleability of the norms. This specific focus, in turn, tells us something important about how young women reckon with different social situations contextually to navigate the tensions between public and secret selves. In foregrounding these tensions, however, I do not intend to depict my interlocutors as fragmented subjects who hold several things to be true and work situationally, nor do I seek to set the self against society as an abstract entity. On the contrary, I conceive my interlocutors as multipositioned gendered selves who seek to combine competing desires for conformity and transgression by inhabiting culturally defined spaces of action. In this sense, close attention to the question of transgression is central to a deeper anthropological understanding of gendered selves, desires, and morality in Muslim life. Especially when coupled with secrecy and silence, girls' transgression is not just *against* moral and societal norms, but requires much moral work. In different ethnographic contexts, Magnus Marsden (2005, 74) and Maria Malmström (2016, 193–94) contend that the desire to keep certain things secret may have different connotations, being central both to their experiences of transgression and to their learning how to become moral and respectable gendered subjects. Ideals of secrecy are not only vital components of young women's immoral actions, cheating, and transgression but also a crucial dimension of gendered moral actions.

With its elaborated etiquettes and standards, transgression, like public conformity, contains within it both moral and immoral dimensions. Mastering the local etiquettes of transgression opens up important rooms for freedom and enhances young women's agentive capacities to live the life they want, as Sanaa said. Concurrently, worries about morality and respectability run deep in the secrecy practices through which my interlocutors circumvent social norms and their family's gendered expectations. Even self-proclaimed transgressive girls like Sanaa—who cunningly hide aspects of their life from her parents to expand their flexible space for freedom—express concern about hurting the feelings of their loved ones. Crucially, such lived concerns, in conjunction with secret infringements of gendered and social expectations, take us beyond the simplistic opposition between transgression and reproduction of the norms.

The focus on the ways in which young women in al-Azaliyya reckon with conflicting desires invites reflection on the broader implications of hidden and open transgressions. As we have seen, hidden transgression is socially tolerated and "could function as a kind of safety valve within the society where political and religious morality has a very important weight" (Chaudat and Lachheb 2018, 20; my translation). In contrast, the reflections of Sanaa and Amal direct our attention to gendered practices that contravene the local etiquettes of transgression with which young women in al-Azaliyya maintain façades while discreetly crossing the line. The open transgression can have important gendered implications, as it emerges vividly in Amal's vicissitudes and in Sanaa's reflections on the affective aspects of lying, on girls' embodiment of societal pressure on preserving virginity, and on the stigma of badness attached to those girls who do not put up a façade. Even though Sanaa was aware that her search for fun and freedom was disapproved of locally, she claimed the normalcy and ordinariness of her desires as part of her youthfulness, thereby calling into question the predominant ideas of femininity and respectability in central Morocco.

Sanaa's desire to get out and have fun is not simply a hedonistic search for pleasure and diversion, but rather gives shape to her vision of the society where she lives. Through her leisure and consumption practices, Sanaa imagined and crafted herself as a specific gendered subject who does not conform to gendered visions of the good girl (*bnt d-dar*), nor to the definition of the pious female subject promoted by local revivalist movements. Resorting to a set of arguments that belong to the contemporary debates on modernity, gender, and cultural authenticity in Morocco, she invoked alternative ways of being a young Muslim woman.

Carved out through hidden and open transgression, "feeling free" is a critical dimension of Sanaa's sense of self. With her friends, she enjoys breaking the social and gendered norms that define the appropriate leisure activities and sexual conduct for girls in al-Azaliyya. For her friend Hafida, too, freedom is central to her sense of self. While Hafida locates her freedom in her economic independence and unmarried status, ultimately Sanaa situates what she calls "total freedom" outside Morocco, in "the outside," which she knows through television and the stories told by returning migrants. In chapter 6, I discuss how a group of university students uses the language of "true love" as a political concept to reflect on the tensions between openness and secrecy and between voice and silence.

6

The Party of Love

A few months before the 2011 revolutions and protests flared up in North Africa and the Middle East, I became involved in the search for "true love" (in French, *le vrai amour*) for Jamila, a twenty-three-year-old student of Islamic studies. I first met her in 2009, in a private language school, where we attended a course in French conversation. After class, we sometimes went out for coffee, and she often invited me to her home, an apartment on the first floor of a two-story building in a low-income neighborhood where she lived with her family. Defining herself as "romantic" (*romantique*), Jamila claimed she wanted to marry for love. She liked talking about love, which she described as "a very interesting and important topic" and "a topic particularly dear to my heart." Wishing to give me insight into the thoughts of the local youth, Jamila introduced me to her friends, a group of university students between the ages of twenty-three and twenty-six. Only a few of them came from the bourgeoisie, while most, like Jamila, had modest socioeconomic and cultural backgrounds yet were pursuing a university education. They all felt they had grown up in a rapidly changing Moroccan society and were searching for a different kind of intimate life from that of their parents, whose marriages were, in their view, without love. Jamila and some of her friends aspired to a relationship with their partner based on personal affinities, shared interests, and "true love." Imagined as integral to their being young and educated, true love expresses authentic emotions and a mode of intimacy based on both emotional and sexual fulfillment, which is worth pursuing both *before* and *after* marriage.

Building on the previous chapter with its focus on the interplay between publicness and secrecy, in this chapter I follow the reflections of Jamila and her male friends to show how their search for true love reveals a powerful vocabulary and imagination through which they reflect upon themselves and their society. As they reckoned with the possibilities and contradictions they encountered in their search, my interlocutors discussed male-female relationships and critically compared changing ideas of masculinity and femininity across generations. Connecting their personal experiences to social and political powers operating in their society, Jamila and her friends also used the language of "true love" to develop a critique of the established authorities, institutions, and ideologies that shape social and intimate lives in al-Azaliyya. Engaging with Michael Hardt's (2011) theorization on the transformative potential of love, as well as with his critics (Berlant 2011; Salih 2016; Wilkinson 2017), I trace how my young interlocutors' search for love—and the difficulties it involves—opens up fundamental horizons for envisioning personal, social, and political transformation. True love emerges here not only as an ideal of intimate attachment and gendered subjectivities but also as a romantic utopia. This is perhaps because, as Iva Illouz (1997, 9) argues, "love is a privileged site for the experience of utopia" insofar as it celebrates the dyad over society and "also opens the possibility of an alternative social order. Love . . . both promises and demands a better world." My interlocutors' quest for love expands the imagination of alternative social order based on different rationality and relationality. Instead of framing premarital love as a dangerous passion to be ruled by reason, as they claim their parents' generation does, they display a different rationality, which includes feelings and passions as a particular way of knowing the self and engaging the world. Imagining themselves as specific gendered subjects in relation to intimate others, they demand a different relationality between men and women and between generations.

Scholars show how, both in colonial times and in the contemporary contexts of globalization and market liberalization, people have engaged with love as a way of challenging traditional forms of power, elaborating generational distinctions, and envisioning different gender relations (Hirsch and Wardlow 2006; Padilla et al., 2007; Cole and Thomas 2009). While my interlocutors' romantic idea of true love, and the intimate and social demands it contains, takes shape in a globalized flow of music, books, movies, and consumer cultures, it cannot be reduced to globalization and the desire to fashion themselves as modern subjects. Rather, I situate their idea of love with respect to the long-standing debates on love marriage with which generations of Moroccans have reimagined political and intimate life since the dawn of independence (see the introduction). However, unlike the generations of human rights activists and leftists who challenged Morocco's authoritarian regime in the 1960s and 1970s, my interlocutors' quest for true love does not impel them to take political action. Nevertheless, their romantic utopia triggers reflection on the limits and possibilities of choice and freedom set by the different powers operating in their lives. Using true love as a social and political concept embedded in the historical context in which they live, Jamila and her friends reflect upon an eminently political silence and secrecy that, in their view, surrounds love and sexuality in Morocco, and they scrutinize the interlocking powers that confines love and sexuality to the spheres of invisibility and unspeakability.

I shall suggest that the connection that Jamila and her friends draw between the search for a voice (to express feelings of love and desire for sexual pleasure) and freedom in their intimate lives takes shape against the backdrop of the changed political climates marked by new freedoms of speech and emerging debates on individual liberties in the post–Hassan II era. Self-censored in public but vividly discussed with friends in the informal spaces of youth sociality, my interlocutors' voices and desires cannot be subsumed under umbrella labels such as "feminist" or "liberal." On the contrary, they are articulated from the standpoint of people who regard themselves as Muslim, if not strictly practicing, and respectful of family ties, but who also want to take control of their intimate and sexual lives. So as to unpack their quest for true love and its political dimensions, let me begin by exploring how Jamila engaged with love to imagine herself as a specifically gendered subject in relation to others.

The Subject of True Love

Dressed in tight blue jeans and T-shirts long enough to cover her hips, Jamila would passionately read me the love poems she wrote in French while sitting in a snack bar crowded with youths. One legacy of the colonial presence in Morocco, French is the language Jamila associated with French literature and romances, and that she considered more apt to express her feelings. Not only did Jamila regard Moroccan Arabic as "too harsh" for talking about love but she also connected the French language—the language of the Moroccan cultural and economic elite—to education and class. In a sense, we can interpret her poetic recitation as a performance of modernity.

Describing the thrilling experience of "falling in love," Jamila celebrated love as a noble state of mind, but she added that she suffered for its absence—perhaps its impossibility—in her life. She often complained that the majority of Moroccan men are not capable of loving a woman with the kind of love that clears any hurdle, the kind she learned about by watching movies and reading romantic novels. "In *Autumn in New York*," she explained, "the protagonist becomes sick with cancer, but her partner stays with her till the end. This type of love is rare in Morocco." Taking this cinematic image as the reality of love relationships in the West, Jamila emphasized the different "mentality" (*mentalité*) of "Moroccans" and "the Westerners," as she put it. This difference, in her view, also emerges in male attitudes to women in the street. Because Jamila was attractive, with piercing black eyes and long curly hair, young men commented on her beauty while we were strolling together in the streets of al-Azaliyya. In addition to facing verbal harassment, Jamila disclosed that she had received sexual proposals from some male acquaintances that had made her feel as though she were looked as just an object of pleasure. She defined the majority of her male peers as "savages" because of their uncontrolled sexuality and their lack of respect for women. Considering herself to be an educated young woman, she aspired to have equal relations with her male peers, by whom she wanted to be respected as a thoughtful person.

When I returned to al-Azaliyya in 2010, I was surprised to see that Jamila had replaced her blouse with a tight-fitting but long-sleeved shirt and covered her hair with a brightly colored veil. When I asked her why she was wearing the veil, she answered conventionally: "You know, according to our religion, a woman should be veiled." Jamila was not interested in delving into her decision, apart from saying that she took it "for the sake of God," but she was keen to talk of love. Changing the subject, she invited me to her home the next day because she wanted to show me the PowerPoint presentation on love that she had prepared for her French class. The next day, we were sitting in front of a computer screen in her sitting room. The presentation provided the opportunity to discuss the hopes and frustrations connected with her quest for true love, as well as opened a reflection on the gendered modalities of masculinity and femininity that, in her view, shape intimate dynamics in al-Azaliyya.

Jamila would read one slide, then explain and comment on it, either referring to her personal experience or sharing with me her general considerations on Morocco. She began with a definition of love (*l'amour*) as a multifaceted sentiment, encompassing the love of God, parents' love of their children, the love of an ideal, and the love of a lover. Then she listed the various states of mind and emotions connected with *l'amour charmant* and *l'amour romantique*, such as intense desire and pleasure, vulnerability and suffering. "In the latter case," she said, "it's better to give up." In the middle of her explanation, her mother entered to serve us mint tea and homemade bread with olive oil. By showing proudly the three rolls of fat around her waist, she invited me to eat more in order to embody local female beauty ideals by repeating: "Eat, my daughter!" Before leaving the room, she turned to me and said: "Moroccans say, 'I love you, I love you,' (*kan-bghik, kan-bghik*), but you never trust them!" I imagined that Jamila's mother might have grasped the subject of our conversation, and, considering me an unmarried woman alone, unfamiliar with local practices and vocabularies, felt compelled to provide maternal advice by warning me against the seductive power of love talk. Her opinion reflects commonsense knowledge in al-Azaliyya, which considers love talk as a means to seduce and enchant girls to obtain a sexual encounter more than an authentic expression of inner feelings. Visibly embarrassed by her mother's comments and advice, Jamila—who embodied the ideal of a slimmer, Western body, suitable for Western dress—felt compelled to excuse her intrusion. Perhaps to explain her mother's statements, she added: "My father and my mother did not know each other before marrying. They just got married, so what is love for them? It's just a habit (*l'habitude*)." Jamila explained that her parents are tied together by a type of feeling that resulted from "getting used to each other" through a life spent together by sharing the duties and responsibilities of marriage and their children's upbringing. "That's why the old generations say that love comes with time," she concluded, evoking the common saying in Morocco that "love comes after marriage." Thinking over a few examples of people who had married for love, she added: "A second marriage is more likely to be based on love. But this situation makes people unhappy."

This episode reveals the different ideas and visions of love underpinning Jamila's and her mother's perspectives, respectively. In her discussion of her parents' marital relationship, Jamila dismisses as "habit" modes of affection and love that are not based on "modern" practices of courtship, leisure, and intimacy, but that entail a process of becoming related to one another over years of a good marriage. Older women's narratives reveal more complex dynamics than Jamila's words suggest. Some women who were married off at an early age affirmed the vital importance of love in marriage and suffered from the lack of it in their own. In chapter 2, I showed that 'Aisha and her husband, like other married couples, developed affection and trust over time.[1] Hasna, too, sees this type of intimate relatedness when looking at parents' relationships. The marriage stories of the older generations of women I collected in Azaliyya show that marital relationships cannot be simply reduced to habit. At times, secret exchanges of gazes and romantic words on the rooftop between kin and neighbors could lead to infatuations and marriage proposals. Besides these exchanges, infatuations also developed in sexual encounters, and scandals were accommodated and forgotten. Some middle-aged couples disclosed that their marriage resulted from a secret romance and recounted how they subtly maneuvered in order to be able to get married or to make their marriage seem to be "arranged." Some other couples surrendered to parental opposition and social constraints but still cherish the vivid memory of their painful stories of unfulfilled romance.

Complicating the opposition Jamila sets between her vision of authentic love and a normative and essentialized vision of traditional marital

---

1. Similarly, Susan Schaefer Davis (1983) notes that couples married by arrangement in a Moroccan village in the 1960s often developed deep feelings of love and care for each other over time.

relations, I am not suggesting that she understated the space for agency and transgression that tradition itself contains and enables. What is worth noting is that love is central to Jamila's desire to mark her way of being a woman, which differs significantly from that of her illiterate mother. Her mother disregarded verbal expression of one's love to the lover, linking love with marriage and taking up responsibility instead. On the contrary, Jamila considered the expression of emotion as an important dimension of intimacy and love between educated couples. Linda-Ann Rebhun (1999) identifies a similar generational difference in her work on the changing dynamics of love in urbanizing Brazil. She notes that young people placed a new emphasis on the verbal expression of love, which they connected to being modern, whereas the older generations experienced love in terms of material care and mutual support (see also Hirsch and Wardlow 2006). It is precisely within the difference between *saying* and *showing* that we can situate Jamila's and her mother's divergent visions of love and marriage.

After her mother had left the room, Jamila reverted to her Power-Point presentation on love by navigating its complexities and nuances. She explained that love between women and men can develop into carnal attraction (*l'amour corporel*) and spiritual love (*l'amour de l'âme*), but she also remarked that, unfortunately, spiritual love is rare in Morocco. Then she paused and, shifting the tone of our conversation, called for a change in the predominant "mentality" of people, especially in men's attitude toward women. She said: "In Morocco, we need a change. Morocco is an extraordinary country, with its culture, traditions, history; the main problem is its inhabitants. People's mentality should change. Men regard women as a piece of meat (*morceau de viande*), they do not love women nor do they want to discuss their ideas with them—they just want to possess their body." With her words, Jamila turns her passionate "phenomenology of love" into a critique of the gender ideologies that shape male-female interactions.

Habiba Chafai (2021) argues that the cultural normalization of sexual harassment in Morocco is connected intimately with gender inequalities and imaginations underlying men's behavior toward girls and women. In al-Azaliyya, verbal and sexual harassment is widespread. "Fishing/hunting the girls" (*tay-seyd l-banat*; to pick the girls up), street displays of hot comments on women, and flirting and romance are all arenas in which young men compete in same-sex gangs and fashion themselves through different masculine performances. Jamila's generalization only captures one facet of the intricate relations between the sexes in central Morocco, and her experience with young men was much more nuanced and complex than she suggested. However, in calling for a different relationality between men and women, based on mutual recognition as equal human beings, Jamila mobilized the language of love to give voice to the changes she hoped for in her intimate and social life. Facing the computer screen displaying her PowerPoint Presentation, Jamila concluded bitterly: "In love relationships, there is nothing we can call love in Moroccan society."

While Jamila found it difficult to build relationships based on equality and true love, friendship enabled her to share ideas and thoughts with some of her male peers, as well as to experience trust with them. In the following sections, I allow her friends to explain in their own voices. Far from considering their viewpoints on love as representative of a generation of young educated men in al-Azaliyya, I trace how love itself is central to their gendered embodiments of, and reflections on, masculinity.

Rethinking Masculinities

One day I received a phone call from Jamila, who invited me to join her for a stroll in the medina with Samir, a master's degree candidate in Rabat who was back in al-Azaliyya to visit his family. Jamila introduced me as an Italian PhD student working on the subject of love in Morocco. While walking toward a youth café, Samir conversed with me casually, asking questions and answering mine. He said that "physical attraction" (l-hobb l-jsd) is the basis of male involvement, but he made clear that it is not enough to build a stable relationship with a woman. As he put it, "Maybe you sleep together, and that's it." Even though Samir did not exclude the possibility that "love at first sight" (l-hobb b-l-awl nadra) might exist, he thought that a love relationship should develop from what he called "intellectual love" (l-hobb taqafy) and "emotional involvement" (l-hobb watif). When I asked him whether he would marry a girl with whom he had a premarital relationship, he replied positively, explaining that knowing each other enables the couple to understand whether they can bear each other's flaws in a life together. However, I felt puzzled when he made clear that he would marry his girlfriend only if she had lost her virginity with him but not in a previous relationship. He considered love a noble sentiment, but he emphasized the importance of maintaining rational control, because, he said, "Today it is not easy to find a serious girl." Samir thought that one has to be careful, as there are girls who are liars (*kddebbat*) or who "do zig-zag" (*dayrin zig zag*)—meaning that they are not honest and serious. Like other young male interlocutors of mine (see chapter 4), Samir complained that female peers store the numbers of many men on their mobile phones, flirting and entertaining several partners to obtain money, gifts, and favors, as, he said, today girls are attracted by money more than by love. Money is, for men, an integral part of the intimate dynamics of caring and taking care in relationships (Cheikh 2009, 2020a), whether marital, extramarital, or premarital. Most of my female interlocutors judged the intensity of their partner's love also by his ability to provide them with money and financial support. They expected their boyfriend to call them, bring them gifts, pay for their outings, and provide for their everyday necessities, actions that they frame as "He takes care of me (*kay-thalla fiya*)." Aymon Kreil (2016) emphasizes the material conditions of love in Egypt, and Sandra Nasser El-Dine (2018) shows how gifting practices are central to making masculinity in the dynamics of intimate exchanges in Jordan. More than just expressing his wish for a nonmonetary basis for love, Samir's words gave voice to general anxiety about changing gender power relations and what he perceived as the commodification of love relationships in a context of global capitalism.[2]

Virginity was a sensitive subject for my young male interlocutors when they thought of their future wife, and Samir was no exception. Unlike him and the other few young men with whom I discussed this issue,

2. Rachel Newcomb (2017, 39) connects men's discourses on women's untrustworthiness with the broader context of the 2004 revisions of the Mudawwana: in other words, the freedom to divorce granted to women has created a climate of fear and suspicion on the part of men that women are marrying and divorcing them to exploit them. I came across similar arguments during my fieldwork.

Rachid, a twenty-four-year-old schoolteacher in a primary school, claimed that he did not regard virginity as an essential criterion in deciding on marriage—mutual trust and a shared mentality were more important. On the afternoon that Jamila showed me her PowerPoint presentation on love, she received a text message from Rachid as she was finishing up. Jamila beeped him back, and, in a few minutes, he was knocking at her front door. Jamila introduced him as "her closest friend" (*mon ami intime*), and when she informed him about the topic of our conversation, Rachid positioned himself as a supporter of the "party of love" (*le parti de l'amour*). Keen to join the conversation, he started his reflection by emphasizing the generational gap between young men and their fathers, which he explained in terms of two different sensibilities and worldviews. He described love as a central dimension of both premarital and married life and argued that today young people aspire to have a different intimate life from that of their parents, which, in his view, was based on pragmatism. "You see," he said, "here in Morocco we have two generations—the former one that considers love as something . . . not concrete . . . that comes after marriage, but is love like getting used to someone? But we, the new generation, talk of love as 'true love' before and after marriage alike."

At first sight, the generational shift Rachid identifies in the opposition of the ideas of "true love" and "pragmatic love" seems to echo Anthony Gidden's (1992) idea of a progression from traditional relationships to romantic love, and then to "pure relationships" based on what he calls "confluent love": a conditional relationship chosen by equal individuals and free from external constraints. Rachid's view complicates such linear progression by showing how different modes of intimate relationships coexist among young people in al-Azaliyya. Even though he opposed the old and the new generations, he recognized that not all young people search for true love, and that there are girls and boys alike who have several relationships simultaneously for the sake of pleasure or money. However, he identified the main difference in terms of a generational gap. Contrasting his father's visions of love with his own ideas, Rachid said: "Love is . . . trust, you find someone with a similar mentality, and age as well. It's not a problem whether she is one year older or younger, but not a big difference. For the older generation, that's normal—men in their mid-thirties looking for girls aged eighteen or fifteen."[3] In contrast, Rachid aspired to a love relationship with a girl his own age, with whom he can share the same mentality, interests, and life projects. However, true love is far from lacking constraints. As Rachid noted, a young man's wish to marry the girl he loves encounters many obstacles: "The problem is that love relationship . . . many times it happens that, even if you love her, you don't get married." When he was in high school, he fell in love with a girl, but he did not dare reveal his feelings because he was still a student and financially dependent on his family. Subsequently, a marriage was arranged for the girl with a man older than Rachid and with a higher social position.

In addition to discussing the question of a young man's financial independence in marriage choice, which is crucial for many lower-class Moroccan youths, Rachid felt he could not share his feelings of love for a woman with his father, who regards love as an ephemeral passion disconnected from the social values upon which marriage should rest. Evoking the unspeakability of the subject between a father and his son, he said: "When you talk of love, you are a weakling—hence, for the older generation, you can't discuss love in front of your father." Not all fathers with whom I discussed this topic opposed the idea of love marriage for their children. Some did explain to me that family life is not based on transient passions and infatuations, but rather on seriousness and responsibility; they complained that young people, especially university students, fall in love and want to marry, but they have neither the social maturity nor the material means to provide for the wedding, the home, or their wife and children. These fathers highlighted the material and economic duties that marriage entails and linked marital love to responsibility (Naguib 2015); they thought they had the necessary experience and wisdom to understand whether the girl is serious, and hence if she might be a fitting wife for their son. The different perspectives of Rachid and his father on love marriage, which also reflects their positions in a man's life trajectory, bring to light different ideas, social constructions, and embodiments of masculinity.

3. Some families arranged marriage between minor girl and a boy although the reformed Mudawwana raised the age of marriage for girls from fifteen to eighteen.

Scholars in North African and Middle Eastern countries show how growing economic precarity, deep social transformations, and changing gender dynamics have contributed to shifting ideas of masculinity (Ghoussoub and Sinclair-Webb 2000; Ouzgane 2003; Inhorn and Isidoros 2022); practices of fatherhood (Inhorn 2012); ideas about breadwinning and migration (Malik 2016; Menin 2016; Elliot 2022); and masculinity and conjugal relations (Inhorn and Naguib 2018). In her fascinating work on men's life trajectory in urban Egypt, Farha Ghannam (2013) traces the complex everyday collective process through which manhood is socially produced, also in the joint effort of men and women, against the backdrop of the broader socioeconomic and political circumstances that shape gender dynamics. Ghannam's approach to manhood and masculinity offers important insights on the processual and relational *becoming* a man in relation to others, including women.

In Morocco, novel social modalities of masculinity (*rajuliya*) have emerged in light of the deep societal changes occurring in the past thirty years, including the societal influence of feminist movements emerging since the 1980s (Conway-Long 2006; Dialmy 2009). Abdessamad Dialmy (2009, 33) argues that the younger generations of Moroccan men, confronted with their undermined power positions and privileges, have called into question the conventional patriarchal vision of masculinity based on the affirmation of virility and the rejection of what is associated with womanhood. In searching for new ways of being men, the few young men with whom I discussed these questions feel confronted with their fathers' conventional ideals of masculinity based on emotional self-control and rationality. This does not mean that the older generations of men do not nurture deep feelings of love for their wives; as we have seen, both men and women connect men's love with everyday acts of providing for, nurturing, and taking care of the wife and children more than with the verbal expression of passionate love, which may be associated with "weakness" (Naamane-Guessous 2013, 16). Today, new local middle-class imaginations of leisure activities and public displays of intimacy have become acceptable for married couples. However, these might still create ambiguity, as Rachid said: "Al-Azaliyya is a small town, and if a man goes out to a restaurant with his wife, people think she is his lover." Many old and middle-aged women, and even some girls, thought that a man who is so affectionate toward his wife to put an apartment in her name must be bewitched (*mshur*). Whereas some young men dismissed this as mere superstition, others interpreted intense love and passion for a girl as a sign of her magic influence. In the contexts in which the public expression of love is associated with the danger of demasculinization, the language of magic enabled some young men I met to voice feelings of passionate attachment to the loved person, and dependency on her, that they might otherwise censor.

Love as a Political Issue

Rachid's discussion of love sheds light on the ways in which certain strands of masculinity are conceptualized, practiced, and reimagined across generations in the Tadla and compels a reflection on love as a constitutive dimension of masculinity itself. Crucially, love also emerged as a political issue during my conversations with Jamila and Rachid. While Rachid put distance between his own views and the older generation's vision of love, Jamila cut in on the conversation by saying something that surprised me: "Nowadays, it is not possible to talk of love if religion is at the forefront . . . it's a matter of power." The tone of our discussion suddenly shifted from a personal to a political level. So far, Jamila had discussed the impossibility of love with respect to men's mentality and gender inequality, but now she was connecting it to the central role that religion as a political power occupies in Moroccan society. Her words took me aback, especially considering her decision to don the veil. Noticing that what she said had captured my attention but also disoriented me, she went on: "I would like to feel free (*horra*) to go out with a friend, to sit in a café, and to love, to love, but in Morocco, and according to religion, you cannot have love relationships before marriage, it's forbidden (*c'est interdit*). Virginity is very important for a woman." In expressing her desire to feel free to love, Jamila evokes virginity as a linguistic device to discuss the limitations to the legitimacy of premarital intimacy. Her invocation of virginity as a cultural and religious duty for girls reveals a critique of societal control over the female body. She went on to emphasize the differential treatment society accords to girls' and boys' premarital sexual activity. "Men can have several liaisons," she said. "There is no equality between men and women, except before God." Rachid nodded in agreement and went a step further by claiming: "Talking of love is talking of power. It's a political issue because you attack . . . you touch on the king, religion, the system."

As these fragments of conversations show, Jamila and Rachid reflected on love not just as a private issue between two individuals, but as something that involves broader religious and state powers. They used love as a "properly political concept," to borrow Michael Hardt's (2011, 676) words, to draw a connection between their intimate worlds and the broader forces that shape them. For Hardt (681), "love is a power, first of all, that operates simultaneously at the most intimate and widest social levels," and, importantly, it is a socially productive concept that potentially blurs the boundaries between political reasoning and affective lives, as well as between reason and passion, and, in so doing, it opens the possibility of both personal and societal transformations. Some scholars have discussed the limits of Hardt's vision of love, highlighting the fundamental questions of ambivalence, power, and inequality that infuse everyday modalities of intimate attachment (Berlant 2011; Salih 2016, 744; Wilkinson 2017). I agree with these scholars, and I have underscored the extent to which ambivalence is a fundamental dimension of love in al-Azaliyya. Nevertheless, I suggest that it is precisely such an idealist vision that leads Jamila and Rachid to imagine true love as a space for transformation. Talking of love, they addressed what was considered taboo topics in Morocco—mainly, politics and religion. In particular, while Jamila discussed the limits set by religion on premarital sex and the ways it affects girls' intimate life, Rachid evoked the historical bonds between the monarchy and Islam (Munson 1993). As we have seen, as a descendant of the Prophet, the king is the "commander of the faithful" (*Amir al-Muminin*), the leader of the Muslim community. The king, who is believed to embody divine grace (*baraka*), was formerly recognized as a "sacred figure" (*muqaddas*), until the constitutional reform that followed the protests of the February 20 Movement in 2011.

Omnipresent in the public sphere, state institutions, and private shops, the image of the king is a constant reminder of the presence of greater powers in people's lives. However, as Susan Ossman (2007) notes, the representation of power in Morocco has significantly changed since the ascent to the throne of Mohammed VI in 1999. The new king helped to bring an end to the "culture of fear" (*taqafa d-l-khof*) that marked the three decades of Hassan's despotic rule by creating a truth commission in 2004 to investigate past state abuses (Slyomovics 2005) and by fostering promises of democracy and freedom of speech. Politically, Mohammed VI broke the image of the patriarchal family by sanctioning gender equality in the reform of Mudawwana in 2004, and privately he chose his wife from a Fasi middle-class family. Unlike his father, Hassan II, who never displayed his wife in public and referred to her as "the mother of my children," the new king's wife, Selma Bennani, became a public figure. Ossman (2007, 526) depicts Mohammed VI's marriage as a groundbreaking performance of modernity and a political statement that, for some interpreters, prepared the way for the reform of the Personal Status Code and the promotion of gender equality.

To some extent, my interlocutors' search for *le vrai amour*, with its meaning of freedom of choice, can be interpreted as a similar performance of modernity. There is a substantial difference, however: the relationship between the royal couple followed a path common to many ordinary Moroccan couples, marked by the passage from a secret romance to a public engagement. On the contrary, by wishing to make public what is supposed to remain secret, my interlocutors' desires for both emotional and sexual freedom take us beyond the social spheres of secrecy and, in so doing, threaten the values on which the Moroccan kingdom is based. As Rachid argues, *speaking* of love and sex out of marriage touches on the king, religion, and the system because in Morocco, as we have discussed in previous chapters, publicity is considered a transgression more so than the secret infringements of the norms. Even though Mohammed VI has encouraged freedom of speech (Vermeren 2006, 2009), some topics remain inviolable—notably, the sanctity and legitimacy of the king, Islam, and the nation. When I asked them, provocatively, "Isn't there freedom of speech?," Rachid replied: "There is freedom of speech, but it's limited." He concluded by reminding me of common sense knowledge among my interlocutors in al-Azaliyya: love, politics, and religion are taboo topics in public life. Precisely because love—a concept that my interlocutors use to refer contextually to an emotion, premarital romance, and sex—is such a powerful force, openly discussing it calls into question other established powers, institutions, fantasies, and ideologies around which the society, and people's lives, are organized (Berlant 1998, 282).

A Place for Love

Samir and Rachid were not the only young men with whom Jamila thought it was worth talking. One afternoon, Jamila and I were relaxing on the sofa at her home when she received a call on her mobile phone from Bader, a medical student in Casablanca in his mid-twenties. She quickly arranged a rendezvous at a youth café in al-Azaliyya and asked me to accompany her, saying that Bader has had many liaisons and could provide important insights. When we arrived at the café, we saw a stylish and attractive young man sitting with his group of male friends. "That's Bader," Jamila whispered. As we approached the group, Jamila introduced me as a friend who was researching young Moroccan people's ideas and experiences of love. Even though Bader found my topic quite bizarre, he agreed that love is a central concern in young people's lives. Like Jamila and Rachid, he emphasized the extent to which young people in al-Azaliyya differ from their parents, who, he stated, "have not experienced love at all!" Bader said that his parents' marriage was arranged by their families and that they did not meet before marrying. In contrast, he argued that today young Moroccans lead their lives in an increasingly globalized world and hence develop new desires and orientations: "When satellite television came, people started seeing what was going on in the world. People watched movies and wanted to experience the same things. Then the Internet arrived. With Facebook, I chat with people around the world, I have many European friends with whom I discuss many things."

Bader's words require context. As I illustrated in chapter 1, the growing liberalization of the Moroccan broadcasting system in the last two decades and the spread of satellite dishes contribute to Moroccan people's access to uncensored news, movies, and entertainment programs. Moreover, the arrival of the Internet in the mid-1990s and the proliferation of internet cafés in both cities and small towns have deepened young people's sense of connectedness to the rest of the world. Thus, with his words, Bader was claiming that watching movies and comparing his experience with that of other youngsters in the world via social media has enabled him to "broaden his mind." At first sight, Bader's reflection evinces the impact of globalized youth cultures on young Moroccans; it also subtly evokes past state censorship of television, which was central to the control of public opinion under Hassan II's authoritarian rule. In this sense, for Bader, the state censorship of the past constrained people's capacity to fully understand their situation, whereas today young people who are connected to the world can envision a better life. In highlighting this rupture, Bader pointed to the tensions that the encounters of local and global cultural practices trigger in young people's lives. "Morocco," he said, "is different from the West. Here there is no place for love. According to Islam, you can't have premarital affairs—you have got to marry. There is no such freedom, *la liberté*, do you understand?" Using "love" to talk of sex, Bader argued that there is no place for love in Moroccan society in the sense that there are no public places for it. As sex out of wedlock is both religiously forbidden and criminalized, young people's sex lives are confined in clandestinity.[4] Far from being neutral, however, transgression has important gendered and class implications (Cheikh 2017).

Like Rachid, Bader claimed that there is no place for love in the relationship between a father and his son, either, as love remains unspeakable there. "You can't go to your parents and say, 'I love this girl,'" he told me. "They wouldn't ever, ever accept it." But while Rachid discussed the economic dimensions of his unfreedom to marry his loved one, Bader emphasized the issues of origin and class. Coming from a well-known family in al-Azaliyya, Bader said that his mother would check on the girl's genealogical origin (*asl*). "Of course, when I meet a girl, I don't know her *asl*, her grandfather's, and so on," he commented. As mothers play a central role in a marriage decision and the selection of a bride, they can be intimate allies

4. Articles 490 and 475 of the Moroccan Penal Code make a man liable to a five-to-ten-year prison sentence for taking a young woman's virginity, even "without violence, threat or fraud, or attempts to do so" and obliges him to marry her (Bakass and Ferrand 2012).

as well as bringing to an end an undesirable love match. Bader's words bring into focus the way that competing ideals of emotional attachment shape marriage dynamics in al-Azaliyya and create tensions in my interlocutors' lives because they involve not only family duty and moral obligations but also essential forms of nurture and affection. Listening carefully to Bader's discussion of the importance of genealogical origin in the selection of his future bride, Jamila came closer to me and whispered: "You see, love does not exist in Morocco!" Whereas Bader and Jamila agreed that transforming premarital love into a love marriage could be complicated, they stressed different facets of the problem. Bader emphasized the role of the family in imposing a social logic that prevents a love marriage, while Jamila seemed to suggest that, by failing to choose true love, young men often contribute to the reproduction of such logics.

As our conversation unfolded, Bader's reflections on the "unspeakability" of love with his father turned into a disclosure of the "unsaid" of his society. Given the division between premarital love and marriage in Morocco, Bader said that prostitution is widespread in al-Azaliyya, and that many married men have affairs with prostitutes and lovers while preserving their respectability in public. The divisions between love and marriage also create a split between sexual pleasure and reproduction, as Bader noted: "The way a man has sex with his lover is different from the way he has sex with his wife . . ." Seeing that I was curious, he added, making Jamila blush, "He might not want to have oral sex with the mother of his children!" Far from describing secret love and sex outside marriage as deviance or moral transgression, Bader suggested that extramarital affairs are part of some men's secrets, which exist alongside conjugality and family responsibilities. The opposition identified by Bader between sex/romance and marriage/family as two naturally different things is common to other ethnographic contexts and closer than expected to modern European societies, which only recently began to tie love and marriage together. In his ethnographic exploration of the disciplining power of heteronormativity associated with Indian modernity, for example, Filippo Osella (2012) makes a similar point by showing how male sociality among Muslim men in South India are crucial spaces where men cultivate secrets and same-sex forms of intimacy as a distinct from public/family marriage domain. In these dynamics, the "public" and the "hidden" are not simply opposed but deeply ingrained in the unfolding of moral, social, and intimate lives in al-Azaliyya. Listening to Bader's words about men's infidelity, once again Jamila leaned over to me and whispered: "This is men's carnal pleasure." In her view, men enjoy their sexual privilege and, with their behavior, reinforce the tension between openness and secrecy, marriage and love, as well as between "good girls" to marry and "bad girls" with whom to experience passionate love. However, pace Jamila, young women and married women are also involved in men's affairs. Interestingly, instead of posing love and sexual pleasure as a potentially subversive power or power's "anti-structure" (Abu-Lughod 1986), Bader and Jamila describe love as a fundamental dimension of people's hidden life that coexist with the public side as long as it remains secret and unspoken. Out-of-marriage love is described by my interlocutors as a "public secret," to use Michael Taussig's (1999, 5) term: a shared repression of information "that is generally known, but cannot be articulated." Taussig's work complicates the Foucauldian theorization on knowledge/power relation by positioning secrecy at the very core of power. It is worth noting that Taussig developed this notion in the context of paramilitarism in Colombia during the 1980s, in which silencing and not-knowing were responses to fear. What is relevant in this context is the pervasiveness and silencing effects of public secrecy that make out-of-marriage love and sex unspeakable. For my interlocutors, the complex coexistence of a conservative public and a secret realm that a focus on love brings to the fore makes love itself an eminently political question in the sense evoked by Rachid above.

Transforming Love

True love provides my young interlocutors with a vocabulary and an imagination that enable them to craft themselves as particular types of gendered subjects, as well as to reflect upon the politics of silence surrounding love and sexuality in al-Azaliyya. By displaying "romantic" sensibilities, they position themselves against their parents and the ideas of love, marriage, and gender relations they express. Confronted by what they depict as the absence, or even impossibility, of true love, they criticize the mentality of the older generations and society in general, with the limits it imposes on and the splits that it engenders in their intimate and affective worlds. The romantic utopia intersecting their idea of true love enables them to discuss the social and political powers that define the limits and possibilities of their search for love. As we have seen, the idea of true love overcomes class divisions and gendered inequalities, whereas, in real-life situations, love does not stand apart from the economic and material worlds. This gap between love as an ideal of intimate attachment and love as a lived experience is what compels Jamila, Bader, and Rachid to reckon with the different powers shaping various dimensions of their lives. Using the language of love to discuss their desires for intimate and sexual freedoms, they reflect on (un)freedom as a specifically gendered condition. This is not only because they encounter the limits and possibilities of freedom in their everyday lives as gendered selves and sexuated bodies but also because "freedom" itself, with its complex relationship with questions of agency, powers, and the limits, entails culturally specific ideas of the (gendered) subject. For Jamila, being free (*horra*) entails the possibility of sitting in a café with her boyfriend without fearing gossip, but also of experiencing emotional and sexual intimacy before marriage without compromising her respectability. For Bader and Rachid, freedom is the possibility of publicly expressing their feelings of love and attachment to a woman without losing their virility or seeming weak. In particular, Bader is more concerned about having sexual relations without slipping into illegality and about not being forced into a prospective marriage, whereas Rachid's argument is about the social and economic possibility of choosing a spouse of his own. Whereas money and financial independence can play a role in young people's capacity to decide on their marriage, this is not always the case, as Bader's discussion of the importance of genealogical origin suggests.

These young people's ideas of freedom resonate with what one Egyptian female interlocutor of Samuli Schielke (2015, 102) called the "freedom of the heart," which is the freedom "to express one's feelings and concerns and to build social relationships without fear and secrecy." Schielke (224) notes that, even though it can also be articulated in a more radical fashion, "freedom" emerges in postrevolutionary Egypt primarily in the conservative sense of choice, "the choice is one that is limited, a choice from a finite range of possible options." Schielke's ethnographic idea of freedom as choice recalls what Fisher and Ravizza call the "freedom to do otherwise" (1993, 6; in Walsh 2002, 453), which is the freedom to have options within a set of limitations. As we have seen, Jamila, Bader, and Rachid also define freedom in these terms. Concurrently, their quest for true love reveals its utopian qualities in its capacity to open horizons for intimate, social, and political transformation. By stating that true love is worth pursuing for its own sake, both before and after marriage, they imagine a different rationality that includes feelings and passions as crucial dimensions of a person's choices and moral reasoning (hooks 2000a; Hardt 2011). While their quest demands a certain degree of autonomy, they do not conceive freedom in terms of independence *from* others (Abu-Lughod 1989). On the contrary, true love evokes and demands a different relationality: the possibility of creating intimate relationships between men and women as well as between father and son that are not based on silence and deference, but on mutual trust and dialogue. In this sense, the demand for freedom that the quest for true love brings to the fore is conceived by my interlocutors not simply in the conservative sense of choice or as the possibility of doing otherwise: to have options and to maneuver and manipulate secrecy and the limits imposed by a given situation. It is also the capacity to imagine otherwise, thereby opening emotional and relational possibilities laden with transformative potentials.

I met Rachid, Bader, and Jamila again when I returned to al-Azaliyya for a short period in the autumn of 2012. Many things had changed in their lives. Bader was starting his specialization in a public hospital in Rabat. Jamila had completed her university studies and was about to marry a Lebanese man she'd met online. Rachid hoped to pass the public competition to become a high school teacher. Talking about the protests across Morocco, Rachid acknowledged that there were moments when he thought that some radical changes seemed about to happen. Soon the rising violence and the unanticipated consequences of the fall of the previous regimes in the neighboring countries made him skeptical about the revolutions in Egypt and Tunisia and even more scared about the evolving civil wars in Libya and Syria. "You see what is happening," he said. "In

Morocco, at least, we still have political stability." His words reflected a feeling widespread among part of the population that the presence of a solid and far-sighted monarchy had helped to avert economic, political, and social disasters in Morocco (Vacchiano 2022, 188). When I said I was surprised by his words on the stabilizing role of the monarchy, he admitted that the revolutions and protests that started in 2011 had changed the horizon of the possible and the sayable in Morocco in unprecedented ways. "Now human rights activists call for the abrogation of Article 490, but this will never happen in a Muslim country," he said. He eventually concluded: "You know, in Morocco, everything changes, but nothing changes." Whereas the Mouvement Alternatif pour les Libertés Individuelles and human rights activists were campaigning for individual freedoms, including sexual freedom, my interlocutors felt that love remained unspeakable in al-Azaliyya, although being vividly discussed in youth socialization spaces. Meanwhile, I could sense the extent to which the spheres of secrecy and invisibility, where premarital romance unfolds, were rapidly expanding thanks to the massive spread of digital technologies. It is precisely on these dynamics that I concentrate in the next chapter.

7

Digital Intimacies

In the narrow lanes of the old city and in the modern sectors of al-Azaliyya, young people strolling in same-sex groups played subtle games of gazes. As the gaze (*nadra*) is deeply sexualized, and skills in its use are much cultivated, the exchange of glances is both a weapon of seduction and an invitation to romance. Following the girls, the boys would whisper sweet words, comment on their beauty, and express the desire to become acquainted with them in the hope of obtaining their phone numbers. At street corners, girls would display shyness and indifference, snubbing the boys as both a gendered performance of moral assertiveness and a strategy to assess their suitors' intentions. If a girl chose to pass on her phone number, a flow of text messages and phone calls could begin, through which occasional encounters in the street could develop into intimate exchanges and premarital romances. In the intimacy of their rooms or on the rooftops of their homes, my young interlocutors received calls from their boyfriends and discreetly exchanged SMS texts or WhatsApp messages. On internet platforms such as chat rooms and Facebook, they would engage in intimate conversations, flirtations, and romances with male friends and intimate strangers beyond the watchful eye of their parents. Exchanges and infatuations could be confined to the online/on-phone sphere, but also develop into face-to-face encounters, long-term secret love relationships, or marriage. While some young women were skeptical about finding a soulmate online, others found love there, and some, as we will see, actively searched for a husband on Muslim matrimonial websites.

In this chapter, I trace the contours of new modes of intimacy and love relationships mediated by digital communication channels that have emerged against the backdrop of the massive remediation of intimate lives in al-Azaliyya. I focus in particular on the ways in which four young women used mobile phones and internet platforms to enact outcomes in their intimate lives and to give the desired shape to their conjugal futures. The mobile phone (in Arabized French, *l-tilifun portable*) and, since 2013–14, smartphones, together with numerous online dating platforms, have become constitutive elements of premarital romance in al-Azaliyya. By making people directly and individually addressable, digital technologies have opened up unprecedented opportunities for male-female interaction and intimate communication. As anthropological and sociological literature shows, the spread of digital technologies in Morocco and the Middle East more broadly has enhanced young women's space of maneuver and their ability to pursue "forbidden desires" for romance without public knowledge (Lee Bowen, Green, and James 2008; Kaya 2009; Sotoudeh Friedland and Afary 2017; Ilahiane 2022), for dating and casual sex (Carey 2012; Hayes 2019, 43), and to add romance to "arranged marriage" (Walter 2021). Whereas some authors emphasize the new possibilities for the transgression of gendered, societal, and religious norms (Pourmehdi 2015; Nevola 2016a), others underscore how these have been paralleled by the reproduction of conventional gendered roles and Islamic normativity (Jyrkiainen 2016) as well as by the strengthening of male surveillance (Hijazi-Omari and Ribak 2008; on Africa in general, see Ling and Horst 2009). Emphasizing the essential ambiguity (Miller and Horst 2012, 4) of digital technologies, scholars show the contradictory effects of these technologies on people's intimate lives (Ling and Donner 2009). Building on this literature, I show how my interlocutors' engagement with mobile phones and internet platforms helps them navigate the unpredictability of intimate relationships by reckoning with specific gendered tensions, aspirations, and moralities as opposed to either transgressing or reproducing conventional norms. Julie Archambault (2017, 23, 24) examines mobile secrecy practices and intimacy by which young people in Mozambique "play with façades . . . in their attempts to craft fulfilling lives" and "cruise through uncertainty." Like Archambault's interlocutors, young women in al-Azaliyya used mobile phones to maneuver through the specific relational and social uncertainties inhabiting their affective worlds.[1] Sometimes, they played with façades via various practices, including cheating, disguise, opacity, and deceit (Carey 2012). In exploring the emotional possibilities opened up by digital communication channels, however, my focus is not so much on the experience of transgression and deceit as it is on the digital practices by which young women seek to combine a quest for love with the affirmation of their moral gendered selves.

This chapter argues that digital communication technologies have radically expanded the social spheres of secrecy, where premarital romance flourishes, and the complex dynamics that precede official marriage proposals unfold. However, the expanded possibilities for secret action afforded by mobile phones and internet platforms do not necessarily entail moral transgression, deceitfulness, or distance from marriage. On the contrary, I show how my interlocutors affirm their respectability and moral selves *through* and not *in spite of* their intimate mediated practices. The four stories I discuss in this chapter go against the grain of the local discourses—held by some of my interlocutors and acquaintances—that digital technologies have made premarital relationships superficial when compared with the past, based, in their view, on hedonistic pleasure and materialistic drives more than on seriousness and the search for a spouse. The young women in this chapter have marriage in mind when they experiment with new intimate connectivity by engaging in online/on-phone romances with male strangers. As I will show, their uses of digital technologies embody and emanate from moral ideas and religious imaginations that, rather than being set apart from or experienced in contrast to their quest for love, are ultimately part and parcel of it. Online relationships emerge here as the spaces where young women fulfill gendered and social expectations and envision and experiment with new intimate dynamics. Reflecting their sensibilities and inclines, my interlocutors invoked different "moral rubrics" (Deeb and Harb 2013), including religious ideas, to discuss their choices and the kind of conjugal future

---

1. Archambault's conceptualization of "navigation" builds on Henrik Vigh's (2006, 2009) notion of "social navigation" as a negotiation of everyday uncertainty.

they wanted. As they used digital technologies to navigate the unpredictability of intimate relationships, they reckoned with the specific possibilities and tensions, between romance and marriage, and between the online and offline realms, surrounding their intimate worlds. Especially when loving couples moved from the secrecy of their online/on-phone encounters to the public promise of marriage, they often encountered the social-cum-transcendental powers involved in the actualization of a marriage. In foregrounding the complexities surrounding the passage from online romance to marriage, I do not suggest a dichotomous vision of online versus offline realms, nor do I counterpoise alleged freedom from societal norms experienced online against an offline world of social and moral constraints. The expanded spheres of secrecy enabled by digital technologies have been paralleled by the emergence of conservative online public realms (Costa 2016b; Costa and Menin 2016). In this process, the boundaries between the online and offline worlds, and between public and secret spheres, have been reshaped in unexpected ways, creating both new online gendered and Islamic normativity and creative, if not cynical (Jyrkiainen 2016), performances of the moral self. What I wish to do in this chapter is explore the limits and possibilities that young women encountered as they moved between secrecy and openness in both online and offline worlds and how they reckoned with the unpredictability of love relationships.

Disembodied Love

I began to realize the fundamental role of the Internet and the mobile phone in young women's intimate lives during a conversation with Najat. In the introduction to this book, I described my first meetings with her in 2009. She was going through a difficult time because her fiancé had become elusive about his marriage commitments after having sworn his love for her. Before I left Morocco in the autumn of 2009, Najat was still suffering from the painful epilogue of her prospected marriage and trying to make sense of it. When I returned to al-Azaliyya in the spring of 2010, Najat updated me about what she had learned through her female networks: not only was Abdelghani having other affairs with other girls while he was dating her but also he eventually married another woman. "I could not believe it," Najat said. "I kept thinking of us, the places where we had been together, the things we had done, our moments of intimacy . . ." Najat explained that Albelghani's behavior upset and hurt her because she felt she did not deserve such treatment. "I phoned him, but he tried to hide his marriage initially. Then, when he realized that I knew of it, he told me that even if people love each other, they do not always succeed in getting married." When I asked her how she felt, she replied that, in spite of her suffering, she had to reckon with God's will: "Maybe it was written (*maktub*), that's what Allah wanted for me." While Najat stressed the wisdom of accepting what God decreed for her, in commenting on Abdelghani's behavior, she offered almost in the same breath alternative interpretations of the end of their love story. By resorting to competing narrative registers, Najat evoked, on the one hand, the classic trope of the lovers thwarted by the family, explaining that his family wanted him to marry a girl with an established social position and a career. "You know, I'm still studying. She has a job and a car," she remarked. On the other, she emphasized his treacherous behavior: "Imagine that he seduced other girls when he was venting his love for me!" This time relying on Moroccan wisdom, she referred to her ex-fiancé as "my loved one, the deceiver (*habiby l-ghddar*)." Najat's polyvocality sheds light on the complexities surrounding premarital relationships and the many unpredictable factors involved in the actualization of a marriage. Far from being mutually exclusive, the alternative registers with which Najat tried to make sense of the failed marriage point to the crucial questions of choice, freedom, and constraints, as well as of sincerity, trust, and cheating in premarital dynamics.

Najat's composed resignation surprised me, considering how hurt she felt by Abdelghani's betrayals and lies. I began to make sense of it when, the next day, we were sitting in the inner garden of a youth café in al-Azaliyya. Chatting over avocado juice, she disclosed that, a few months before, she had started a relationship with a young Moroccan man she met on the Internet. Najat got closer to me and sighed with dreamy eyes: "Love on the Internet does exist . . . Yes! Love exists for educated and religious young women." She said: "Initially, we began chatting on the Arab chat line *chatiw* [translatable as "Let's chat"], then we exchanged mobile phone numbers." Starting from an initial dialogue through SMS texts and timid phone calls, she said, "Now he sends me very romantic messages. You know, 'My loved one, have you slept well?' 'You are my soul (*nty ruhy*),' and so on. Every day we spend hours talking about love and the feelings between us."

Like instant messaging, the mobile phone enables simultaneity and individual addressability but also provides "the emotional immediacy of the voice" (Madianou and Miller 2011, 269). This helped Najat and her boyfriend develop a deeper level of communication, which, in turn, transformed the quality of their relationship and the intensity of their emotional involvement. The shift from online to mobile phone chatting to make a relationship more intimate is typical of the dynamics of the online encounters I could follow during my stay in al-Azaliyya. Like Najat, my interlocutors would often move between diverse types of social media and communication styles to develop deeper levels of intimacy: from a generic chat and online flirtation into a more individualized, personal, and regular exchange on the phone.

Crucially, Najat's story provides several interesting insights into premarital love that I could not grasp before. First, it foregrounds the growing importance of digital technologies in making intimate lives in al-Azaliyya, as a strategy to mediate competing desires and explore emotional possibilities. Even before the advent of smartphones and applications such as WhatsApp, mobile phones allowed for a new kind of disembodied intimacy constructed through the exchange of simple texts and phone calls. Moreover, Najat's story invites us to appreciate how the emerging forms of digital intimacy, crafted in a subtle game of distance and closeness, are imagined by my interlocutors as halal. Najat told me that her boyfriend lived in Casablanca, hence they had not yet met, but she confided that she often found herself fantasizing about him or imagining herself kissing him. In her view, the mediation of digital technology enabled her to develop an intimate dialogue and feel in love with an intimate stranger beyond physicality. Even though Najat presented herself as a religiously committed girl, she did not deny the importance of physical attraction and intimacy in a love relationship. She said: "Men and women can be bound by spiritual love and physical love, both of which I've experienced." Najat thought that carnal pleasure should not be pursued for its own sake but ought to be based on a solid relationship. "Physical love exists," she said. "I'm an educated woman, and I can't say that it doesn't exist. But spiritual love must be the basis of physical love." While opening room for premarital intimacy, she made clear: "There are limits, and the first is virginity." In discussing the limits set by religion, she clarified that the boundaries of what is licit in premarital intimacy are located according to different religious sensibilities and interpretations of Islam. "There are several types of *zina*," she explained.[2] "*Zina*, for me, is the penetrative sexual act, the direct contact between the male and the female genital organs. There are other types of *zina*, such as kissing and touching each other's bodies. For some people even talking is *zina*. Modern educated women have a different view—they are more open-minded."

Far from framing her viewpoint as a transgression, Najat invoked the alternative interpretations of the Islamic notion of *zina* to draw the boundaries of what she considered licit in premarital romances. By positioning herself as a modern, religious, and educated girl, she defined *zina* as penetrative sexual intercourse, thus leaving room for other sexual practices. While Najat argued for the leicity of a certain degree of physical intimacy in premarital relationships, she also explained that the end of her earlier story had made her aware of its dangers. She disclosed that they would kiss passionately in his office but regretted having accepted his invitation to his home: "I was so naive when I agreed to go to his home . . . when I went to his place, I touched him . . . I could control myself, but the man thinks that the girl is available."

Women and girls always warned me about the dangers of accepting men's invitations, that venturing alone into a man's place is considered unsafe because the man interprets acceptance as sexual availability. Even though Abdelghani was dating other girls while declaring his love for

2. *Zina* indicates unlawful sexual intercourse: both adultery and fornication. The Qur'an prescribes being stoned to death, whipped, or exiled as possible punishments but requires the witnessing of the illicit act by four male adults of established moral quality. Historically, such sentences have been applied rarely in Muslim contexts (Esposito 2004, 348). For a discussion of *zina* law and its revival in the twentieth century, see Hamzić and Mir-Hosseini (2010).

her—as Najat later found out—and his family seemingly hindered their marriage, she speculated that his invitation was a way to test her, and that her acceptance led him to change his mind regarding their marriage. Contrasting her passionate and physical relationship with Abdelghani with her current one, Najat said: "On the Internet or the phone, my boyfriend and I can discuss our thoughts. We declare our love for each other, but there is a physical distance." Even though Najat considered physicality as integral to premarital relationships, her words reveal the ambivalence surrounding her desire for intimacy and draw attention to the way digital technologies enabled her to develop emotional closeness while maintaining a physical distance.

I met Najat in 2012 when we were traveling on a coach directed to Casablanca: I was going to the airport, while she was going to Rabat to take part in an open competition for a public-service job. During the five-hour journey, she told me how emotionally intense her first meeting with her boyfriend had been, and how excited she was to meet him again. As the "disembodied love" she had developed via digital technologies was about to incarnate in a face-to-face meeting, she said jokingly: "I will not accept an invitation to go to his place this time!"

As with Najat, other girls think that their boyfriend or fiancé might test them by trying to seduce and have sex with them. They are aware that while some young men like Samir (whom we met in chapter 6) claim that they would marry the girl who has lost her virginity to him—but not in previous relationships—others think that "if the girl sleeps with me, she will sleep with anyone." As we have seen throughout this book, these gendered dynamics not only make (sexual) intimacy, in girls' eyes, potentially dangerous, albeit exciting and desired, but also contribute to a generalized mutual suspicion between the sexes that renders trust (*tiqa*) difficult to be built. Matthew Carey (2017) argues that mistrust, as "a general sense of the unreliability of a person or thing," is the basis of particular ideas of personhood, communication practices, and assumption of unknowability, which rules social, affective, and intimate lives in Moroccan High Atlas. My interlocutors, too, consider a person's *niya*, translatable here as the "real" intention or hidden purpose (Rosen 1984, 47–56), hard to grasp if not unknowable, at least initially; they often underline people's opacity and think that only a gullible person can trust anyone. However, they do not regard untrustworthiness as an intrinsic feature of Moroccan people and still believe that trust can be built over time through mutual respect and dialogue. Deeply aware of the complexity of premarital love relationships, my interlocutors often sought to test their partner in various ways to dissipate the opacity of their intentions. As I will discuss, digital technologies can help young women assess their suitor's intentions, trustworthiness, and even the couple's compatibility before a formal engagement.

Testing Compatibility

Veiled and elegantly dressed in modest but fashionable clothes that concealed her shape, Zahra was twenty-two when she started a two-year vocational course at a private school in al-Azaliyya in 2009. I was in a petit taxi back to hay el-Mounia when Zahra got in and started a casual conversation. As we lived in the same neighborhood, we decided to exchange mobile phone numbers and, from time to time, she invited me to her home for an afternoon tea, to stroll in the medina, or to accompany her on her errands. During a walk, Zahra told me that a young man named Abdelqader had approached her in the street, asking if he could make her acquaintance. Since Zahra felt that his request was polite, she agreed to exchange phone numbers, thereby opening emotional and relational possibilities.

That same evening, she received Abdelqader's first text message, which she ignored because she did not want him to think she was willing to flirt. The next day, he sent other text messages saying that he could not stop thinking about her. Eventually, she beeped him, and he promptly phoned back. From their first conversation on the phone, Abdelqader overwhelmed Zahra with daily texts and phone calls. Through a flow of texts and calls exchanged discreetly, away from the watchful eye of her brothers, Zahra and Abdelqader could create a space of intimate exchange around which they crafted romantic fantasies and gendered expectations. Zahra expected Abdelqader to call and text her as proof of his love and care. Lavish attention expressed through texts and calls is integral to the flirtatious rituals by which young men try to seduce girls and win their trust and through which girls, in turn, assess their suitors' commitment.

Although Zahra was wary about boys' use of "love talk" to enchant them while just wanting sex, she also believed that phone calls and texts materialize the admirer's feelings. She said: "You feel the man thinks of you if he phones you before sleeping or in the morning just to ask you how you slept. When he calls you every hour, why should he do so if there is nothing between you?" In a subtle game of seduction, Zahra used the mobile phone tactically to prolong "relationally productive uncertainty" by keeping Abdelqader "in a state of suspense where a vast range of possibilities remain open" (Carey 2012, 200). She often snubbed his calls by saying: "If he is interested, he will call again and again. You don't have to be always there for him!"

Through her informed use of mobile communication, she controlled her self-image by displaying modesty and shyness but also by using tactical distance and elusiveness to fuel her suitor's interest. Even though Zahra often fantasized about future encounters, she declined Abdelqader's invitations to meet up by saying that she was busy with her studies and domestic chores, as a "good girl" was expected to do. Zahra wished to know about Abdelqader's personality before dating him, but she also thought that Moroccan men get bored with girls who are "available." She commented bitterly: "You see, women always have to veil their feelings. They have to say no, even though, inside their heart, they feel the opposite." Even though the dynamics of seduction and courtship remained grounded in conventional gendered expectations, Zahra's comments reveal a subtle critique of the gendered practices that constrain girls' emotional freedom and expression of agency in order not to pass for "bad girls." Zahra tried to assess Abdelqader's seriousness and test their compatibility before getting involved in a relationship by maintaining a distance while developing emotional closeness through secret exchanges on the mobile phone.

After one month, Zahra agreed to meet Abdelqader in the presence of her female cousin and myself to affirm her respectability by following the Islamic prescription of a go-between (*maharam*) in premarital interactions. "According to Islam," she explained, "you should meet your potential husband—getting to know each other (*ta'aruf*) before marriage is essential to testing mutual understanding and compatibility." Under the pretext of errands to run, Zahra proposed to meet in the medina. After a few polite exchanges, Zahra and Abdelqader began walking side by side, while her cousin and I discreetly followed them a step behind. After about an hour, Zahra said she had to get back home. Two weeks later, they met again in an ice cream parlor frequented by youths and unmarried couples, this time alone. Having previously asked me to act as a go-between, I asked her why she decided to meet him alone. Zahra replied: "It is not sinful to meet in a public place. According to Islam, you should not be alone in isolated places. You should not date for ages but should be limited to the time necessary to understand if you want to get married." Not all of my religious interlocutors agreed that it is licit to meet alone in public. Even though Zahra thought it was, she was always careful not to be seen by relatives or neighbors. Like other young women, Zahra did not regard dating as contrary to Islam, provided that it follows certain rules, such as meeting in public (not isolated) places, avoiding both physical contact and improper topics of conversation. She also made it clear that meeting up was aimed at testing mutual compatibility for marriage. While the mobile phone helped Zahra engage in "halal dating," she considered meeting in person, also alone, as essential to understanding a suitor's personality.

Zahra's relationship with Abdelqader did not last long. One day she told me that, while they were sitting in a café, he grabbed her mobile phone from her bag to check her incoming calls and texts. Although annoyed by his behavior, Zahra initially interpreted *ghyra* (jealousy) as a sincere expression of his feelings. As this happened repeatedly, Zahra felt increasingly uncomfortable with what she described as Abdelqader's "controlling behavior." He would complain about her dress style, saying that he wanted his wife to wear a traditional jellaba instead of jeans, as Zahra used to do (although long loose blouses covered her bodily shape). She also realized that he had begun shadowing her to control her movements and interactions at school. For Zahra, Abdelqader's actions denoted his lack of trust in and respect for her, which she considered the basis of a love relationship. She said: "When you feel that a man is jealous (*tay-ghyr 'alik*), you can say that he loves you, but this should not go beyond a certain point, or it becomes something else." Offering a different angle on the jealousy-love connection illustrated so far, Zahra interpreted Abdelqader's excessive jealousy as an expression of self-assertion and dominance rather than love and protection, which, in her view, reflected his "traditional mentality" ('*aqliya taqlidiya*). Crucially, Zahra resorted to a religious language to criticize his behavior, claiming that Islam invites the married couple to cultivate affection, dialogue, mutual understanding, respect, and companionship. In her view, Abdelqader's behavior precluded the possibility of egalitarian respect and trust between them and provided a glimpse into what being his wife might entail. This led Zahra to reflect on their mutual compatibility, and she eventually decided to break up with him, as they had "two different mentalities" and visions of what a love relationship should be.

Zahra's story powerfully shows the centrality of the mobile phone in the making and breaking of her love relationship. Initially, it enabled Zahra to create a private, direct space of communication with a male stranger met by chance in the street, in which subtle, digitally mediated flirtatious exchanges helped her assess her admirer's intentions. Creating emotional intimacy through phone calls and texts while carefully balancing physical distance, Zahra controlled her self-image and asserted her respectability. The transition from online interactions to offline encounters was particularly revealing for her. With its physicality (Ginzburg, Abu-Lughod, and Larkin 2002, 19), the mobile phone became a crucial "actor" in face-to-face meetings by making palpable their divergent visions of a love relationship. Abdelqader's checking of her mobile phone materialized critical aspects of his personality and attitude, which eventually led Zahra to end their relationship. Emphasizing his traditional mentality, Zahra criticized her boyfriend's behavior as incompatible with her rather than as immoral or wrong per se. In this sense, their contrasting visions of gender and love relationships reveal broader transformations in female-gendered aspirations and the role of a revivalist vocabulary and imagination in shaping novel desires and expectations in intimate lives.

A Soulmate Online

Digital technologies have been rapidly incorporated into existing practices of flirting, seduction, and romance and, in turn, have contributed to reshaping premarital dynamics in unexpected ways. The mediation of mobile phones and internet platforms has created new romantic expectations and enabled specific modes of intimate connectedness to emerge. Like Najat, my interlocutors regarded regular chatting on the Internet and the frequent exchange of phone calls or text messages with an intimate stranger as having a relationship (*dir shy 'alaqa*), even though this led to face-to-face encounters only occasionally. Such intimate connectedness was built through numerous daily romantic SMS texts and calls, or one long phone call, either daily or whenever possible, according to the situation. One particular way in which young women in al-Azaliyya navigated the relational possibilities opened by digital communication channels is by actively searching for a husband on a matrimonial website, as in Samira's story. Samira was a friend of Hasna, and the two of them visited often, sometimes staying overnight at one another's place or meeting in the city for a stroll. With Hasna, Samira shared ambitions and frustrations, like being still unmarried and having a precarious job despite her university degree. Samira was considered a *bnt n-nas* in the *sha'bi* neighborhood where she lived with her family.[3] Although she had a good reputation, she was nearing her thirties and was still unmarried, a situation that generated anxieties regarding her conjugal future. On a hot evening in the summer of 2009, I was sitting on a bench in a public garden with Samira when she disclosed that she had received a marriage proposal from Mohammed, a Moroccan man she had met six months earlier on the Muslim matrimonial website www.mon-bled.com. When I said I hadn't known she was in a relationship, Samira clarified: "I've never, ever, wanted a relationship (*'alaqa*). I hoped for a marriage, God willing."

Mixing the French language (*mon*/my) and the Moroccan dialect (*bled*/country), the matrimonial website mon-bled.com offers "Muslim encounters with chat (*rencontres musulmanes avec chat*)" or, more specifically, the possibility of meeting, for marriage purposes, other Maghrebi Muslims who live either in North African countries or abroad. The website guarantees the seriousness of such online encounters and promises to

---

3. This idiomatic expression indicates a girl of excellent character, who cares about her reputation and gets along well with others.

help unmarried people in the search for a soulmate for a lifelong love relationship, declaring: "Among hundreds, thousands, of profiles with photos of singles, you will find women and men who share your tastes and values. Mon-bled is the ideal place to make a beautiful Muslim meeting." On such websites, you enter your profile and select a partner with the specific characteristics you are seeking: for example, age, education, nationality, and religiosity. The matrimonial website claims to "create your personal meeting announcement in a few minutes and help your destiny (in French, *aidez votre mektoub*)." The idea that one can help her destiny by using a matrimonial website captures the ways my young interlocutors try to participate in and precipitate their hoped conjugal future (Elliot 2016, 492).

In telling me the dynamics of her encounter with Mohammed, Samira made it clear that she was not looking for a husband, but "friends" (*asdiqa*, pl. of *sadiq*).[4] Perhaps Samira wanted to affirm the morality of her intention when she registered on the Muslim matrimonial website, completed her profile, and scanned the male profiles. Among those available on this website, Samira came across Mohammed, who seemed to be potentially compatible with her because, she said, "We both are practicing Muslims, university educated, and of a similar age." These features, which Samira regarded as essential for mutual understanding between a married couple, along with the fact that Mohammed was from the Tadla, prompted her to get in touch. He replied, and they gradually started an exchange of messages on the matrimonial website, eventually moving on to emails and messages via Messenger. When their relationship strengthened, they started using Skype to hear each other's voices. Telling me about their exchanges, Samira sighed with dreamy eyes: "Before sleeping and soon as I get up, I read all his SMS texts, every day, and I feel happy."

Together with the morality of their intention, the disembodied dynamics of their online exchanges and the morally appropriated contents of their conversations rendered their mutual acquaintance coherent, in

4. In Moroccan Arabic, the terms *sadiq dialy* and *sahby* (my friend) are used interchangeably among male friends; in contrast, in cross-sex interactions, *sahby* assumes a sexualized connotation and indicates a "boyfriend."

Samira's eyes, with Islamic values. Unlike young women like Najat, who enjoyed online romantic conversations with an intimate stranger, Samira considered it improper to speak of love with a man who was neither her fiancé nor her husband. For six months, during which they got to know each other, Mohammed had never mentioned love, nor had he asked Samira to turn on the camera on Skype. On the contrary, she added: "I'd met young men looking for virtual sex, who displayed their genitals on the webcam and a young man who seemed polite at first but suddenly started talking about sex and love. I deleted contacts immediately." In other words, more than the mere mediation of digital technologies itself, for Samira, their moral use of such mediation made her relationship with Mohammed morally appropriate. Samira would reiterate that Mohammed's respectful behavior convinced her of his moral qualities and religious ideas. This was more important than seeing him on camera. I jokingly asked: "Isn't physical appearance important to you? What if he was ugly?" She replied that, after a few months, they had exchanged pictures, and she liked him, but she made it clear that they had turned on the camera only after Mohammed had expressed his desire to ask her hand in marriage.[5] On this occasion, he revealed that he was an emigrant living in Germany. Samira explained that Mohammed had not put this information in his online profile because he feared that many girls would only take an interest in him to get a visa to go abroad. In a context like the Tadla, where migration occupies such a powerful place in young people's imagination, marrying a migrant is a common strategy for girls to pursue social-cum-geographical mobility (Elliot 2016). Samira forgave this omission on his part, understanding that he might want to avoid girls in search of a "marriage of interest (*zawej dyal mslaha*)." She was glad to imagine her future conjugal life in Europe.

Samira's enthusiasm about her prospective marriage crumbled when she said that Mohammed's parents opposed their marriage. Farmers in a small rural village in the Tadla, they did not consider her a suitable wife

---

5. My interlocutors were careful about exchanging photos, as they feared that these could be misused to undermine their reputation and even for magic influence.

for their son because they believed that an educated woman nearing her thirties did not fit in with their ideal. They wanted for their son a younger bride, whom they expected to move to their home after the wedding and work in the fields and around the house. In their eyes, Samira was too old and independent for their son and too educated and urbanized to deal with the hardships of country life. Although Mohammed was economically independent (ideally a requirement for a man to marry), he wanted his parents' consent to marriage.

A few months passed, and the stillness of the situation made Samira uncertain about its future developments. Doubtful about whether she should wait for a positive twist or surrender to the situation, Samira prayed the *salat al-istikhara* to seek God's guidance.[6] In Morocco, as in the Muslim world, *istikhara* is performed to seek God's guidance in focal events in life and in situations marked by uncertainty, when the believer is confused about two possible choices (Edgar and Henig 2010; Edgar 2011; Mittermaier 2011; Louw 2010; Menin 2020). God's response may manifest itself through signs or dreams. Anthropological literature has long emphasized the central role of dreams in both everyday and mystical religiosity in Morocco and beyond (Crapanzano 1975; Kilborne 1978). The performance of *salat al-istikhara* is recommended before accepting or rejecting a marriage proposal, but, in real-life situations, the timing of its performance can vary, and, as with Samira, my interlocutors performed it when they were unsure about what decision to make in critical moments.

6. Literally meaning "seeking the best," this special Islamic prayer to seek God's direction when one is uncertain about two permissible courses of action and consists of two ritual cycles or *rakaa* followed by the prayer: "Oh Allah, I seek Your help in finding out the best course of action by invoking Your knowledge; I ask You to empower me by virtue of Your Power. You alone have the absolute power, while I have no power. You alone know it all, while I do not. You are the Knower of the unseen realms (*'allamu al-ghuyub*). Oh Allah, if You know this thing [I am embarking on] is good for me in my religion, my sustenance, and my ultimate destiny, then decree it for me and facilitate it for me. And if You know this thing is bad for me in my religion, my livelihood, and my ultimate destiny, turn it away from me, and turn me away from it, and decree what is good for me, wherever it may be and then make me satisfied with it."

Moroccan people have long sought the intercession and blessing (*baraka*) of saints by performing *salat al-istikhara* at shrines (Crapanzano 1975), and some continue to do so, as Araceli Gonzalez-Vazquez (2014) shows. Conversely, Samira did not seek human intercession, but tried to establish a direct connection with God through the individual performance of *istikhara*. Against the backdrop of the increased influence of the Islamic revival, this long-standing practice of dream incubation has been promoted globally on television, on the Internet, and in local religious circles. In al-Azaliyya, booklets on *istikhara* were available on the stalls of Islamic books and on the Internet. Like Samira, other young women I knew resorted to this prayer to seek God's guidance before accepting a marriage proposal, starting a job, or choosing a university course. The performative power of the dream vividly emerged in young women's narratives in which divinely inspired dreams were invoked to decline an undesirable marriage proposal or, as in Samira's case, to precipitate the actualization of a conjugal future.

"After praying *istikhara*," Samira said, "I had a dream in which I saw the celebration of my wedding with Mohammed. We were surrounded by our families and relatives in a joyful atmosphere." The dream persuaded Samira that the conflicts between Mohammed and his father would be overcome and that their marriage would happen. Samira reported her dream to Mohammed, who faced his father again. Samira's "active engagement with the dreaming imagination" (Bulkeley 2002, 4) reveals not only the centrality of Islam in envisioning and visualizing her conjugal future but also the performative powers of the divinely inspired dream in prompting people to act (Mittermaier 2012, 249).

A few months later, Mohammed returned to Morocco. He and Samira first met in al-Azaliyya in the presence of Hasna, who remarked that they were so shy that they could hardly say a word or look into each other's eyes. Persuaded by Samira's impeccable behavior, Mohammed insisted to his parents that she was a serious girl, and that he would not marry any other girl but her. Perhaps the weight of Mohammed's remittances to his family's income led his father to reconsider his fierce opposition and eventually to agree to the marriage. Mohammed's female kin visited

Samira's family informally, and then the men discussed the practicalities of the marriage agreements (the bridewealth, wedding ceremony, and marriage contract, which included the condition that Samira would join her husband abroad). In 2012, I participated in Samira's henna party with her closest female friends. We girls helped her bake cookies for her engagement party, which she celebrated at her family home with her female friends, relatives, and neighbors. When I returned in 2013, Samira told me that her relationship with Mohammed became more intimate after the betrothal. He would send her money when she needed to visit a doctor or buy medicines. He paid for the installation of a high-speed internet connection at Samira's home, so they could chat on Skype every day, making online technologies both a powerful mediator of their distant relationship and a materialization of his caring for her.

Samira's story offers insights into the ways in which young women in al-Azaliyya try to "help their destiny" by exploring relational possibilities on a matrimonial website. Samira did not wish to wait for a potential husband to come and propose to her family, nor did she want to rely on the neighborhood-based female networks or a female matchmaker (samsara) to find a husband. On the contrary, she aspired to find a husband with precise characteristics, such as education, age, and religiosity, which she considered essential for mutual understanding (tfahum) in married life. She managed to keep her online premarital relationship secret from her parents, by making it seem like a conventional marriage. Although she considered having a digitally mediated, disembodied love relationship with the ultimate goal of marriage as halal, according to Islam, she was afraid that her parents would consider her online exchanges as shameful (hshuma). Samira succeeded in marrying her beloved one, but love does not always suffice in actualizing the desired marriage. In revealing the tensions between online and offline dynamics, Samira's story reminds us of the many factors involved in the actualization of marriage. In this case, Mohammed did not surrender to parental opposition without struggling for the sake of their love, nor did Samira accept his hesitation without prompting him to act with the help of God. In what follows, I continue to discuss the manifold factors that may hinder a love marriage and how my young interlocutors use digital technologies to navigate the unpredictability of premarital relationships.

"If marriage is written . . ."

One evening, when I was back to Morocco in 2012, Lina (met in chapter 3) came to visit Hasna after dinner. I noted immediately that, while she was chatting with us, she was impatiently checking the screen of Hasna's PC. As I learned, she was waiting for Samir, a young emigrant from the Tadla, to call her on Skype. She did not have an internet connection at home and did not want to be seen in the smoky *cyber* of Rabi'a. Lina had met Salem in a chat room some months earlier, and, after chatting on the Internet for two months, they exchanged phone numbers. She said: "Our friendship evolved into a mutual feeling of love. He said that he wanted to get married, but added that his economic situation in Spain was unstable." Since the global financial crisis of 2008–9, many emigrants in southern Europe have lost their jobs and returned to Morocco, while others have stayed abroad waiting for the situation to get better. When I returned in the spring of 2013, Lina was increasingly doubtful about Samir's intention or ability to marry her without involving his family in the choice of his bride. During my field trip in al-Azaliyya in the fall of 2014, Lina recounted that when Salem was planning his return to Morocco for summer, she had suggested that he could visit her family—meaning that he could ask them for her hand in marriage. "He replied that he could not do so just then and asked me to be patient," Lina said. Samir's hesitation, which he justified in terms of his economic precarity, instilled doubts in Lina about his intentions because, she said, "I did not ask him to marry me, but to visit my family and formalize our engagement. Then I would wait until his economic situation was stable."

To make sense of Salem's delaying, Lina resorted to the language of kinship and suggested that his family may be already arranging his marriage in his native village in the Tadla where his mother might be looking for a wife. "I know how it is going to end," she said bitterly. "Eventually his mother will choose his wife. I'm in love with him, but I'm already thirty-one and did not want to prolong this relationship for years without a formal engagement." Lina's concerns intensified when a female colleague informed her that her brother Omar wanted to request her hand in marriage. "I've met him only twice. I cannot accept a marriage proposal from a man I'm not acquainted with. I insisted on meeting him in person. He hesitated, but then agreed to meet up alone in a café in the city center." I asked how their rendezvous was. "Hmm," she said, thinking it over, clearly unconvinced, and added: "He described his social position and his job and listed what he could provide: a small house, a car, and a simple but comfortable life." Lina paused and then continued: "We discussed aspects of our future married life, such as housing arrangements, the number of children we would like, and the possibility of me continuing to work." Although Omar's credentials qualified him as a suitable husband, Lina felt she and he were too different. She was not in love with him. "He was satisfied with our meeting," she said. "In his view, it confirmed his idea. For me, it was not enough to get to know his personality." Lina had the impression that he was not interested in getting to know her as a person with unique attributes and qualities, but that he was looking for a wife with specific features and considered her a good girl to marry. Omar would text her regularly to inquire about her health and family, following the conventional etiquette of polite conversation. Compared to her on-phone relationship with Salem, which was based on intense and intimate dialogue, Lina felt that their impersonal exchange did not help her get to know Omar. Despite her invitation to meet up, they only met a few times in cafés because he was reluctant to meet her alone, as a way of displaying his respect for her.

Determined to ask for her hand, Omar persistently requested a formal meeting with her family. Initially, Lina asked him to wait seeking various excuses, and continued to keep in touch with Salem, hoping that he would ask for her hand in marriage. When she could no longer delay his insistent requests, she informed Salem about the marriage proposal, to prompt him to act. His palpable disappointment notwithstanding, Salem repeated that he could not marry her right away. "Only God knows what is better for you," he said to her. "If this is written (*ila maktub*), it will happen." Perhaps Salem used the language of destiny to suggest that the future developments of their love were beyond his control. Lina, in contrast, interpreted Salem's evocation of destiny as his passive acceptance of the social circumstances. As she said: "Marriage is *maktub*. Only God knows what a person's destiny is. But each one should work for her destiny and not wait idly." After a two-year relationship, Lina expected Salem to take up his responsibility by asking for her hand in marriage; hence, his inaction led her to question his determination to marry her.

Lina's attempts to discern Salem's intention prompted specific digital actions, which, in turn, generated moral dilemmas vis-à-vis him, her family, and Omar. While awaiting the unfolding of events, she continued her double on-phone relationships, but the condition of waiting for her conjugal future to manifest itself was painful, and Lina oscillated between guilt and confusion. "I feel I'm going mad," she often said during the conversations that followed the one at Hasna's home. Unable to choose between the uncertain possibility of a secure love marriage, Lina prayed *salat al-istikhara* twice to seek God's guidance, but she was unable to discern a clear answer. Confronted by the social pressure to marry and the limited power she felt over her conjugal future, Lina phoned Salem to tell him of her decision to accept Omar's proposal. "I want a family and children, but I cannot wait for years. I am in Morocco, not in Europe," she explained to me. She changed her SIM card to end her relationship with him definitively.

What captured my attention in Lina's story was not just the possibilities of moral transgression that digital communication channels make possible (Archambault 2017; Carey 2012). Undoubtedly, the mobile phone made it easy for Lina to maintain a relationship with two men simultaneously. What, in my view, makes her story ethnographically and conceptually compelling is that Lina's digital practices reveal the specific anxieties that infuse young women's conjugal futures. These anxieties are connected with the centrality of marriage in the social definition of womanhood in a context where financial uncertainty forces many young men into a condition of material and existential stillness. This is particularly true at a historical time when the possibility of building a future in "the outside" had become a very precarious enterprise. After two decades of prosperity in the Tadla connected to emigration to Italy and Spain, the aftermaths of restricting migration laws and the financial crisis had generated material and existential stagnation in young people's lives and instilled deep uncertainties about their conjugal futures. Lina's story also reveals specifically gendered tensions triggered by the gap between the expanded horizons of possibility and material constraints in young women's lives. While Lina imagined her future married life with a man with whom she is in love, eventually she decided to secure a family and children with the man with serious intentions. In 2016, Lina gave birth to her first baby. Despite the difficulties of everyday life, over the years she has built a good relationship with her husband. Her love for Omar developed after marriage, she said, through sharing the joys and worries of life.

Navigating Online-Offline Relationships

Taking us into the digital worlds of young women in central Morocco, a focus on the different digital practices of Najat, Zahra, Samira, and Lina reveals the emergence of novel intimate dynamics and experiences of love mediated by digital communication channels. The mobile phone and the Internet are distinct media with specific, intrinsic qualities that are interpreted, appropriated, and understood locally (Horst and Miller 2006; Miller et al. 2016). My interest, however, was less in the Internet and the mobile phone as specific media than in the intimate and social dynamics that their varying uses and appropriations have triggered in al-Azaliyya. As I have argued, digital communication channels have contributed to expanding the social spheres of secrecy where premarital romances unfold, and, in so doing, they have engendered new relational modalities of intimacy. Digital technologies have opened up the possibility for girls to chat with male strangers just for fun, to search for love on matrimonial websites, to cheat on a partner in mobile phone relationships, to create fantasy avatar-like versions of themselves, and to explore emotional possibilities without the social implications of venturing into a man's house.

Precisely because of the expanded secrecy afforded by digital technologies, the Internet and the mobile phone are often blamed for instigating illicit liaisons and transgressive and immoral behaviors. Going against the grain of public discourse on the alleged immorality of digital technologies, I have shown how, for the young women in this chapter, it is the use of such mediation that defines the moral quality of male-female exchanges. In different ways, Najat, Zahra, Samira, and Lina use digital technologies to combine a quest for love with the enactment of a gendered moral self. As they navigate emotional possibilities with intimate strangers and search for a suitable husband beyond the conventional rules of courtship, they use internet platforms and mobile phones to initiate or deepen disembodied relationships whose ultimate goal is marriage. In particular, Najat uses the mediation of these technologies to craft a chaste, disembodied love that helps her avoid the dangers of physical intimacy. Zahra affirms her respectability and complies with her boyfriend's expectations of sexual purity in courtship rituals while she evaluates mutual compatibility carefully before committing herself to a formal engagement. Samira actively seeks a husband on a Muslim matrimonial website to secure a romantic marriage in accordance with Islamic values. Lina, in turn, uses the mobile phone to carry on two relationships simultaneously to maximize the opportunities to combine love and marriage. In many ways, my interlocutors' digitally mediated, gendered performances mirror conventional gender dynamics, with their specific courtship rituals and expectations. Concurrently, within the process of exploring the relational possibilities afforded by digital technologies, new types of intimacy and dynamics of intimate exchanges have emerged.

A common feature of digital intimacies emerging from the four stories discussed in this chapter is young women's uses of digital technologies to develop emotional intimacy while keeping physical distance. Before the Internet and mobile phones, other forms of mediation, like love letters, contributed to love relationships based on both physical distance and emotional closeness. Compared with the exchange of love letters, however, the dynamics illustrated are marked by the immediacy of the mediation, which contributes to shifting the qualities of intimate interactions and the dynamics of intimacy-building.

Crucially, the young women in this chapter understand their digital practices as compatible with moral and religious ideas, and their digital practices contribute to delineating new intimate dynamics *within* an Islamic and moral frame. Instead of concentrating on the contradictions between romantic aspirations and religious values (Schielke 2009; Fortier,

Kreil, and Maffi 2016), I have directed attention to these young women's conceptualizations and enactments of religiously and morally inflected notions of intimacy. In her work on the use of social media in Turkey, Elisabetta Costa (2016a, 2016b) makes a similar point when she argues that Islamic morality and premarital romance, rather than being mutually exclusive, can be theorized as two constitutive aspects of the same mediated practices. Creatively combining romance with pious pursuits, my interlocutors navigate the emotional possibilities opened by the new digital communication channels to initiate and cultivate what Nancy Smith-Hefner calls "new Muslim romances" (2005, 456–57; 2019, chap. 6). With this term, Smith-Hefner identifies romances aimed at marriage and marked by adherence to a neo-orthodox vision of Islam that entails, for example, the decision to forgo courtship, strict avoidance of physical contact between the couple, and the presence of a go-between to avoid their being alone together. Focusing in particular on normatively conservative Muslim young people in Indonesia, Smith-Hefner (2019, 145) maintains that such models of courtship and marriage are "illustrative of a distinctive pattern of individuality within modernity, one that is morally embedded rather than self-constructively 'free.'"

The intimate practices of Najat, Zahra, Samira, and Lina reveal a morally embedded self. However, within the secret dynamics of online/on-phone romance, they display a wide range of gendered performances and act within the specific moral boundaries they draw according to their religious sensibilities and other ideas. In other words, their digital practices are not merely molded by a specifically Islamic normativity, but by a "diffuse Islam" (Marsden and Retsikas 2013, 12), in which a variety of "moral registers" (Schielke 2009) or "moral rubrics" (Deeb and Harb 2013), as well as their personal religiosity, are evoked contextually to reckon with moral constraints and emotional possibilities present in their lives and evaluate the suitability of potential husbands. Even though they all consider premarital romances, within varying boundaries, as compatible with respecting and embodying religious values, they display different visions of morality, Islam, and love relationships more broadly. While Samira hesitated to appear on camera before her fiancé asked for her hand, Najat did not confine the experience of physical intimacy to marriage and resorted to the Islamic notion of *zina* to discuss the boundaries of what is "licit" in premarital relationships. While affirming the normalcy of her desire, she was aware of the dangers of premarital intimacy. Najat talked passionately of love with her boyfriend, while Samira considered speaking of love improper and avoided physical contact with her boyfriend before marriage. Far from interpreting her online exchanges as moral or gendered transgressions, Samira believed that the disembodied dynamics of these contacts with her fiancé, ultimately aimed at marriage, rendered their mutual acquaintance coherent with Islamic values. Some young women, like Zahra, experimented with "halal dating": meetups in public places whose ultimate goal was to get to know each other and test mutual compatibility for marriage. In other words, instead of resorting to abstract Islamic normativity, they used a variety of sources, including but not limited to religious ideas, to negotiate contemporary desires and evaluations. While they emphasized that the moral use of such mediation made these romances a proper avenue to marriage, their parents did not always agree on the morality of digital romances, and hence the premarital dynamics that precede an official marriage proposal often remained, albeit not always, secret and unspoken of within their family. Close attention to the secret dynamics of premarital romance shows that behind a couple there is often "conglomerate of confidants" (Fioole 2021) that helps them build their conjugal futures.

Ultimately, in a context in which marriage is understood as the result of both social circumstances and subtle maneuverings, of human agency and divine destiny, the massive remediation of premarital dynamics via mobile phones and internet platforms has enhanced young women's agentive capacities and their ability to manage intimate and affective lives. Without their skilled use of digital technologies, my interlocutors might have not been able to craft a sense of emotional intimacy with male strangers met on the Internet or the streets of al-Azaliyya. However, the passage from online/on-phone romance and marriage reveals the gendered tensions that inhabit young women's intimate and affective worlds. These tensions relate to the gap between evolving ideas of femininity and gender relations and the persistence of powers operating at different scales in young women's lives, which they discussed through the languages of deceit, destiny, and kinship. Young women's digitally mediated romances offer a glimpse into the complex ways in which gendered (Islamic) moralities and romantic desires, social and transcendental powers, are navigated and remediated between the online and offline realms. The Internet and the mobile phone not only function as powerful mediators between constraints and possibilities but also become integral to the ways in which young women reflect on and act in their intimate and moral worlds. A focus on digital technologies enables us to show how young women's intimate lives are inhabited and intimately shaped by power relations, moral concerns, and gendered normativity, as well as by the hidden dynamics in which they seek to "stretch the boundaries of their social worlds and creatively re-imagine emotional and sexual possibilities" (Costa and Menin 2016, 140).

In the past decade, digital communication technology has rapidly evolved: messaging and social media applications like WhatsApp, Facebook, Instagram, Tinder, and other dating applications available on smartphones have become more and more central to young people's intimate and social lives in Morocco (Hayes 2019). What kind of intimacy is taking shape in such a constant connectivity? How are new mobile applications and technologies remolding young people's experiences of premarital romance and sex? Further ethnographic research is needed to trace new developments and changes in the ways in which premarital love and gender dynamics are negotiated, experienced, and reinvented through digital technologies.

Conclusion

On a gloomy day in 2017, I received the very sad news that Naima had passed away. The departure of this old woman of extraordinary wisdom and dignity suddenly brought me back to the lively atmosphere and emotional warmth of her home in Rabi'a. I recalled the shared experiences, thoughts, and jokes with her daughters and granddaughters over glasses of mint tea, sitting on the colorful carpets in her living room. Before departing, however, Naima was able to see many of her grandchildren settled down with a job and a family. Hasna won the public competition that she had entered repeatedly to become a schoolteacher, celebrated her marriage, and had two children. She achieved what she had hoped for, but initially her married and family life was not always easy, due to the burden of housework and a full-time job, the tensions with her mother-in-law, and the responsibility of two little kids. As with Hasna, the lives of the young women who shared my days in al-Azaliyya have changed in the past decade: they have grown older, gotten married, had children, relocated to a new town, emigrated abroad, or found new jobs. The spread of smartphones and mobile applications, especially WhatsApp, has made it easier and cheaper for us to keep in touch. I came to know that, upon obtaining family reunification visa, Samira reached her husband in Germany, but in her first few years there, she experienced loneliness and the difficulties of childbearing and raising two children far from her female relatives and friends. Being a strong-willed and resourceful person, Samira managed to cope with the situation and found a part-time job to contribute to her family's income and send remittances to her natal family. In spite of her search for an eventful life, Sanaa was not able to find a way to migrate to Italy. She married her boyfriend, had a child, and continued to work. Her friend Amal and her child eventually moved with her husband to his family home after her father-in-law died.

In the last decade, not only have the lives of the women in this book changed but also the political and cultural life of the country has undergone important changes. During my trip to al-Azaliyya in 2014, some of my interlocutors were following these developments with deep interest. They felt that the 2011 protests had brought about important changes in the country, making people more conscious of their own power. For example, Ghizlan said: "Our generation was raised with the fear of politics and the police, but the younger generation is now living in a different political culture." She was doubtful, however, about the impact of the February 20 Movement on the larger population. Crucially, Ghizlan underlined how the spread of literacy, the end of state monopoly on television, and the arrival of satellite television and the Internet influenced people's political understanding of their country. "Morocco is in transition," she said. "It is not the same as before, but there is neither total freedom nor full democracy—there are still many problems and limitations." Moroccan society has also witnessed continuous debates on the questions about abortion, violence against women, unachieved gender equality (formally recognized by Article 19 of the 2011 Moroccan Constitution), and individual liberties, including the depenalization of out-of-marriage sex and homosexuality. In 2014–15, the debate on the depenalization of abortion, initiated in the 1990s, accelerated significantly (Gruénais 2017). The king's intervention, which led to a minor softening of the law, did not halt the demands for more radical reforms (Borrillo 2016, 411). The issue of individual freedoms has become central in campaigns, debates, and protests beyond the initial mobilization of the February 20 Movement for dignity, freedom, and social justice (2016). The Mouvement Alternatif pour les Libertés Individuelles has been particularly vocal in this regard. In addition to human rights organizations and associations campaigning on individual freedoms, some intellectuals, filmmakers, writers, and artists have taken a stand in these debates. In 2019, Leila Slimani, author of *Sexe et mensonges: La vie sexuelle au Maroc* (2017), and filmmaker Sonia Terrab launched the manifesto *Hors-la-loi* (Out of Law) to promote the abolition of Article 490 of Moroccan Penal Code, which punishes out-of-marriage sex with sentences of up to one year of imprisonment, and abortion.[1] Contrary to Rachid's skepticism about more radical changes, on July 30, 2022, the king's royal speech called for the strengthening of freedoms in Morocco and a reform of the Mudawwana and the Penal Code. A multidisciplinary group formed in the spring of 2022 drew up a document titled "Les Libertés Fondamentales au Maroc: Propositions de Réformes" (Fundamental Freedoms in Morocco: Proposals for Reforms),[2] which includes, but is not limited to, questions of out-of-marriage sex, abortion, and freedom of conscience.[3]

The emergence of public debates on such critical issues, which affect intimate dimensions of young people's lives—young women's, in particular—tells us something important about the transformations that Moroccan society has undergone in the decades *before* the revolutionary moment and its aftermath. As Ghizlan has said, current changes are rooted in a longer history, which interweaves with that of the recent protests and debates in complex ways. Moving the focus of attention away from the public and political debates, I have traced in this book how broad societal transformations have inflected young women's sense of self, their desires, aspirations, and hopes for the future in a middle-sized town in central Morocco. I have focused on the ways in which they engage in a quest for love by navigating competing desires, gendered imaginations, and moralities. I have conceptualized love not just in terms of gender and sexuality, nor of freedom and choice, or of engaging with modernity, although these are all crucial aspects of my analysis. On the contrary, I have theorized

---

1. The manifesto was signed by 490 men and women and followed by mobilization of the defense of journalist Hajar Raissouni, who had been sentenced to prison for illegal abortion and sexual relations outside marriage. As representatives of Collectif 490, Leila Slimani and Sonia Terrab were awarded the Simone de Beauvoir Prize for Women's Freedoms on January 9, 2020 (Bras 2019).

2. The group includes Moroccan Islamic feminist and physician-by-training Asma Lamrabet, who discussed the main point of the document in a recent interview on May 2, 2023, in *Jeune Afrique* magazine, https://www.jeuneafrique.com/1436750/societe/sexualite-liberte-de-conscience-le-maroc-doit-evoluer/ (accessed September 1, 2023).

3. Available at https://medias24.com/content/uploads/2023/03/13/libertes_fondamentales_DP_VF.pdf?x40396 (accessed September 1, 2023).

love as a *quest* that opens up huge ethical, existential, and cosmological questions and allows my interlocutors to work out their relationships with those questions and with a range of contexts, issues, dilemmas. The idea of love as a quest highlights the dimensions of danger and pleasure, hope and disillusionment, unknowing and discovering, navigation and experimentation—all dimensions that ultimately make their intimate quest a journey of learning and personal growth, self-reflexivity and transformation.

By engaging in a quest for love, my interlocutors rethink themselves and their society, giving voice to new desires in their intimate and social lives. Such desires, discussed discreetly among friends and in youth socializing spaces, have taken shape within long-lasting processes of social and political change, which precede and interweave with the 2011 protests and revolutions. As we have seen, love acquires a central place, and a variety of meanings, in the everyday lives and imaginations of the young women whom I met at a crucial historical and biographical conjuncture. After three decades of violent political repression and state violence under Hassan II's regime (1961–99), the arrival of Mohammed VI in 1999 fueled hopes of political change. The new king initiated crucial reforms: from promoting freedom of expression to reforming the Mudawwana and establishing a truth commission in 2004 to investigate state violence during Hassan II's despotic rule. These historical developments have intertwined with deep transformations at both societal and biographical levels. Since the 1980s, increased female school attendance has postponed the age of marriage and provided new opportunities for gender-mixed socializing and premarital romance to emerge.

The young women in this book have experienced new emotional possibilities and the existential tensions connected with the expanded temporality between girlhood and womanhood. In addition to the neighborhood and gender-mixed schools, new socializing places have emerged in al-Azaliyya and in online settings, where young people can meet, flirt, and fall in love away from the family's watchful eyes. Young women's access to education, the possibility of transnational migration, TV cultures, and the spread of digital media and communication technologies have all contributed to the emergence of novel aesthetics, desires, and orientations, which they negotiate along with, and against, the increased influence of the Islamic Revival. As we have seen, the Islamic Revival in al-Azaliyya has promoted the ethical reform of religious subjectivities and sociability, as well as alternative imaginations of social and intimate lives. It also created a sense of a gap, noted worldwide, between consciously Muslim children and allegedly traditional parents, who sometimes are accused by the former of blind traditionalism instead of correct Islamic practice. Against the backdrop of this complex scenario, I have tried to understand why love was described as a problem, and, perhaps most importantly, what young women's engagement in a quest for love could tell us about emerging gendered selves, desires, and intimate dynamics.

Hasna, Sanaa, Ghizlan, Jamila, and the other young women in this book have experienced these entrenched dynamics as deep generational ruptures. Unlike the older generations of women in their family, they could attend high school or pursue a university education despite their poor and lower-middle-class backgrounds. They desired professional and conjugal lives that differed from that of their illiterate or poorly educated mothers and grandmothers. While the latter described marriage as an inevitable fate and a deep fracture in their life as a girl, the younger generations imagined it as a choice of love to pursue along with the search for self-fulfillment and professional careers. These generational ruptures reveal the growing significance that conjugal love and intimacy have acquired in central Morocco in the past few decades. While most young women in this book searched for love with marriage in mind, others, such as Sanaa, Amal, and Jamila, also wanted to experience love *beyond* marriage as part of being young and educated. Far from representing change as a linear trajectory, however, a generational lens reveals critical ruptures as well as significant continuities in the embodiment of love practices and understandings throughout the last decades in central Morocco. Comparing their experiences with those of their mother and grandmothers, my interlocutors were acutely aware of the major freedoms they enjoy in their social and intimate lives. At the same time, they experienced the contradictions and tensions triggered by the clash between the vast imaginative horizons available to them and the material and moral constraints they encountered in their everyday lives. Alongside the emergence of new desires and visions of married life, enduring gender imaginations and ideologies of intimate attachment continued to shape young women's paths of self-fulfillment and their dynamics with young men. For example, the investment in education and the searches for qualified jobs in a context of economic uncertainty contributes to prolonged celibacy or makes it difficult to find a man who lives up to their expectations. In central Morocco, where womanhood is defined by marriage status, prolonged singlehood was experienced with ambivalence because of the social pressures on girls to marry but also because being a wife and mother was central to the idea that most of my interlocutors had of themselves in the future. Crucially, some young women contested the inevitability of marriage and claimed singlehood as a legitimate choice. In other words, premarital relationships were one crucial site where young women negotiated the tensions and possibilities triggered by broader societal transformations. Concurrently, their quest for love became a powerful trigger of intimate, social, and imaginative dynamics.

Building on my interlocutors' theorizations of love and their love practices, I have explored love as a social concept, grounded in local ideas of gendered self and relationships, which engages with the demands of everyday norms and is enabled by the agentive investments of the young women themselves. Central in the performance of the gendered selves, love is engendered in sexual and gender politics at the very core of the emergence of gendered subjectivities and heteronormativity. However, the quest for love exceeds the normative orders that produce it and the powers that seek to contain it and opens up a space for self-exploration and reflexivity. In this sense, as I have argued, the quest for love goes beyond the search for the loved one, as love itself becomes a quest for the self: while many girls in this book seek a moral, joyful Muslim subjectivity, others, like Sanaa, define their gendered selves beyond a religious frame. While my interlocutors often experienced ambivalence and "fragmented desires" (Ozyegin 2015), theirs are not necessarily fragmented selves; rather, I have conceptualized these young women as multipositioned gendered subjects who navigate shifting gendered roles and imaginative possibilities to craft meaningful lives. As they searched for creative ways to keep together several distinct grounds of self-making and subjectivation (e.g., family affection, faith, television, religious discourse, friendship groups), they also experienced the tensions that this process entails. Such tensions, in turn, led them to reflect upon themselves as gendered subjects in relation to intimate others and to recognize the broader gendered and sexualized orders operating in everyday norms, gestures, discourses, affects, relationships, and embodied practices. Through the language and the imagination of love, the young women in this book reconsidered gendered and societal norms and reflected on how society draws the boundaries of desirable female and male selves. They discussed the place they occupy in the family and society, thereby offering their viewpoint on the working of power *within* their affective and intimate worlds. In other words, love is not only conceived of just as the intimate site of the reproduction of gendered power and heteronormativity but also as the site from where to imagine different relational modalities of masculinity and femininity, as well as alternative social orders. This is perhaps because the quest for love contains within it the potential to open imaginative horizons for both personal and social transformations. Inhabiting love as a horizon for transformation, the young women in this book searched for and envisioned an alternative relationality between men and women. This does not necessarily entail a move away from religion, but it reveals the complex coexistence of worldly and religious horizons in young women's everyday life. Indeed, many young women in this book searched for love along with piety and elaborated ideas and practices of love within an Islamic frame, thereby giving shape to new intimate and social dynamics. Some young women, for example, endeavored to make their intimate life moral by balancing physical distance and emotional closeness through the relational possibilities opened by digital communication technologies or, like Samira, searched for an Islamic avenue toward marriage with the help of a Muslim matrimonial website. They experienced new communication technologies as a strategy, a desire, a possibility, and even a space to inhabit in a variety of unanticipated ways.

Crucially, the quest for love engenders radically different imaginations of intimate, social, and political forms of life: from the revivalist cultivation of conjugal love and the "Islamization" of private and public lives in al-Azaliyya (chapter 3) to the hope for an alternative social order based on a different rationality, one that includes emotions and passions as relevant dimensions of a person's choices and moral reasoning (chapter 6). At times, the quest for love takes the shape of a romantic utopia that brings into focus the connection between intimate, social, and political realms.

My focus on the imaginative and utopian qualities of the quest for love does not suggest a detachment from reality, but rather a particular way of engaging the everyday. Jamila, Bader, and Rachid also used love as a "properly political concept" (Hardt 2011) to bring under scrutiny the power structures and institutions that touch on and regulate people's intimate worlds in their society. Rachid, in particular, talked of love itself as a power able to destabilize other established political and religious powers. The argument for the destabilizing power of love is not new. Notably, Fatema Mernissi (1975) contends that love and desire are described in literary traditions as dangerous forces to be ruled by reason because the seductive power of women is thought to create *fitna* (chaos or social disorder; literally, "temptation") and hence to divert men's attention from social and religious duties.[4] Criticizing Mernissi for locating negative interpretations of love and sexuality within the religious tradition, Lila Abu-Lughod (1986, 144) argues instead that the Awlad 'Ali regard love and sexuality as dangerous because they challenge the gender and generational hierarchies on which the social order relies. Although Abu-Lughod (1990) later softens her argument on the anti-structural quality of love, she writes that "[love] poetry as a discourse on defiance of the system symbolizes freedom" (1989, 252), conceived in terms of autonomy from domination by, and dependency on, others (79). Ultimately, the imagination that infuses both the oral poetry studied by Abu Lughod, as well as classic tales of unfulfilled romance, is "inherently conservative, teaching one how to accept the loss" (Nevola 2016a, 162). Jamila and Bader's quest for love, in contrast, is potentially *transformative* not only because it is centered on personal and social transformations but also because it "allows one to want something, to want a world" (Berlant 2011, 687).

The language and the imagination of love enabled my interlocutors to discuss the different social-cum-transcendental powers that impinge

---

4. Mernissi (1975, 31) notes: "*Fitna* also means a beautiful woman-the connotation of the femme fatale who makes men lose their self-control."

on their lives and to reflect on the degree of choice and freedom they can exert. Sometimes, when discussing their society and the changes they wanted, young women gave voice to demands for major freedom and choice in their intimate and social lives. Dealing with such demands anthropologically, however, is far from being unproblematic. This is not only because anthropology's focus on the social and cultural forces shaping people's lives and actions has long eluded a theoretical and ethnographic engagement with freedom (Laidlaw 2013, 1–44) but also because, as Abu-Lughod (2013, 101) reminds us, assuming that Muslim women and girls want "what we want—love, choice, and sexual freedom" forecloses the possibility of grasping their wish to be dutiful daughters and devoted wives, or their aspiration to fashion themselves as pious Muslims. Mahmood's work on the bodily and ethical practices of the pietist women involved in a mosque movement in Cairo is a committed and brilliant example of the limitations that such an ideological framing poses to an anthropological understanding of women's aspirations to fashion themselves as pious subjects submitted to the law of God. Interrogating the universality of women's desire for freedom, Saba Mahmood (2001, 2005) offers a compelling critique of feminist and liberal tendencies to naturalize and assume a priori such desire.

Mahmood's and Abu-Lughod's invitations to take seriously women's desires to fashion themselves as pious subjects, as well as their concern about the ideological and political implications of mainstream Western conceptualizations of freedom, make me aware of the dangers inherent in exploring love as a universal experience centered on the Western idea of free choice. Nevertheless, I have resisted the idea that my interlocutors' quest for love is just "the sign of a new liberal mystery, a secular religion" (Povinelli 2006, 191) and instead have foregrounded the imaginative possibilities and the "noise ambivalences" (Berlant 2011) it generates and contains. I have inquired what love, with its complicated connections with ideas of choice and freedom, has meant for a generation of women that have experienced a highly complex landscape of different strivings, promises, and limitations. In different ways, lower-class religious young women like Hasna, who regard themselves as dutiful daughters and care about family's respectability, do engage in a quest for love and craft different ideas of "freedom" and "choice" to reflect on constraints and possibilities in their intimate and social worlds. The quest for love is not necessarily in opposition with piety and gendered moralities, nor is the desire for major choice and freedom in their lives unavoidably identifiable with liberal, Western thought. In his critical dialogue with Saba Mahmood, Samuli Schielke (2015, 224) notes that "just as there is no reason to assume a priori that people want freedom, there is no reason to assume a priori that freedom means individual autonomy." The young women in this book do not think of themselves as autonomous, self-possessed subjects of modern continental philosophy. On the contrary, they regard themselves as connected gendered selves whose lives are embedded in the webs of family and social relations that contribute to giving them a place in the everyday world they inhabit. As Suad Joseph (1999, 11) contends, family connectivity within which people's sense of self is rooted does not deny the possibility of autonomy and personal agency—nor, I add, of imagining and carving out a flexible space for experiencing various degrees of personal choice and freedom. For example, when Hasna, in chapter 1, talked of the patriarchal society embodied by her younger brother's controlling behavior, or when she said that a girl represses her desires because of family and social control, she was not simply claiming an autonomous self; she was reflecting on the complex ways in which power and love, protection and control interweave within her relationships with the people she loves. Sharing with me her gaze on the intimate power relations in which she was involved, she was also giving voice to her demand for an existential and emotional space of her own.

When young women overtly connected their quest for love to freedoms and constraints, the former was not conceived as the abstract freedom imagined by Western political debates and popular imagination, nor was the latter identified with family/tradition/religion/society in unproblematic ways. Some young women, like Jamila, claimed the freedom to experience romance without secrecy and the fear of losing respectability. Her male friends would like to feel free to express their feelings without inviting doubts about their virility or to have sex without slipping into illegality. Distancing themselves from their parents, they were seeking alternative ways of being men beyond the jealousy/care/control dynamics.

More than enacting or searching for a (sexual) revolution (Mahdavi 2009), the young people in this book conveyed an idea of freedom mainly as having choices within a limited range of possibilities (Jackson 2011; Schielke 2015, 224). Secrecy practices or digital technologies helped them work within, maneuver, and manipulate the limits imposed by a given situation to carve out a flexible space for individual choice and freedom. They were acutely aware that they could help their destiny, but not radically change the social-cum-transcendental powers imbricated in their lives. Far from regarding themselves as "self-constructively free" (Smith-Hefner 2019, 145), they conceived of themselves as subjects ultimately dependent on the bounty of God, although they displayed different religious feelings and visions of Islam. In Sanaa's experience, the search for freedom acquires the meanings of a rupture with the gendered and societal norms. She described feeling free as fulfilling her desires to have a boyfriend, travel, and have fun without being judged as a bad girl. Mariém Cheikh (2020b) argues that such desires for fun and freedom should not be situated in a normative framework and interpreted as transgression, but as integral to emerging youth subjectivities and cultures in contemporary Morocco. Even though I agree with Cheikh's emphasis on the normalcy of premarital love and sex in urban youth cultures, this ethnography also shows that behaviors that break the norms in al-Azaliyya were tolerated as long as they were confined in the social spheres of secrecy and invisibility. "There is everything in Morocco, everything is hidden (*kulshy kayn f-l-maghrib, kulshy mkhabby*)," Sanaa would say to refer to the interplay between public and secret spheres of life. And it is Sanaa herself who reflected on the consequences faced by young women who do not conform to gendered ideas of modesty and respectability, especially when their sexual transgressions become socially visible. Sanaa felt that her personal freedom was constrained by what she interprets as social hypocrisy and by the difficulties in achieving economic independence and, ultimately, placed "total freedom" elsewhere outside Morocco: in "the outside" imagined through television and the local experience of migration.

Young women's demands of choice, and even freedom, brought to the fore by their engagement in a quest for love, cannot be dismissed easily as the result of the global installment of neoliberal subjectivity, but requires

careful ethnographic explorations (Freeman 2020). Far from being simply the reverberation of Western liberal traditions, these demands reveal
gendered selves and desires emerging in a transitional society where the
questions of individual freedom, women's rights, and gender equality have
been integral to ongoing debates and political struggles within Morocco.
A struggle for freedom of conscience animated the generations of political
activists and students during Hassan II's regime and has continued to be
demanded by the human rights movements that have emerged from Morocco's postcolonial history of state violence and political repression (Rollinde 2002; Slyomovics 2005). As we have seen, the question of "freedom,"
with its different semantic and historical permutations (Abu-'Uksa 2016),
has become central to the unfolding events following the revolutions and
uprisings in North Africa and the Middle East. Perhaps most importantly,
in contrast to academic search and critique of freedom as something
identified with liberal, Western thought, young women in al-Azaliyya interrogate the very meanings of choice and freedom in a context where
human actions, desires, and intentionality encounter greater powers. This
emerges forcefully in Ghizlan's story, where the encounter with love's
unexpected outcomes triggers a reflection on the fragility of the human
condition, but also on the space left open by social-cum-transcendental
powers. This space, which Ghizlan calls "free will," is the human condition to act within the limits set by divine and social powers. Confronted
with the forces and powers that transcend one's ability to control their
life, one can still seek to live with and work through them. Far from being
centered on the absence of limits, this idea of freedom is rooted in the
experience of the limits and entails the capacity to turn to the best events
and situations beyond personal control and intentionality. In this sense,
Ghizlan's encounter with the limits of human agency in the face of greater
powers reconfigures love as a fundamental learning ground, a high-stakes
game that, if one learns to play well, will shape her into a person who can
handle the changes, challenges, tensions, and ambivalences of life. Love,
indeed, compels people to reckon, practically and existentially, with questions of unpredictability and unknowability.

Young women's encounter with the unpredictability of love powerfully
brings to the fore the creative tensions between acting and being acted

upon (Mittermaier 2011) that infuse the imagination of intimate life in al-Azaliyya. Premarital love is experienced as a risky and exciting adventure made of dreams and hopes, hazards, and strivings, whose outcomes remain unpredictable. A distinctive trait of premarital relationships in al-Azaliyya, love's unpredictability was variously articulated through the language of destiny, kinship, deceit, or a combination of the above. These languages were mobilized contextually by my interlocutors to speak of the different powers that touch on intimate dimensions of their lives. The language of destiny was often invoked to talk of hopes about the future and conjugal plans or to make sense of unfulfilled love; in all cases, it pointed to situations that go beyond human control and even understanding as a powerful reminder that greater powers are at play. Evoking destiny, however, did not translate into an absence of agency and free will vis-à-vis a mighty God. My interlocutors' creative engagements with the ideas of destiny elicit the imagination of human life in which major elements in life, including marriage, ultimately depend on the will of God. Far from erasing the possibility of human agency in the face of a powerful God, however, destiny requires, and even propels, action (Elliot 2016; Elliot and Menin 2018). As we have seen, young women always sought to help their destiny, as Samira's Muslim marriage website puts it, to actualize their hoped-for marital future and criticized those men who passively surrender to adverse situations instead of seeking to reverse them.

While, ultimately, love's outcomes are not in one's hands, destiny requires human action and striving to accomplish itself. As young women cruised through the unknowability and unpredictability of love to give shape to their conjugal futures, they could also encounter the powers of their parents to hinder a love marriage. Especially during the transition from secret love to marriage, the unpredictability of premarital relationships emerged vividly. This is perhaps because love is often imagined as the seductive dream of an elective union between two individuals, which presses against the backdrop of other modes of love and relatedness. In real-life situations, however, it manifests itself as a battleground between competing powers and desires, affections and allegiances, expectations, and ideologies of attachment. As we have seen, some families do support a choice of love and generally, unmarried couples seek to combine romance and parental approval. In any event, the language of kinship speaks of the enduring tensions between marital love and family love and directs our attention toward the many powers and intentionalities involved in the transition from a secret relationship to a marriage. In addition to the divine and human powers, the trope of male deceit evokes the gendered construction of young men as potential deceivers (*ghddar*) to be wary of because they may "play at love" to pass time or try to win the girl's trust to obtain a sexual encounter without serious intentions. The young men we encountered, in turn, maintained that it is not easy to find a girl they can trust. For example, Rachid's and Samir's complaints about the monetary basis for love shed light on the economic dimension of the practices and ideas that sustain premarital relationships and on male fears about being hustled and exploited by girls. Looking more closely, girls are not just passive victims of male deceptions, nor are young men just victims of female *quelb*—namely, the tricks to bind and manipulate a man. Both girls and boys can play with the other's expectations and the rules of seduction. Nevertheless, the language of men's deceit speaks of the persistence of gender inequalities and the implications of the legal, social, and cultural gender constructions on intimate and affective dynamics, including the ways in which trust between the sexes is built.

Because of the different scales of unknowability and unpredictability surrounding premarital love in central Morocco, searching for it requires the ability to navigate the specific possibilities and tensions it engenders between love and marriage, open and hidden realities, online and offline, and destiny and freedom. One way in which young women in al-Azaliyya sought to negotiate the unpredictability of intimate relationships and carve out a space for enacting their desires was by moving between revealing and hiding. A focus on young women's secrecy practices, conceived as gendered social practices (Hardon and Posel 2012; Ryan-Flood and Gill 2010), invites us to move beyond the question of normativity and transgression. It reveals instead how young women try to keep together and inhabit creatively the competing, and at times conflicting, gendered moralities, desires, and self-images shaping their everyday worlds. A close examination of how young women inhabit the malleability of the norms shows that the specific gendered tensions encountered by my interlocutors cannot be easily reduced to sharp oppositions: between personal desires and family expectations, conformity and transgression, freedom and social constraints. These tensions are difficult to handle precisely because they touch on the ways in which my interlocutors imagine themselves both as gendered selves who are part of a web of family relationships where people feel deeply involved in each other's lives, as well as self-reflexive subjects who want to keep their intimate and social lives into their hands.

Exploring the ways in which young women pursue a quest for love between secrets and silences, and between conformity and transgression, is key in broadening our understanding of the aspirations, hopes, and desires at the core of alternative reading of Muslim subjectivities in Morocco. In this sense, the quest for love generates a vantage point from which to scrutinize the complex negotiations, navigations, and uncertainties involved in the making of intimate lives at a historical time of deep transformations in the ways gendered selves and relationships are practiced, contested, and reimagined. By bringing together the intimate and the political, the worldly and the transcendental, the imaginative and the concrete, their quest foregrounds "love," with the tensions and possibilities it triggers, as a productive ethnographic concept for thinking through contemporary social, intimate, and political life in Morocco and beyond.

Glossary

Bibliography

Index

Glossary

asl	one's origin, genealogical origin
'a'yla	"the big family," family
'ayb	shame
'alaqa	relationship
'alaqa jinsiya	sexual intercourse
'aqd dyal zawej	marriage contract
'aris	groom
'arosa	bride
'ars	wedding
'asry	modern, contemporary
brra	literally meaning "outside," is used to refer to migration destinations in Europe
brrani	(f. sing. *barraniya*) outsiders
bayra	spinster
bled	natal villages, country
bnt (**pl.** *bnat*)	daughter, girl, virgin, unmarried woman
cyber	internet café
dhaza	dowry
din	religion
dars	lessons
dar	house
fatiha	the first Sura of the Qur'an, communal marriage ceremony not registered officially
gandora	traditional Moroccan gowns
gawry	(f. *gawriya*, pl. *gwer*) the Westerner
ghyra	protective jealousy
hay	neighborhood
hedga	capable, housekeeper

215

halal	that which is permitted and lawful
hammam	public steam bath
haram	that which is forbidden and unlawful
hobb	most general term for love
hadith	sayings and deems of the Prophet Muhammad
heya	shyness, modesty, timidity
jellaba	the traditional loose-fitting outdoor dress with wide sleeves and hood
jora	residential proximity
jam'a	mosque
khotoba	formal engagement
khimar	long dark veil that cover the head and extends over the torso
l-medina l-qadima	the old city
medina	the city
maktub	that which is written
makhzen	the government, administration, authority
mr'a	adult, married woman, woman
murahaqa	adolescence
musalsala	soap opera
nafs	carnal self, psyche
niqab	face veil
niya	intention, good intention, naivete
qada' wa-l-qadar	destiny and predestination
qalb	heart
qasba	fortified city
qarib	close; also indicates closeness between people
rada'a	milk-kinship
siher	magic
sadiq (f. *sadiqa*)	friend
sahb	male friend or boyfriend in cross-sex relations
salat al-istikhara	special prayer before taking important decisions
sdaq	bridewealth
shari'a	moral discourses and legal procedures, "Islamic law"
shikhat	female performers who sing and dance in festivity
shaytan	the devil
shahadat al-'uzoba	certificate of virginity, often required for marriage

sodfa	coincidence
sum'a	reputation
tiqa	trust
umma	community of Muslims
wali	marriage guardian
waseta	social connections
zina	adultery, fornication
zif	general name for the Moroccan foulard
zufry	single man
zwej or zawej	marriage

Bibliography

Abaza, Mona. 2007. "Shifting Landscapes of Fashion in Contemporary Egypt." *Fashion Theory* 11 (2–3): 281–97.

Abu-Lughod, Lila. 2013. *Do Muslim Women Need Saving?* Cambridge, MA: Harvard Univ. Press.

———. 2005. *Drama of the Nationhood: The Politics of Television in Egypt*. Chicago: Univ. of Chicago Press.

———. 1993. *Writing Women's Worlds: Bedouin Stories*. Berkeley: Univ. of California Press.

———. 1990. "The Romance of Resistance: Tracing Transformations of Power through Bedouin Women." *American Ethnologist* 17 (1): 41–55.

———. 1989. "Zones of Theory in the Anthropology of the Arab World." *Annual Review of Anthropology* 18:267–306.

———. 1986. *Veiled Sentiments. Honor and Poetry in a Bedouin Society*. Berkeley: Univ. of California Press.

Abu-Lughod, Lila, ed. 1998. *Remaking Woman. Feminism and Modernity in the Middle East*. Princeton, NJ: Princeton Univ. Press.

Abu-Lughod, Lila, and Catherine Lutz, eds. 1990. *Language and the Politics of Emotion*. New York: Cambridge Univ. Press.

Abu-'Uksa, Wael. 2016. *Freedom in the Arab World: Concepts and Ideologies in Arabic Thought in the Nineteenth Century*. Cambridge: Cambridge Univ. Press.

Afary, Janet. 2009. *Sexual Politics in Modern Iran*. Cambridge: Cambridge Univ. Press.

Ahearn, Laura M. 2001. *Invitations to love: Literacy, Love Letters, and Social Change in Nepal*. Ann Arbor: Univ. of Michigan Press.

Ahmadi, Azal. 2016. "Recreating Virginity in Iran: Hymenoplasty as a Form of Resistance." *Medical Anthropology Quarterly* 30 (2): 222–37.

Ahmed, Leila. 1992. *Women and Gender in Islam: Historical Roots of a Modern Debate*. New Haven, CT: Yale Univ. Press.

Aksikas, Jaafar. 2009. *Arab Modernities: Islamism, Nationalism, and Liberalism in the Post-Colonial Arab World*. New York: Peter Lang.

Allen, Roger. 2000. *An Introduction to Arab Literature*. Cambridge: Cambridge Univ. Press.

Allouche, Sabiha. 2019a. "Love, Lebanese Style: Toward an Either/And Analytic Framework of Kinship." *Journal of Middle East Women's Studies* 15 (2): 157–78.

———. 2019b. "Queering Heterosexual (Intersectarian) Love in Lebanon." *International Journal of Middle East Studies* 51 (4): 547–65.

Al-Samman, Hanadi, and El-Ariss, Tarek. 2013. "Queer Affects: Introduction." *International Journal of Middle East Studies* 45 (2): 205–9.

Altorki, Soraya. 1986. *Women in Saudi Arabia: Ideology and Behavior among the Elite*. New York: Columbia Univ. Press.

———. 1980. "Milk-Kinship in Arab Society: An Unexplored Problem in the Ethnography of Marriage." *Ethnology* 19 (2): 233–44.

Altorki, Soraya, and El-Solh, Camilla Fauzi, eds. 1988. *Arab Women in the Field: Studying Your Own Society*. Syracuse, NY: Syracuse Univ. Press.

Amer, Paul. 2011. "Middle East Masculinity Studies: Discourses of 'Men in Crisis.'" *Journal of Middle East Women's Studies* 7 (3): 36–70.

Andersen, Ditte; Signe Ravn, and Rachel Thomson. 2020. "Narrative Sense-Making and Prospective Social Action: Methodological Challenges and New Directions." *International Journal of Social Research Methodology* 23 (4): 367–75.

Archambault, Julie Soleil. 2017. *Mobile Secrets: Youth, Intimacy, and the Politics of Pretense in Mozambique*. Chicago: Univ. of Chicago Press.

Babayan, Kathryn, and Najmabadi Afsaneh, eds. 2008. *Islamicate Sexualities: Translations across Temporal Geographies of Desire*. Cambridge, MA: Harvard Univ. Press.

Badran, Sammy Zeyad. 2022. *Killing Contention: Demobilization in Morocco during the Arab Spring*. Syracuse, NY: Syracuse Univ. Press.

Bakass, Fatima, and Michele Ferrand, 2013. "L'entrée en sexualité à Rabat: les nouveaux arrangements entre les sexes." *Population* 68:41–65.

Baron, Beth. 1993. "The Making and Breaking of Marital Bonds in Modern Egypt." In *Women in Middle Eastern History: Shifting Boundaries in Sex and Gender*, edited by Nikki R. Keddie and Beth Baron, 275–91. New Haven, CT: Yale Univ. Press.

Bayat, Asef. 2007. "Islamism and the Politics of Fun." *Public Culture* 19 (3): 433–59.

Beatty, Andrew. 2014. "Anthropology and Emotion." *Journal of the Royal Anthropological Institute* 20 (3): 545–63.

Beaumont, Valérie, Corinne Cauvin Verner, and François Pouillon, eds. 2010. "Sexe et sexualités au Maghreb. Essais d'ethnographies contemporaines." *L'Année du Maghreb* 4:5–268.

Benchemsi, Ahmed. 2012. "Morocco: Outfoxing the Opposition." *Journal of Democracy* 23 (1): 57–69.

Ben Moussa, Mohamed. 2019. "Rap It Up, Share It Up: Identity Politics of Youth 'Social' Movement in Moroccan Online Rap Music." *New Media & Society* 21 (5): 1043–64.

Bennani-Chraïbi, Mounia. 1995. *Soumis et rebelles: les jeunes au Maroc*. Paris: Cnrs.

Berlant, Lauren. 2011. "A Properly Political Concept of Love: Three Approaches in Ten Pages." *Cultural Anthropology* 26 (4): 683–91.

———. 1998. "Intimacy." *Critical Inquiry* 24 (2): 281–88.

Berriane, Yasmine. 2013. *Femmes, associations et politique à Casablanca*. Rabat: Centre Jacques Berque.

Billaud, Julie. 2015. *Kabul Carnival: Gender Politics in Postwar Afghanistan*. Philadelphia: Univ. of Pennsylvania Press.

Boddy, Janice. 1989. *Wombs and Alien Spirits: Women, Men, and the Zar Cult in Northern Sudan*. Madison: Univ. of Wisconsin Press.

Borrillo, Sara. 2016. "Egalité de genre au Maroc après 2011? Les droits sexuels et reproductifs au centre des récentes luttes de reconnaissance." In *Emerging Actors in Post-Revolutionary North Africa: Gender Mobility and Social Activism*, edited by Anna Maria Di Tolla and Ersilia Francesca, 398–418. Naples: Il Torcoliere.

Bouasria, Abdelilah. 2015. *Sufism and Politics in Morocco: Activism and Dissent*. Abingdon: Routledge.

Boufraioua, Leila. 2017. "L'émergence d'une sexualité juvénile hors mariage chez les jeunes de Sidi Ifni (Maroc)." *L'Année du Maghreb* 17:31–48.

Bouhdiba, Abdelwahab. 1975. *La sexualité en Islam*. Paris: Presses universitaires de France.

Bourdieu, Pierre. 2000. *Esquisse d'une théorie de la pratique: Précédé de "Trois études d'ethnologie Kabyle."* Paris: Éditions du Seuil.

———. 1998. *La Domination masculine*. Paris: Éditions du Seuil.

Bousbaa, Amal. 2022. "La maternité célibataire au Maroc: pour une approche dynamique de l'expérience." *L'Année du Maghreb* 28 (2): 127–40.

———. 2017. "Les conditions des mères célibataires face aux défaillances des politiques sociales au Maroc." *Revue des politiques sociales et familiales* 124:53–61.

Bras, Pierre. 2019. "Le Collectif 490 des Hors-la-loi du Maroc reçoit le prix Simone-de-Beauvoir pour la liberté des femmes 2020." *L'Homme & la Société* 209 (1): 9–12.

Brinkman, Inge, Mirjam de Bruijn, and Hiham Bilal. 2009. "The Mobile Phone, 'Modernity,' and Change in Khartoum." In *Mobile Phones: The New Talking Drums of Africa*, edited by Mirima de Bruijn, Francis Nyamnjoh, and Inge Brinkman, 69–91. Leiden: African Studies Centre.

Bruner, Jerome. 1987. "Life as Narrative." *Social Research* 54 (1): 11–32.

Bubandt, Nils, Mikkel Rytter, and Christian Suhr. 2013. "A Second Look at Invisibility: Al-Ghayb, Islam, Ethnography." *Contemporary Islam* 13:1–16.

Bulkeley, Kelly. 2002. "Reflections on the Dream Traditions of Islam." *Sleep and Hypnosis* 4 (1): 1–11.

Buskens, Léon. 2003. "Recent Debate on Family Law Reform in Morocco: Islamic Law as Politics in an Emerging Public Sphere." *Islamic Law and Society* 10 (1): 70–129.

Butler, Judith. 1997. *The Psychic Life of Power*. Stanford, CA: Stanford Univ. Press.

———. 1993. *Bodies That Matter: On the Discursive Limits of "Sex."* London: Routledge.

Capelli, Irene. 2021. "Undutiful Daughters Claiming Their Futures and the Uncertainties of Non-Marital Love in Casablanca." *EtnoAntropologia* 9 (1): 61–80.

Capello, Carlo. 2008. *Le prigioni invisibili. Etnografia multisituata della migrazione marocchina*. Milan: Franco Angeli.

Carey, Matthew. 2017. *Mistrust: An Ethnographic Theory*. Chicago: Hau.

———. 2012. "'The Rules' in Morocco? Pragmatic Approaches to Flirtation and Lying." *HAU: Journal of Ethnographic Theory* 2 (2): 188–204.

———. 2010. "Entre rencontres et rendez-vous: stratégies marocaines de sexualité hors marriage." *L'Année du Maghreb* 4:171–87.

Carsten, Jane. 2004. *After Kinship*. Cambridge: Cambridge Univ. Press.

Cavatorta, Francesco. 2016. "Morocco: The Promise of Democracy and the Reality of Authoritarianism." *International Spectator* 51 (1): 86–98.

Cavatorta, Francesco, and Emanuela Dalmasso. 2009. "Liberal Outcomes through Undemocratic Means: The Reform of the Code de statut personnel in Morocco." *Journal of Modern African Studies* 47 (4): 487–506.

Chafai, Habiba. 2021. "Everyday Gendered Violence: Women's Experiences of and Discourses on Street Sexual Harassment in Morocco." *Journal of North African Studies* 26 (5): 1013–32.

Chappatte, André. 2014. "Nightlife in Urban Mali: Being a Muslim Maquisard in Bougouni." *Journal of the Royal Anthropological Institute* 20 (3): 526–44.

Charrad, Mounira. 2001. *States and Women's Rights: The Making of Post-Colonial Tunisia, Algeria, and Morocco.* Berkeley: Univ. of California Press.

Chaudat, Philippe, and Monia Lachheb, eds. 2018. *Transgresser au Maghreb: la normalité et ses dépassements.* Paris: Karthala.

Cheikh, Mériam. 2020a. *Les filles qui sortent. Jeunesse, sexualité et prostitution au Maroc.* Brussels: Éditions de l'Université de Bruxelles.

———. 2020b. "The Intimate Life of the Disenfranchised and Criminalised Moroccan Working-Class Youth." *Hesperis Tamuda* 55 (3): 431–48.

———. 2017. "De l'ordre moral à l'ordre social. L'application des lois pénalisant la sexualité prémaritale selon des lignes de classe." *L'Année du Maghreb* 17:49–67.

———. 2009. "Échanges sexuels monétarisés, femmes et féminités au Maroc: une autonomie ambivalente." *Autrepart* 1 (49): 173–88.

Cohen, Shana. 2004. *Searching for a Different Future: The Rise of a Global Middle Class in Morocco.* Durham, NC: Duke Univ. Press.

Cohen, Shana, and Larabi Jaidi. 2006. *Morocco: Globalization and Its Consequences.* London: Routledge.

Cole, Jennifer, and Lynn M. Thomas, eds. 2009. *Love in Africa.* Chicago: Univ. of Chicago Press.

Conway-Long, Don. 2006. "Gender, Power, and Social Change in Morocco." In *Islamic Masculinities*, edited by Lahucine Ouzgane, 145–60. New York: Zed.

Costa, Elisabetta. 2016a. "The Morality of Premarital Romances: Social Media, Flirting, and Love in Southeast Turkey." *Middle Eastern Journal of Culture and Communication* 9 (2): 199–215.

———. 2016b. *Social Media in Southeast Turkey: Love, Kinship, and Politics.* London: Univ. College London.

Costa, Elisabetta, and Laura Menin. 2016a. "Introduction: Digital Intimacies— Exploring Digital Media and Intimate Lives in the Middle East and North Africa." *Middle East Journal of Culture and Communication* 9 (2): 137–45.

Costa, Elisabetta, and Laura Menin, eds. 2016b. "Digital Intimacies: Exploring Digital Technologies and Intimate Lives in North Africa and the Middle East." *Middle East Journal of Culture and Communication* 9 (2): 133–241.

Crapanzano, Vincent. 2014. "Half Disciplined Chaos: Thoughts on Destiny, Contingency, Story, And Trauma." In *Genocide and Mass Violence: Memory, Symptom, and Recovery*, edited by D. E. Hinton, and A. L. Hinton, 157–72. Cambridge: Cambridge Univ. Press.

———. 2004. *Imaginative Horizons: An Essay in Literary-Philosophical Anthropology*. Chicago: Univ. of Chicago Press.

———. 1985. *Tuhami: Portrait of a Moroccan*. Chicago: Univ. of Chicago Press.

———. 1975. "Saints, Jnun, and Dreams: An Essay in Moroccan Ethnopsychology." *Journal for the Study of Interpersonal Processes* 38 (2): 145–59.

Cuno, Kenneth M. 2015. *Modernizing Marriage: Family, Ideology, and Law in Nineteenth- and Early Twentieth-Century Egypt*. Syracuse, NY: Syracuse Univ. Press.

D'Angelo, Lorenzo. 2019. "God's Gifts: Destiny, Poverty, and Temporality in the Mines of Sierra Leone." *Africa Spectrum* 54 (1): 44–60.

Daadaoui, Mohamed. 2011. *Moroccan Monarchy and the Islamist Challenge: Maintaining Makhzen Power*. New York: Palgrave Macmillan.

Davis, Douglas A. 1995. "Modernizing the Sexes: Changing Gender Relations in a Moroccan Town." *Ethos* 23:69–78.

Davis, Susan Schaefer. 1983. *Patience and Power: Women's Lives in a Moroccan Village*. Cambridge, MA: Schenkman.

Davis, Susan Schaefer, and Douglas Davis. 1989. *Adolescence in a Moroccan Town: Making Social Sense*. New Brunswick, NJ: Rutgers Univ. Press.

———. 1995a. "The Mosque and the Satellite: Media and Adolescence in a Moroccan Town." *Journal of Youth and Adolescence* 24 (5): 577–93.

———. 1995b. "Possessed by Love: Gender and Romance in Morocco." In *Romantic Passion: A Universal Experience?*, edited by William Jankowiak, 219–38. New York: Columbia Univ. Press.

De Cillis, Maria. 2014. *Free Will and Predestination in Islamic Thought: Theoretical Compromises in the Works of Avicenna, Ghazali, and Ibn Arabi*. New York: Routledge.

De Lauretis, Teresa. 1990. "Eccentric Subjects." *Feminist Studies* 16:115–50.

Deeb, Lara. 2015. "Thinking Piety and the Everyday Together: A Response to Fadil and Fernando." *HAU: Journal of Ethnographic Theory* 5 (2): 93–96.

———. 2006. *An Enchanted Modern: Gender and Public Piety in Shi'i Lebanon*. Princeton, NJ: Princeton Univ. Press.

Deeb, Lara, and Dina al-Kassim, eds. 2011. "Middle East Sexualities." *Journal of Middle East Women's Studies* 7 (3): 1–132.

Deeb, Lara, and Jessica Winegar, eds. 2012. "Anthropologies of Arab-Majority Societies." *Annual Review of Anthropology* 41 (1): 537–58.

Deeb, Lara, and Mona Harb. 2013. *Leisurely Islam: Negotiating Geography and Morality in Shiʻite South Beirut.* Princeton, NJ: Princeton Univ.Press.

Devika, J. 2021. "The Kiss of Love Protests: A Report on Resistance to Abjection in Kerala." In *Sexuality, Abjection, and Queer Existence in Contemporary India*, edited by Pushpesh Kumar, 131–48. London: Routledge.

Dialmy, Abdessamad. 2019. "Transitional LGBT in Morocco LGBT between Islam and Human Rights." In *Dynamics of Inclusion and Exclusion in the MENA Region: Minorities, Subalternity, and Resistance*, edited by Hamza Tayebi and Jochen Lobah, 249–72. Rabat: Hanns Seidel Foundation Morocco/Mauritania.

———. 2017. *Transition sexuelle: entre genre et Islamisme.* Paris: L'Harmattan.

———. 2014. *Sociologie de la sexualité arabo-musulmane.* Paris: L'Harmattan.

———. 2009. *Vers une nouvelle masculinité au Maroc.* Dakar: Codesria.

———. 2005. "Sexuality in Contemporary Arab Society." *Social Analysis* 49 (2): 16–33.

———. 2003. "Premarital Female Sexuality in Morocco." *Al-Raida* 20 (99): 74–83.

———. 1988. *Sexualité et Discours au Maroc.* Casablanca: Afrique Orient.

Dieste, Josep Lluìs Mateo. 2013. *Health and Ritual in Morocco: Conceptions of the Body and Healing Practices.* Leiden: Brill.

Dwyer, Daisy Hilse. 1978. *Images and Self-Images: Male and Female in Morocco.* New York: Columbia Univ. Press.

Edgar, Iain R. 2011. *The Dream in Islam: From Quranic Tradition to Jihadist Inspiration.* New York: Berghahn.

Edgar Iain, and David Henig. 2010. "Istikhara: The Guidance and Practice of Islamic Dream Incubation through Ethnographic Comparison." *History and Anthropology* 21 (3): 251–61.

Eickelman, Dale. 1981. *The Middle East: An Anthropological Approach.* New York: New York Univ. Press.

———. 1976. *Moroccan Islam: Tradition and Society in a Pilgrimage Center.* Austin: Univ. of Texas Press.

Eickelman, Dale, and Jon W. Anderson, eds. 1999. *New Media in the Muslim World: The Emerging Public Sphere.* Bloomington: Indiana Univ. Press.

El Aji, Sanaa. 2018. *Sexualité et célibat au Maroc: Pratiques et verbalization.* Casablanca: La Croisee Des Chemins.

El-Dine, Sandra Nasser. 2018. "Love, Materiality, and Masculinity in Jordan: 'Doing' Romance with Limited Resources." *Men and Masculinities* 21 (3): 423–42.

El Feki, Shereen. 2013. *Sex and the Citadel: Intimate Life in a Changing Arab World*. New York: Pantheon.

El Guabli, Brahim. 2012. "Reflections on the Unfolding Debate about Sexual Freedom in Morocco." Reset Doc. Accessed April 20, 2022. https://www.reset doc.org/story/reflections-on-the-unfolding-debate-about-sexual-freedom-in -morocco/.

Elliot, Alice. 2022. "Repeating Manhood: Migration and the Unmaking of Men in Morocco." In *Arab Masculinities: Anthropological Reconceptions in Precarious Times*, edited by Marcia C. Inhorn and Konstantina Isidoros, 97–115. Bloomington: Indiana Univ. Press.

———. 2021. *The Outside: Migration as Life in Morocco*. Bloomington: Indiana Univ. Press.

———. 2016. "The Makeup of Destiny: Predestination and the Labor of Hope in a Moroccan Emigrant Town." *American Ethnologist* 43 (3): 488–99.

Elliot, Alice, and Laura Menin, eds. 2018. "For an Anthropology of Destiny." *HAU: Journal of Ethnographic Theory* 8:292–99.

Eltahawy, Mona. 2015. *Headscarves and Hymens: Why the Middle East Needs a Sexual Revolution*. New York: Farrar, Straus & Giroux.

Esposito, John L., ed. 2004. *The Oxford Encyclopedia of the Islamic World*. New York: Oxford Univ. Press.

Fabietti, Ugo. 2012. "Errancy in Ethnography and Theory: On the Role of Discovery in Anthropological Research." In *Serendipity in Anthropological Research: The Nomadic Turn*, edited by Haim Hazan and Esther Hertgoz, 15–30. New York: Routledge.

Fadil, Nadia, and Mayanthi Fernando. 2015. "Rediscovering the 'Everyday' Muslim: Notes on an Anthropological Divide." *HAU: Journal of Ethnographic Theory* 5 (2): 59–88.

Fioole, Annerienke. 2021. "Publicity, Discretion, and Secrecy through Becoming a Moroccan Couple." PhD diss., Universiteit van Amsterdam.

———. 2020. "Evidently Married: Changing Ambiguities in Creating Family Ties in Morocco." *Hawwa* 20 (1–2): 34–54.

Fortier, Corinne, Aymon Kreil, and Irene Maffi, eds. 2018. *Reinventing love: Gender, Intimacy, and Romance in the Arab World*. Bern: Peter Lang.

———. 2016. "The Trouble of Love in the Arab Worlds: Romance, Marriage. and the Shaping of Intimate Lives." *Arab Studies Journal* 24 (2): 96–148.

Foster, Angelina. 2002. "Young Women's Sexuality in Tunisia: The Consequences of Disinformation among University Students." In *Everyday Life in the Muslim Middle East,* edited by Donna Lee Bowen, Evelyn E. Early, and Becky Schulthies, 98–110. Bloomington: Indiana Univ. Press.

Foucault, Michael. 1975. *Surveiller et punir: Naissance de la prison.* Paris: Gallimard.

Franzosi, Roberto. 1998. "Narrative Analysis—or Why (and How) Sociologists Should Be Interested in Narrative." *Annual Review of Sociology* 24 (1): 517–54.

Friedl, Erika. 1989. *Women of Deh Koh: Lives in an Iranian Village.* Washington, DC: Smithsonian Institution.

Friedland, Roger, Janet Afary, Paolo Gardinali, and Cambria Naslund. 2016. "Love in the Middle East: The Contradictions of Romance in the Facebook World." *Critical Research on Religion* 4 (3): 229–58.

Gaibazzi, Paolo, and Marco Gardini. 2015. "The Work of Fate and Fortune in Africa." *Critical African Studies* 7 (3): 203–9.

García-Andrade, Adriana, Lena Gunnarsson, and Anna Jónasdóttir. 2018. *Feminism and the Power of Love: Interdisciplinary Interventions.* London: Routledge.

Geertz, Hildred. 1979. "The Meaning of Family Ties." In *Meaning and Order in Moroccan Society: Three Essays in Cultural Analysis,* edited by Clifford Geertz, Hildred Geertz, and Lawrence Rosen, 363–77. Cambridge: Cambridge Univ. Press.

Ghannam, Farha. 2013. *Live and Die Like a Man: Gender Dynamics in Urban Egypt.* Stanford, CA: Stanford Univ. Press.

Gidden, Anthony. 1992. *The Transformation of Intimacy: Sexuality, Love, and Eroticism in Modern Societies.* Stanford, CA: Stanford Univ. Press.

Ginsburg, Faye D., Lila Abu-Lughod, and Brian Larkin. 2002. "Introduction." In *Media Worlds: Anthropology on New Terrain,* edited by Faye D. Ginsburg, Lila Abu-Lughod, and Brian Larkin, 1–36. Berkeley: Univ. of California Press,

Glassé, Cyril, and Huston Smith. 2003. *The New Encyclopedia of Islam.* New York: Rowman Altamira.

Gonzalez-Vazquez, Araceli. 2014. "Dreaming, Dream-Sharing, and Dream-Interpretation as Feminine Powers in Northern Morocco." *Anthropology of the Contemporary Middle East and Central Eurasia* 2 (1): 97–108.

Gruénais, Marc-Éric. 2017. "La publicisation du débat sur l'avortement au Maroc. L'État marocain en action." *L'Année du Maghreb* 17:219–34.

Guessous, Nadia. 2020. "Feminist Blind Spots and the Affect of Secularity: Disorienting the Discourse of the Veil in Contemporary Morocco." *Signs: Journal of Women in Culture and Society* 45 (3): 605–28.

———. 2011. "Genealogies of Feminism: Leftist Feminist Subjectivity in the Wake of the Islamic Revival in Contemporary Morocco." PhD diss., Columbia Univ.

Habib. Samar. 2007. *Female Homosexuality in the Middle East: Histories and Representations*. New York: Routledge.

Hafez, Sherine. 2014. "The Revolution Shall Not Pass through Women's Bodies: Egypt, Uprising, and Gender Politics." *Journal of North African Studies* 19 (2): 172–85.

————. 2011. *An Islam of Her Own: Reconsidering Religion and Secularism in Women's Islamic Movements*. New York: New York Univ. Press.

Hamdy, Sherine F. 2009. "Islam, Fatalism, and Medical Intervention: Lessons from Egypt on the Cultivation of Forbearance (*Sabr*) and Reliance on God (*Tawakkul*)." *Anthropological Quarterly* 82 (1): 173–96.

Haraway, Donna. 1988. "Situated Knowledge: The Science Question in Feminism and the Privilege of Partial Perspective." *Feminist Studies* 14 (3): 575–99.

Hardon Anita, and Deborah Posel. 2012. "Secrecy as Embodied Practice: Beyond the Confessional Imperative." *Culture, Health & Sexuality* 14 (1): 1–13.

Hardt, Michael. 2011. "For Love or Money." *Cultural Anthropology* 26 (4): 676–82.

Harrami, Noureddine, and Mahdi Mahdi. 2008. "Mobilité transnationale et recomposition des valeurs sociales dans la société rurale marocaine d'aujourd'hui." In *Le Maroc aujourd'hui*, edited by Paola Gandolfi, 261–81. Venezia: Il ponte.

————. 2006. "Mobilité internationale et dynamique de changement dans les sociétés de depart." In *Mediterraneo e migrazioni oggi*, edited by Emanuela Trevisan Semi, 35–50. Venezia: Il Ponte.

Hart, Kimberly. 2007. "Love by Arrangement: The Ambiguity of 'Spousal Choice' in a Turkish Village." *Journal of the Royal Anthropological Institute* 13 (2): 345–62.

Hassa, Samira. 2012. "Projecting, Exposing, Revealing Self in the Digital World: Usernames as a Social Practice in a Moroccan Chatroom." *Names* 60 (4): 201–9.

Hasso, Frances Susan. 2010. *Consuming Desires: Family Crisis and the State in the Middle East*. Stanford, CA: Stanford Univ. Press.

Hasso, Frances Susan, and Zakia Salime, eds. 2016. *Freedom without Permission: Bodies and Space in the Arab Revolutions*. Durham, NC: Duke Univ. Press.

Hayes, Shannon. 2019. "Hexes and Exes: Navigating Romantic Relationships in Fez, Morocco." M.A. Diss. Georgetown Univ.

Hegasy, Sonja. 2007. "Young Authority: Quantitative and Qualitative Insights into Youth, Youth Culture, and State Power in Contemporary Morocco." *Journal of North African Studies* 12 (1): 19–36.

Herding, Maruta. 2014. *Inventing the Muslim Cool: Islamic Youth Culture in Western Europe*. Bielefeld: Transcript Verlag.

Herrera Linda, and Asef Bayat, eds. 2010. *Being Young and Muslim*. Oxford: Oxford Univ. Press.

Hibou, Béatrice. 2011. "Le mouvement du 20 février, le Makhzen et l'antipolitique. L'impensé des réformes au Maroc." *Les dossiers du CERI* 1 (12). www.ceri-sciencespo.com/archive/2011/mai/dossier/art_bh2.pdf (accessed October 5, 2023).

———. 2006. "Maroc: d'un conservatisme à l'autre." *Legs colonial et gouvernance contemporaine* 2:154–96.

Hibou, Béatrice, and Mohamed Tozy. 2002. "De la friture sur la ligne des réformes. La libéralisation des télécommunications au Maroc." *Critique international* 14 (1): 91–118.

Hijazi-Omari, Hiyam, and Rivka Ribak. 2008. "Playing with Fire: On the Domestication of the Mobile Phone among Palestinian Teenage Girls in Israel." *Information, Communication & Society* 11 (2): 149–66.

Hirsch, Jennifer Sue, and Holly Wardlow. 2006. *Modern Loves: The Anthropology of Romantic Courtship and Companionate Love*. Ann Arbor: Univ. of Michigan Press.

Hirschkind, Charles. 2006. *The Ethical Soundscape: Cassette Sermons and Islamic Counterpublics*. New York: Columbia Univ. Press.

hooks, bell. 2000a. *All about Love: New Visions*. New York: HarperCollins.

———. 2000b. *Feminism Is for Everybody: Passionate Politics*. Cambridge, MA: Pluto.

Hoodfar, Homa. 1997. *Between Marriage and the Market: Intimate Politics and Survival in Cairo*. Berkeley: Univ. of California Press.

Horst, Hether, and Daniel Miller. 2006. *The Cell Phone: An Anthropology of Communication*. Oxford: Berg.

Howe, Marvine. 2005. *Morocco: The Islamist Awakening and Other Challenges*. Oxford: Oxford Univ. Press.

Huq, Maimuna. 2008. "Reading the Qur'an in Bangladesh: The Politics of 'Belief' among Islamist Women." *Modern Asian Studies* 42 (2–3): 457–88.

Ilahiane, Hsain. 2022. *The Mobile Phone Revolution in Morocco: Cultural and Economic Transformations*. Lanham, MD: Rowman & Littlefield.

———. 2020. "Mobile Phones and the Making and Unmaking of Gender and Place on the Fly in Morocco." *Hespéris-Tamuda* 55 (4): 197–212.

———. 2019. "The Berber House of the World Leaked: Mobile Phones, Gender Switching, and Place in Morocco." In *Location Technologies in International*

Context, edited by Rowan Wilken, Gerard Goggin, and Heather A. Horst, 54–66. London: Routledge.

Ilkkaracan, Pinar. [2008] 2016. *Deconstructing Sexuality in the Middle East: Challenges and Discourses*. London: Routledge.

Illouz, Eva. 1997. *Consuming the Romantic Utopia: Love and the Cultural Contradictions of Capitalism*. Berkeley: Univ. of California Press.

Inhorn, Marcia C. 2012. *The New Arab Man: Emergent Masculinities, Technologies, and Islam in the Middle East*. Princeton, NJ: Princeton Univ. Press.

———. 1996. *Infertility and Patriarchy: the Cultural Politics of Gender and Family Life in Egypt*. Philadelphia: Univ. of Pennsylvania Press.

Inhorn, Marcia C., and Nancy J. Smith-Hefner, eds. 2021. *Waithood: Gender, Education, and Global Delays in Marriage And Childbearing*. New York: Berghahn.

Inhorn, Marcia C., and Nefissa Naguib, eds. 2018. *Reconceiving Muslim Men: Love and Marriage, Family, and Care in Precarious Times*. Oxford: Berghahn.

Isidoros, Konstantina, and Marcia C. Inhorn, eds. 2022. *Arab Masculinities: Anthropological Reconceptions in Precarious Times*. Bloomington: Indiana Univ. Press.

Jabbour, Jana. 2017. "Winning Hearts and Minds through Soft Power: The Case of Turkish Soap Operas in the Middle East." In *Media in the Middle East*, edited by Nele Lenze, Charlotte Schriwer, and Zubaidah Abdul Jalil, 145–63. Cham: Palgrave Macmillan.

Jackson, Michael. 2011. *Life within Limits: Well-Being in a World of Want*. Durham, NC: Duke Univ. Press.

Jankowiak, William, ed. 2008. *Intimacies: Love and Sex across Culture*. New York: Columbia Univ. Press.

———. 1995. *Romantic Passion: A Universal Experience?* New York: Columbia Univ. Press.

Jankowiak, William, and Edward F. Fischer. 1992. "A Cross-Cultural Perspective on Romantic Love." *Ethnology* 31 (2): 149–55.

Jones, Carla. 2010. "Materializing Piety: Gendered Anxieties about Faithful Consumption in Contemporary Urban Indonesia." *American Ethnologist* 37 (4): 617–37.

Joseph, Suad. 2005. "Learning Desire: Relational Pedagogies and the Desiring Female Subject in Lebanon." *Journal of Middle East Women's Studies* 1 (1): 79–109.

Joseph, Suad, ed. 1999. *Intimate Selving in Arab Families: Gender, Self, and Identity*. Syracuse, NY: Syracuse Univ. Press.

———. 1994. "Brother/Sister Relationships: Connectivity, Love, and Power in the Reproduction Of Patriarchy in Lebanon." *American Ethnologist* 21 (1): 50–73.

———. 1993. "Connectivity and Patriarchy among Urban Working-Class Arab Families in Lebanon." *Ethos* 21 (4): 452–84.

Juntunen, Marko. 2002. "Between Morocco and Spain: Men, Migrant Smuggling, and a Dispersed Moroccan Community." PhD diss., Helsinki Univ.

Jyrkiainen, Senni. 2016. "Online Presentation of Gendered Selves among Young Women in Egypt." *Middle Eastern Journal of Culture and Communication* 9 (2): 182–99.

Kahf, Mohja. 1999. *Western Representations of the Muslim Woman: From Termagant to Odalisque*. Austin: Univ. of Texas Press.

Kandiyoti, Daniz, ed. 1996. *Gendering the Middle East: Emerging Perspectives*. London: I. B. Tauris.

Kandiyoti, Daniz. 1988. "Bargaining with Patriarchy." *Gender & Society* 2 (3): 274–90.

Kapchan, Deborah. 2007. *Traveling Spirit Masters: Moroccan Gnawa Trance and Music in the Global Marketplace*. Middletown, CT: Wesleyan Univ. Press.

———. 1996. *Gender on the Market: Moroccan Women and Revoicing Tradition*. Philadelphia: Univ. of Pennsylvania Press.

Kaya, Laura Pearl. 2009. "Dating in a Sexually Segregated Society: Embodied Practices of Online Romance in Irbid, Jordan." *Anthropological Quarterly* 82 (1): 251–78.

Keddie, Nikki. 1989. "Problems in the Study of Middle Eastern Women." *International Journal of Middle East Studies* 10 (2): 225–40.

Kilborne, Benjamin. 1978. *Interprétation du rêve au Maroc*. Grenoble: La Pensée sauvage.

Kondo, Dorinne. 1990. *Crafting Selves: Power, Gender, and Political Discourses of Identity in a Japanese Workplace*. Chicago: Univ. of Chicago Press.

Kraidy, Marwan M. 2009. *Reality Television and Arab Politics: Contention in Public Life*. Cambridge: Cambridge Univ. Press.

Kreil, Aymon. 2016. "The Price of Love: Valentine's Day and Its Enemies in Egypt." *Arab Studies Journal* 24 (2): 128–46.

Kriem, Maya S. 2009. "Mobile Telephony in Morocco: A Changing Sociality." *Media, Culture, and Society* 31 (4): 617–32.

Kottak, Conrad Phillip. 2016. *Prime-Time Society: An Anthropological Analysis of Television and Culture*. London: Routledge.

Laidlaw, James. 2013. *The Subject of Virtue: An Anthropology of Ethics and Freedom*. New York: Cambridge Univ. Press.

Laouni, Nour-Eddine. 2022. "Cyberactivism and Protest Movements: The February 20th Movement—the Forming of a New Generation in Morocco." *Journal of North African Studies* 27 (2): 296–325.

Lee Bowen, Donna, Alexia Green, and Christiaan James. 2009. "Globalization, Mobile Phones, and Forbidden Romance." *Journal of North African Studies* 13 (2): 227–41.

Liechty, Mark. 2020. *Suitably Modern*. Princeton, NJ: Princeton Univ. Press.

Liberatore, Giulia. 2017. *Somali, Muslim, British: Striving in Securitized Britain*. London: Bloomsbury Academic.

———. 2016. "Imagining an Ideal Husband: Marriage as a Site of Aspiration among Pious Somali Women in London." *Anthropological Quarterly* 89 (3): 781–812.

Lindholm, Charles. 2006. "Romantic Love and Anthropology." *Etnofoor* 19 (1): 5–21.

———. 1998. "Love and Structure Anthropology." *Theory, Culture, and Society* 15:243–63.

Ling, Rich, and Heather Horst. 2009. "Mobile Communication in the Global South." *New Media & Society* 13 (3): 363–74.

Ling, Rich, and Jonathan Donner. 2009. *Mobile Communication: Digital Media and Society Series*. London: Polity.

Louw, Maria Elizabeth. 2010. "Dreaming Up Futures: Dream Omens and Magic in Bishkek." *History and Anthropology* 21 (3): 277–92.

Lutz, Catherine A., and Geoffrey M. White. 1986. "The Anthropology of Emotions." *Annual Review of Anthropology* 15:405–36.

Lutz, Catherine A., and Lila Abu-Lughod, eds. 1990. *Language and the Politics of Emotion*. Cambridge: Cambridge Univ. Press.

Decker, Corrie. 2015. "Love and Sex in Islamic Africa." *Africa Today* 61 (4): 1–103.

Madianou, Mirca, and Daniel Miller. 2011. "Crafting Love: Letters and Cassette Tapes in Transnational Filipino Family Communication." *South East Asia Research* 19 (2): 249–72.

Maghraoui, Driss. 2011. "Constitutional Reforms in Morocco: Between Consensus and Subaltern Politics." *Journal of North African Studies* 16 (4): 679–99.

———. 2009. "Ilmaniyya, Laicité, Sécularisme/Secularism." In *Words in Motion: Toward a Global Lexicon*, edited by Carol Gluck Anna and Lowenhaupt Tsing, 109–28. Durham, NC: Duke Univ. Press.

Mahdavi, Pardis. 2009. *Passionate Uprisings: Iran's Sexual Revolution.* Palo Alto, CA: Stanford Univ. Press.

Maher, Vanessa. 1989. *Il potere della complicità: Conflitti e legami delle donne nordafricane.* Turin: Rosemberg & Sellier.

————. 1974. *Women and Property in Morocco: Their Changing Relation to the Process of Social Stratification in the Middle Atlas.* Cambridge: Cambridge Univ. Press.

Mahmood, Saba. 2009. "Religious Reason and Secular Affect: An Incommensurable Divide?" *Critical Inquiry* 35 (4): 836–62.

————. 2005. *Politics of Piety: The Islamic Revival and the Feminist Subject.* Princeton, NJ: Princeton Univ. Press.

————. 2001. "Feminist Theory, Embodiment, and the Docile Agent: Some Reflections on the Egyptian Islamic Revival." *Cultural Anthropology* 6 (2): 202–36.

Mains, Daniel. 2017. "Too Much Time: Changing Conceptions of Boredom, Progress, and the Future among Young Men in Urban Ethiopia, 2003–2015." *Focaal* 78:38–51.

Malik, Aisha Anees. 2016. "Of Migration, Marriage, and Men: Rethinking the Masculinity of Transnational Husbands from Rural Pakistan." In *Gender and Sexuality in Muslim Cultures*, edited by Gul Ozyegin, 71–88. London: Routledge.

Malmström, Maria Frederika. 2016. *The Politics of Female Circumcision in Egypt: Gender, Sexuality, and the Construction of Identity.* New York: I. B. Tauris.

Marsden, Magnus, and Konstantinos Retsikas. 2013. "Introduction." In *Articulating Islam: Anthropological Approaches to Muslim Worlds*, edited by Magnus Marsden and Konstantinos Retsikas, 1–32. Dordrecht: Springer.

Marsden, Magnus. 2007. "Love and Elopement in Northern Pakistan." *Journal of Royal Anthropological Institute* 13:91–108.

————. 2005. *Living Islam: Muslim Religious Experience in Pakistan's North-West Frontier.* Cambridge: Cambridge Univ. Press.

Masquelier, Adeline. 2007. "When Spirits Start Veiling: The Case of the Veiled She-Devil." *Africa Today* 54 (3): 39–64.

Maqsood Ammara. 2021. "Love as Understanding: Marriage, Aspiration, and the Joint Family in Middle-Class Pakistan." *American Ethnologist* 48 (1): 93–104.

McMurray, David A. 2001. *In and Out of Morocco: Smuggling and Migration in a Frontier Boomtown.* Minneapolis: Univ. of Minnesota Press.

McNay, Lois. 2000. *Gender and Agency: Reconfiguring the Subject in Feminist and Social Theory.* Cambridge: Polity.

Menin, Laura. 2020. "'Destiny Is Written by God': Islamic Predestination, Responsibility, and Transcendence in Central Morocco." *Journal of the Royal Anthropological Institute* 26 (3): 515–32.

———. 2018. "Texting Romance: Mobile Phones, Intimacy, and Gendered Moralities in Central Morocco." *Contemporary Levant* 3 (1): 66–78.

———. 2016. "'Men Are Not Scared! (*rijjala ma tay-khafosh*)': Luck, Destiny, and the Gendered Vocabularies of Clandestine Migration in Central Morocco." *Archivio Antropologico Mediterraneo* 18 (1): 25–36.

———. 2011. "Bodies, Boundaries, and Desires: Multiple Subject-Positions and Micro-Politics of Modernity among Young Muslim Women in Milan." *Journal of Modern Italian Studies* 16 (4): 504–15.

Mernissi, Fatema. 2011. *Les 50 noms de l'amour*. Rabat: Les Edition Marsam.

———. 2009. *L'amour dans les pays musulmans*. Casablanca: Editions Le Fennec.

———. 2001. *Le harem et l'Occident*. Paris: Albin Michel.

———. 1994. *Dreams of Trespass: Tales of a Harem Girlhood*. New York: Addison Wesley.

———. 1993. Interview with Terry Gross on *Fresh Air*, National Public Radio, December 15, 1993.

———. 1982. "Virginity and Patriarchy." *Women's Studies International Forum* 5 (2): 183–91.

———. *Beyond the Veil: Male-Female Dynamics in a Modern Muslim Society*. Cambridge: Schenkman.

Mesbahi, Nima. 2018. "The Victimization of the 'Muslim Woman': The Case of Amina Filali, Morocco." *Journal of International Women's Studies* 19 (3): 49–59.

Miller, Catherine. 2012. "Mexicans Speaking in Dariia (Moroccan Arabic): Media, Urbanization, and Language Changes in Morocco." In *Arabic Language and Linguistics*, edited by Reem Bassiouney and E. Graham Katz, 169–88. Washington, DC: Georgetown Univ. Press.

Miller, Catherine, and Mériam Cheikh. 2010. "Les mots d'amour: dire le sentiment et la sexualité au Maroc. De quelques matériaux." *EDNA, Estudios de dialectología norteafricana y andalusí* 13:173–99.

Miller, Daniel, 2009. "What Is a Mobile Phone Relationship?" In *Living with the Information Society in Asia*, edited by Erwin Alampay, 24–35. Singapore: Institute of Southern Asian Studies/International Development Research Centre.

Miller, Daniel, and Heather Horst. 2012. "The Digital and the Human: A Prospectus for Digital Anthropology." In *Digital Anthropology*, edited by Heather Horst and Daniel Miller, 3–38. London: Berg.

Miller, Laura, and Jan Bardsley, eds. 2005. *Bad Girls of Japan*. New York: Palgrave Macmillan.

Mir-Hosseini Ziba, and Vanja Hamzić. 2010. "Control and Sexuality: The Revival of Zina Laws in Muslim Contexts." Women Living under Muslim Laws. Accessed October 5, 2023. https://www.wluml.org/2010/01/03/control-and-sexuality-the-revival-of-zina-laws-in-muslim-contexts.

Mittermaier, Amira. 2014. "Bread, Freedom, Social Justice: The Egyptian Uprising and a Sufi Khidma." *Cultural Anthropology* 29 (1): 54–57.

———. 2012. "Dreams from Elsewhere: Muslim Subjectivities beyond the Trope of Self-Cultivation." *Journal of the Royal Anthropological Institute* 18 (2): 247–65.

———. 2011. *Dreams That Matter: Egyptian Landscapes of the Imagination*. Berkeley: Univ. of California Press.

Moll, Yasmin. 2012. "Storytelling, Sincerity, and Islamic Televangelism in Egypt." In *Global and Local Televangelism*, edited by Thomas Pradip Ninan and Philip Lee, 21–44. New York: Palgrave Macmillan.

———. 2010. "Islamic Televangelism: Religion, Media, and Visuality in Contemporary Egypt." *Arab Media & Society* 10:1–27.

Moore, Henrietta. 2011. *Still Life: Hopes, Desires, and Satisfactions*. Cambridge: Polity.

———. 2007. *The Subject of Anthropology*. Cambridge: Polity.

———. 1994. *A Passion for Difference: Essays in Anthropology and Gender*. Bloomington: Indiana Univ. Press.

Moors, Annelies, and Emma Tarlo. 2013. *Islamic Fashion and Anti-Fashion: New Perspectives from Europe and North America*. London: Bloomsbury Academic.

Moors, Annelies. 2007. "Fashionable Muslims: Notions of Self, Religion, and Society in Sanà." *Fashion Theory: The Journal of Dress Body & Culture* 11 (2–3): 319–46.

———. 2003. "Islam and Fashion on the Streets of San'a, Yemen." *Etnofoor* 16 (2): 41–56.

Munson, Henry, Jr. 1993. *Religion and Power in Morocco*. New Haven, CT: Yale Univ. Press.

Naamane-Guessous, Soumaya. 2013. *Nous les femmes, vous les hommes: chroniques*. Rabat: Marsam.

———. 1991. *Au delà de toute pudeur: La sexualité feminine au Maroc*. Casablanca: Ediff.

Naamane-Guessous, Soumaya, and Chakib Guessous. 2005. *Grossesses de la honte: enquête raisonnée sur les filles mères et les enfants abandonnés au Maroc*. Casablanca: Editions Le Fennec.

Nagi, Mariam. 2018. "Islam, Sexualities, and Education." In *Handbook of Islamic Education*, vol. 7, edited by Holger Daun and Reza Arjmand, 263–87. Cham: Springer International.

Naguib, Nefissa. 2015. *Nurturing Masculinities: Men, Food, and Family in Contemporary Egypt*. Austin: Univ. of Texas Press.

Najmabadi, Afsaneh. 2005. *Women with Moustaches and Men without Beards: Gender and Sexual Anxieties of Iranian Modernity*. Berkeley: Univ. of California Press.

Nevola, Luca. 2018. "Destiny in Hindsight: Potentiality and Intentional Action in Contemporary Yemen." *HAU: Journal of Ethnographic Theory* 8 (1–2): 300–13.

———. 2016a. "Blood Doesn't Lie: Hierarchy and Inclusion/Exclusion in Contemporary Yemen." PhD diss., Univ. of Milano Bicocca.

———. 2016b. "Love, Mobile Phones, and the Codification of Intimacy." *Middle Eastern Journal of Culture and Communication* 9 (2): 147–64.

Newcomb, Rachel. 2017. *Everyday Life in Global Morocco*. Bloomington: Indiana Univ. Press.

———. 2008. *Women of Fes: Ambiguities of Urban Life in Morocco*. Philadelphia: Univ. of Pennsylvania Press.

Ochs, Elinor, and Lisa Capps. 2001. *Living Narrative: Creating Lives in Everyday Storytelling*. Cambridge, MA: Harvard Univ. Press.

Orlando, Valerie. 2009. *Francophone Voices of the "New" Morocco in Film and Print: (Re)Presenting A Society In Transition*. New York: Palgrave Macmillan.

Osella, Caroline. 2012. "Desires under Reform: Contemporary Reconfigurations of Family, Marriage, Love, and Gendering in a Transnational South Indian Matrilineal Muslim Community." *Culture and Religion* 13 (2): 241–64.

Osella, Filippo. 2012. "Malabar Secrets: South Indian Muslim Men's (Homo) Sociality across the Indian Ocean." *Asian Studies Review* 36 (4): 531–49.

Osella, Filippo, and Caroline Osella. 2007. "Muslim Style in South India Fashion Theory." *Journal of Dress, Body & Culture* 11 (2–3): 233–52.

Ossman, Susan. 2007. "Cinderella, CVs, and Neighborhood Nemima: Announcing Morocco's Royal Wedding." *Comparative Studies of South Asia, Africa, and the Middle East* 27 (3): 525–35.

———. 2002. *Three Faces of Beauty: Casablanca, Paris, Cairo*. Durham, NC: Duke Univ. Press.

———. 1994. *Picturing Casablanca: Portraits of Power in a Modern City*. Berkeley: Univ. of California Press.

Ouzgane, Lahoucine, ed. 2006. *Islamic Masculinities*. New York: Zed.

Ozyegin, Gul. 2015. *New Desires, New Selves: Sex, Love, and Piety among Turkish Youth*. New York: New York Univ. Press.

Ozyegin, Gul, ed. 2016. *Gender and Sexuality in Muslim Cultures*. New York: Routledge.

Padilla, Mark B., Jennifer S. Hirsch, Miguel Munoz-Laboy, Robert E. Sember, and Richard G. Parker, eds. 2007. *Love and Globalization: Transformations of Intimacy in the Contemporary World*. Nashville, TN: Vanderbilt Univ. Press.

Pandolfo, Stefania. 2018. *Knot of the Soul: Madness, Psychoanalysis, Islam*. Chicago: Univ. of Chicago Press.

———. 2007. "'The Burning': Finitude and the Politico-Theological Imagination of Illegal Migration." *Anthropological Theory* 7 (3): 329–63.

———. 2000. "The Thin Line of Modernity: Some Moroccan Debates on Subjectivity." In *Questions of Modernity*, edited by T. Mitchell, 115–47. Minneapolis: Univ. of Minnesota Press.

———. 1997. *Impasse of the Angels: Scenes from a Moroccan Space of Memory*. Chicago: Univ Pearl. of Chicago Press.

Pepicelli, Renata. 2016. "Being Young and Post-Feminist in Morocco: The Emergence of a New Women's Activism." In *Emerging Actors in Post-Revolutionary North Africa: Gender Mobility and Social Activism*, edited by Anna Maria Di Tolla and Francesca Ersilia, 419–46. Naples: Il Torcoliere.

Personal Narratives Group. 1989. *Interpreting Women's Lives: Feminist Theory and Personal Narratives*. Bloomington: Indiana Univ. Press.

Piela, Anna. 2011. "Piety as a Concept Underpinning Muslim Women's Online Discussions of Marriage And Professional Career." *Contemporary Islam* 5 (3): 249–65.

Pourmehdi, Mansour. 2015. "Globalisation, the Internet, and Guilty Pleasures in Morocco." *Sociology and Anthropology*, (9): 456–66.

Povinelli, Elizabeth. 2006. *The Empire of Love: Toward a Theory of Intimacy, Genealogy, and Carnality*. Durham, NC: Duke Univ. Press.

Prefol, Pierre. 1986. *Prodiges de l'irrigation au Maroc: la développement exemplaire du Tadla, 1936–85*. Paris: Nouvelles Editions Latines.

Pussetti, Chiara. 2005. "Introduzione. Discorsi sulle emozioni." *Annuario Antropologia "Emozioni"* 6: 5–14.

Rabinow, Paul. 1977. *Reflections on Fieldwork in Morocco*. Berkeley: Univ. of California Press.

Rassam, Amul. 1980. "Women and Domestic Power in Morocco." *International Journal of Middle East Studies* 12 (2): 171–79.

Rausch, Margaret. 2001. *Bodies, Boundaries, and Spirit Possession: Moroccan Women and the Revision of Tradition*. London: Transaction.

Rebhun, Linna-Anne. 1999. *The Heart Is Unknown Country: Love in the Changing Economy of Northeast Brazil*. Stanford, CA: Stanford Univ. Press.

Reddy, William M. 1999. "Emotional Liberty: Politics and History in the Anthropology of Emotions." *Cultural Anthropology* 14 (2): 256–88.

Robbins, Joel. 2012. "On Becoming Ethical Subjects: Freedom, Constraint, and the Anthropology Of Morality." *Anthropology of This Century* 5. http://aotcpress.com/articles/ethical-subjects-freedom-constraint-anthropology-morality/ (accessed August 14, 2023).

————. 2007. "Between Reproduction and Freedom: Morality, Value, and Radical Cultural Change." *Ethnos: Journal of Anthropology* 72 (3): 293–314.

Rollinde, Marguerite. 2002. *Le mouvement marocain des droits de l'homme: entre consensus national et engagement citoyen*. Paris: Karthala Éditions.

Rozario, Santi. 2011. "Islamic Piety against the Family: From 'Traditional' to 'Pure' Islam." *Contemporary Islam* 5:285–308.

Ryan-Flood, Róisín, and Rosalind Gill. 2010. "Introduction." In *Secrecy and Silence in the Research Process: Feminist Reflections*, edited by Róisín Ryan-Flood and Rosalind Gill, 1–13. New York: Routledge.

Rock, Aaron. 2010. "Amr Khaled: From Daʿwa to Political and Religious Leadership." *British Journal of Middle Eastern Studies* 37 (1): 15–37.

Rosaldo, Michelle. 1984. "Toward an Anthropology of Self and Feeling." In *Culture Theory: Essays on Mind, Self, and Emotion*, edited by Richard Shweder and Robert Levine, 137–57. Cambridge: Cambridge Univ. Press.

Rosen, Lawrence. 1984. *Bargaining for Reality: The Construction of Social Relations in a Muslim Community*. Chicago: Univ. of Chicago Press.

Roy, Oliver. 2004. *Globalized Islam: The Search for a New Ummah*. New York: Columbia Univ. Press.

Sadeghi, Fatemeh. 2010. "Negotiating with Modernity: Young Women and Sexuality in Iran." In *Being Young and Muslim*, edited by Linda Herrera and Asef Bayat, 273–90. Oxford: Oxford Univ. Press.

Sahlins, Marshall. 2011. "What Kinship Is (Part One)." *Journal of the Royal Anthropological Institute* 17:2–19.

Said, Edward. 1978. *Orientalism*. New York: Pantheon.

Salih, Ruba. 2016. "Bodies That Walk, Bodies That Talk, Bodies That Love: Palestinian Women Refugees, Affectivity, and the Politics of the Ordinary." *Antipode* 49:742–60.

———. 2003. *Gender in Transnationalism: Home, Longing, and Belonging among Moroccan Migrant Women*. New York: Routledge.

Salime, Zakia. 2016. "Embedded Counterpublics: Women and Islamic Revival in Morocco." *Frontiers: A Journal of Women Studies* 37 (3): 47–73.

———. 2014. "New Feminism as Personal Revolutions: Micro Rebellious Bodies." *Signs: Journal of Women in Culture and Society* 40 (1): 14–20.

———. 2012. "New Feminism? Gender Dynamics in Morocco's February Twentieth Movement." *Journal of International Women's Studies* 13:100–114.

———. 2011. *Between Feminism and Islam: Human Rights and Sharia Law in Morocco*. Minneapolis: Univ. of Minnesota Press.

———. 2009. "Revisiting the Debate on Family Law in Morocco: Context, Actors and Discourses." In *Gender and Family Laws in a Changing Middle East and South Asia*, edited by Kenneth M. Cuno and Manisha Desai, 45–62. Syracuse, NY: Syracuse Univ. Press.

Sakr, Naomi. 2001. *Satellite Realms: Transnational Television, Globalization, and the Middle East*. London: I. B. Tauris.

Salamandra, Christa. 2012. "The Muhannad Effect: Media Panic, Melodrama, and the Arab Female Gaze." *Anthropological Quarterly* 85 (1): 45–77.

Saoudi, Nour-eddine. 2007. *Voyage au-delà des nuits de plomb*. Rabat: Synergie civique.

Scheper-Hughes, Nancy. 1992. *Death without Weeping: The Violence of Everyday Life in Brazil*. Berkeley: Univ. of California Press.

Schielke, Samuli. 2015. *Living in a Future Tense: Hope, Frustration, and Ambivalence in Egypt, before and after 2011*. Bloomington: Indiana Univ. Press.

———. 2009. "Being Good in Ramadan: Ambivalence, Fragmentation, and the Moral Self in the Lives of Young Egyptians." *Journal of the Royal Anthropological Institute* 15:24–40.

———. 2008. "Boredom and Despair in Rural Egypt." *Contemporary Islam* 2:251–70.

Schulz, Dorothea E. 2006. "Promises of (Im)Mediate Salvation: Islam, Broadcast Media, and the Remaking Of Religious Experience in Mali." *American Ethnologist* 33 (2): 210–29.

Sehlikoglu, Sertaç. 2021. *Working Out Desire: Women, Sport, and Self-Making in Istanbul.* Syracuse, NY: Syracuse Univ. Press.

Sehlikoglu, Sertaç, and Asli Zengin. 2015. "Introduction: Why Revisit Intimacy?" *Cambridge Journal of Anthropology* 33 (2): 20–25.

Sehlikoglu, Sertaç, and Asli Zengin, eds. 2016. "Everyday Intimacies in the Middle East." Special issue, *Journal of Middle East Women's Studies* 12 (2): 139–245.

Sehlikoglu, Sertaç, and Frank G. Karioris. 2019. *The Everyday Makings of Heteronormativity: Cross-Cultural Explorations of Sex, Gender, and Sexuality.* London: Lexington.

Sinclair-Webb, Emma, and Mai Ghoussoub, eds. 2000. *Imagined Masculinities: Male Identity and Culture in the Middle East.* London: Saqi.

Singerman, Diane. 2013. "Youth, Gender, and Dignity in the Egyptian Uprising." *Journal of Middle East Women's Studies* 9 (3): 1–27.

Skalli, Loubna Hanna. 2014. "Young Women and Social Media against Sexual Harassment in North Africa." *Journal of North African Studies* 19 (2): 244–58.

Skouri, Hassan. 2015. "The Effect of Arab Satellite Entertainment Channels on Moroccan University Students." *Revue de Gestion et d'Économie* 3 (3): 358–76.

Slimani, Leila. 2017. *Sexe et mensonges: La Vie sexuelle au Maroc.* Paris: Les Arenes.

Slyomovics, Susan. 2005. *The Performance of Human Rights in Morocco.* Philadelphia: Univ. of Pennsylvania Press.

Smith-Hefner, Nancy J. 2019. *Islamizing Intimacies: Youth, Sexuality, and Gender in Contemporary Indonesia.* Honolulu: Univ. of Hawai'i Press.

———. 2005. "The New Muslim Romance: Changing Patterns of Courtship and Marriage among Educated Javanese Youth." *Journal of Southeast Asian Studies* 36 (3): 441–59.

Soares, Benjamin, and Filippo Osella. 2009. "Islam, Politics, Anthropology." *Journal of the Royal Anthropological Institute* 15 (1): 1–23.

Sopranzetti, Claudio. 2016. "Framed by Freedom: Emancipation and Oppression in Post-Fordist Thailand." *Cultural Anthropology* 32 (1): 68–92.

Sotoudeh, Ramina, Roger Friedland, and Janet Afary. 2017. "Digital Romance: The Sources of Online Love in the Muslim World." *Media, Culture & Society* 39 (3): 429–39.

Spadola, Emilio. 2014. *The Calls of Islam: Sufis, Islamists, and Mass Mediation in Urban Morocco*. Bloomington: Indiana Univ. Press.

Swearingen, Will Davis. 1987. *Moroccan Mirages: Agrarian Dreams and Deceptions, 1912–1986*. Princeton, NJ: Princeton Univ. Press.

Tarlo, Eemma. 2010. *Visibly Muslim: Fashion, Politics, Faith*. Oxford: Berg.

Taussig, Michael. 1999. *Defacement: Public Secrecy and the Labor of the Negative*. Stanford, CA: Stanford Univ. Press.

———. 1991. "Tactility and Distraction." *Cultural Anthropology* 6 (2): 147–53.

Tozy, Mohammed. 1999. *Monarchie et islam politique au Maroc*. Paris: Presses de Sciences Po.

Troin, Jean-François, ed. 2002. *Maroc: Regions, pays, territoires*. Paris: Maisonneuve & Laros.

Tsuda, Takeyuki. 2015. "Is Native Anthropology Really Possible?" *Anthropology Today* 31 (3): 14–17.

Uberoi, Patricia. 2006. *Freedom and Destiny: Gender, Family, and Popular Culture in India*. Oxford: Oxford Univ. Press.

Vacchiano, Francesco. 2022. *Antropologia della dignità: aspirazioni, moralità e ricerca del benessere nel Marocco contemporaneo*. Verona: Ombre Corte.

van Nieuwkerk, Karin. 2008. "Creating an Islamic Cultural Sphere: Contested Notions of Art, Leisure, and Entertainment. An Introduction." *Contemporary Islam* 2 (3): 169–76.

Venkatesan, Soumhya, Jeanette Edwards, Rane Willerslev, Elizabeth Povinelli, and Perveez Mody. 2011. "The Anthropological Fixation with Reciprocity Leaves No Room for Love: 2009 Meeting of the Group for Debates in Anthropological Theory." *Critique of Anthropology* 31 (3): 210–50.

Vermeren, Paul. 2009. *Le Maroc de Mohamed VI: La Transition Inachevée*, Paris: La Découverte.

———. 2006. *Histoire du Maroc depuis l'indépendance*. Paris: La Découverte.

———. 2002. *Le Maroc en transition*. Paris: La Découverte.

Vigh, Henrik. 2009. "Motion Squared: A Second Look at the Concept Of Social Navigation." *Anthropological Theory* 9 (4): 419–38.

Walsh, Andrew. 2002. "Responsibility, Taboos, and 'The Freedom to do Otherwise' in Ankarana, Northern Madagascar." *Journal of the Royal Anthropological Institute* 8 (3): 451–68.

Walter, Anna-Maria. 2021. *Intimate Connections: Love and Marriage in Pakistan's High Mountains*. New Brunswick, NJ: Rutgers Univ. Press.

Watt, William Montgomery. 1948. *Free Will and Predestination in Early Islam*. London: Luzac.

Wikan, Unni. 1996. *Tomorrow, God Willing: Self-Made Destinies in Cairo*. Chicago: Univ of. Chicago Press.

Wilkinson, Eleanor. 2017. "On Love as an (Im)Properly Political Concept." *Environment and Planning D: Society and Space* 35 (1): 57–71.

Wynn, Lisa L. 2018. *Love, Sex, and Desire in Modern Egypt: Navigating the Margins of Respectability*. Austin: Univ. of Texas Press.

———. 2016. "'Like a Virgin': Hymenoplasty and Secret Marriage in Egypt." *Medical Anthropology* 35 (6): 547–59.

———. 2015. "Writing Love, Affect, and Desire into Ethnography." In *Phenomenology in Anthropology: A Sense of Perspective*, edited by Kalpana Ram and Christopher Houston, 224–47. Bloomington: Indiana Univ. Press.

Wynn, Lisa L., and Saffaa Hassanein. 2017. "Hymenoplasty, Virginity Testing, and the Simulacrum of Female Respectability." *Signs* 42 (4): 893–917.

Yassine, Abdessalam. [1994] 2003. *The Muslim Mind on Trial: Divine Revelation versus Secular Rationalism*. Iowa City: Justice & Spirituality.

———. [1998] 2000. *Winning the Modern World for Islam*. Iowa City: Justice & Spirituality.

Ze'evi, Dror. 2006. *Producing Desire: Changing Sexual Discourse in the Ottoman Middle East, 1500–1900*. Berkeley: Univ. of California Press.

Zeghal, Malika. 2008. *Islamism in Morocco: Religion, Authoritarianism, and Electoral Politics*. Princeton, NJ: Markus Wiener.

Zigon, Jarrett. 2009. "Within a Range of Possibilities: Morality and Ethics in Social Life." *Ethnos* 74 (2): 251–76.

Žvan Elliott, Katja. 2015. *Modernizing Patriarchy: The Politics of Women's Rights in Morocco*. Austin: Univ. of Texas Press.

Zyskowski, Kathryn, ed. 2014. "Everyday Islam." Cultural Anthropology Online. https://journal.culanth.org/index.php/ca/catalog/category/everyday-islam (accessed May 10, 2023).

Index

243

Laura Menin is an associate researcher in the School of Global Studies, University of Sussex. A social anthropologist specializing in North Africa, she has worked in Morocco and Europe on love and intimate relationships, migration and racism, and political violence and cultural production emerging from the "Years of Lead" (1961–99) in Morocco.